ANDY MURRAY

Eleanor Preston is a respected writer and broadcaster who has travelled on the men's, women's and junior circuits for the past six years. She covers the sport for a range of publications worldwide, including the *Sunday Herald* and *The Guardian*, and is also co-president of the International Tennis Writers Association. She lives in London.

Rob Robertson lives in Edinburgh and is an award-winning sportswriter for *The Herald*. He has travelled extensively with Andy Murray over the past year, following his rise to stardom.

Rob Robertson and Eleanor Preston

ANDY MURRAY

The Story So Far . . .

MAINSTREAM
PUBLISHING

EDINBURGH AND LONDON

First published in Great Britain in 2006 by
MAINSTREAM PUBLISHING COMPANY
(EDINBURGH) LTD
7 Albany Street
Edinburgh EH1 3UG

ISBN 1 84596 172 2

A catalogue record for this book is available from
the British Library

Typeset in Apollo and Hamilton

Printed in Great Britain by
William Clowes Ltd, Beccles, Suffolk

This book is dedicated to the memories of
Antony and William Preston, and to the late Brian Meek,
one of Scotland's greatest ever sports writers.

ACKNOWLEDGEMENTS

ROB:

To Kirsten and Clare Robertson for making me smile and being my best friends. Also to Carolyn W for all her support and to Robin Leith and Fiona Crombie for their words of wisdom. Many thanks to Herald sports editor Donald Cowey as well as George Cheyne, Denis Campbell and Mark McSherry for all their encouragement and photographers Fred and Susan Mullane, Roger Parker, Alan Peebles, Rob Eyton Jones and Chris Watt for their magnificent work.

ELEANOR:

With love and gratitude to Mum; Matt and Emma; Katie and Paul and to my nephews, nieces, godchildren and their parents. Thanks to Denise for a lifetime of support and friendship and to Alix, Ivan and

Leeann, Stevie B, Calamity James and Nic for being such good mates. And to Rob, for giving me the chance to do this.

Both of us would like to thank Paul Murphy and Graeme Blaikie at Mainstream, Leon Smith, Colin Banks, Faye Andrews, Mark Hodgkinson, Charlie Wyett and everyone who helped with this book. Last but not least, our thanks go to Andy for giving us so much to write about!

CONTENTS

1

THE EARLY YEARS

ANDREW BARRON MURRAY WAS BORN IN THE QUEEN MOTHER'S HOSPITAL IN GLASGOW on 15 May 1987, the second son of Judy and Willie Murray. Their first son Jamie had been born on 13 February 1986, also in Glasgow. Judy's mum and dad, Shirley and Roy Erskine, who were from the beautiful cathedral town of Dunblane, and Willie's mum and dad, Ellen and Gordon, who were from Kilsyth, were delighted to have two grandsons.

The boys were sporty, and, unusually for youngsters from Scotland, they both excelled at tennis. Because of the dreadful Scottish weather and lack of decent facilities, the country did not have a great legacy of top-class tennis players. Ross Matheson and Zambian-born Miles Maclagan flew the flag for Scotland, up until Murray came along, with limited success. Maclagan's claim to fame came when he was two sets up and had match point in the first round at Wimbledon against Boris Becker in 1999, only for the German to come back to win the match. Despite his limited success as a player, Maclagan went on to become a respected top-class coach.

The ladies' game in Scotland also struggled until recent years, but Judy Murray was one of the best players of her generation north of the border. She won the 1981 British Hardcourt Doubles Championships with her friend Ellinore Lightbody and also played for Great Britain in the World Student Games in Bucharest, Romania, in the same year. In total, she won 64 Scottish titles at junior and senior levels in both doubles and mixed doubles. She also had the chance to go to America on a tennis scholarship when she was 16 years old, but, at that stage, there was no real support network in place to help her. Her mum and dad had her two brothers Keith and Niall to look after at home. For 15 months, she thought long and hard about joining the tennis tour. However, by her own admission, she was not tough enough to hack around the world by herself and decided against taking up a career as a player.

Her own experience back then had a lasting affect, and she swore that if Andy and Jamie were good enough to be professional players, she would do all in her power to make their dreams come true. As it turned out, it was her drive and support which have helped Andy on his way towards the top of the world game.

Andy was a boisterous child, and with Jamie being 15 months older, Judy and Willie had their work cut out early on to bring up the two young boys. The family lived in Dunblane, a small, picturesque town situated off the M9 motorway on the way to the Highlands. One of the most historic places in Scotland, Dunblane was founded in AD 602 by the Celtic missionary St Blane from whom the town derives its name. Today, Dunblane still exudes an 'olde worlde' charm with examples of seventeenth- and eighteenth-century architecture blending with Victorian and more contemporary buildings. The centrepiece is the beautiful cathedral, about which

John Ruskin, the English writer and painter, wrote, 'He was no common man who designed the cathedral of Dunblane. I know of nothing so perfect in its simplicity and so beautiful in all Gothic with which I am acquainted.' The small town was a great place for two boys to live as they had excellent sporting facilities on their doorstep and the great outdoors was never far away.

Judy was an accomplished tennis coach and tennis correspondent for the Scottish national broadsheet newspaper *The Herald*, while Willie worked in the retail trade. Their house was 200 yards from Dunblane Sports Club, which included tennis and squash courts. It was here that the Murray brothers played their first games, and the club quickly became a second home for them.

Nowadays, there is a small framed picture in the clubhouse of Andy as a youngster, and there are other photos of Jamie and Judy. There is also a picture of Andy with the US Open boys' singles trophy on another wall. Judy coached at the club from 1989, when Andy was two and Jamie three, up until she became the Scotland national coach in 1995. She also voluntarily ran the Dunblane primary and high school team.

A racket was thrust into Andy's hand at the age of two, and he used to run around the garden at their home occasionally managing to hit the odd ball or two. At other times, the family used to play Swingball together in their back garden.

From the age of three, Andy would toddle around at the side of the courts at Dunblane Sports Club with Jamie as Judy carried out her coaching sessions. They didn't play short or mini-tennis, as many children do nowadays, and were not competing with each other to any great degree, although that would soon change. At that age, all they wanted to do was hit the ball over the net. Andy played his first tournament when he was five years old in an Under-10 competition in Dunblane, and although he played three one-set matches, the results are lost in the mist of time.

He was just one of many youngsters in Dunblane who flocked to the sports club to play tennis and invariably found himself in small groups with other five and six year olds who took turns at hitting the ball across the net to each other. It was easy to see he was enjoying himself in such a playful environment, and he had as much fun playing football matches at the side of the court as anything else. The children also enjoyed water-bomb fights in the summer, and although they were taught the disciplines of tennis, they were also taught to have fun when playing the sport.

Back then, Jamie was the better player of the two brothers. He could hit the ball better than Andy, and Judy had to spend a lot of time throwing balls to Andy to improve his coordination. Jamie was a much more natural player, and Andy had to work hard to keep up with his older brother. In those days, he hit every shot, forehand and backhand, double-handed. The fact that Jamie was the better player worked well for Andy. Jamie went on all the tennis trips before Andy did and set the standards that his younger brother wanted to meet.

As the months progressed, Andy got better and better, and his competitive spirit started to kick in. The best example of that came when he made his debut for Dunblane Sports Club third team at the tender age of eight. He was playing with the respected architect John Clark, who went on to design the Skye Road Bridge and who was in his early 50s. They were playing on one of the bottom courts at the club, and Judy remembers well what her young son said to the man more than 40 years his senior. 'I remember watching the game,' said Judy. 'It was about the time that Andy was starting to show real promise. The game was just a few points in, and Andy walked up to the net and said to him, "You're standing a bit close to the net. You should stand back a bit as you might get lobbed if I decide to serve and volley." It was a laugh at the time, and John was brilliant with him, but it showed us all how confident Andy was becoming in his ability.'

THE EARLY YEARS

Not surprisingly, there were a number of players in the Central District Tennis League who didn't appreciate playing an eight year old, and there was talk of bringing in an age limit which would ban Andy from participating. Such a move was defeated and older players from other clubs now dine out on the time they played against the eight-year-old Andy Murray.

Away from tennis, Murray was trying every sport going. He played football at primary school and also tried his hand at golf, mini-rugby and gymnastics, the latter improving his suppleness.

As a youngster, he was a bit of a contradiction, being both stubborn and laid back. He was stubborn on the tennis court, because he knew exactly what he did or didn't want to do, which made it quite difficult to teach him at times, but at home he was really laid back. He was also a big football supporter and a member of Hibs Kids, the youth wing of his favourite football team Hibernian, the Scottish Premier League side that his grandfather Roy had played for. However, when his dad took him to his first game, he asked to leave at half-time, partly because he was freezing cold but mostly because Hibs were being beaten. As well as liking football, he was a big fan of American wrestling and often used to watch it on television and video.

Andy attended Dunblane Nursery School and then Dunblane Primary School. He enjoyed the primary school, which had an excellent reputation and the largest school roll in the Central region of Scotland with 640 pupils. The school buildings at the time were spread over a large site and a number of classrooms were housed in huts away from the main building.

It was here on 13 March 1996, when Andy was eight years old, that an evil act was perpetated by Thomas Hamilton, who killed sixteen beautiful children and their teacher in the school gym. It was an act of unquestionable evil which sent shock waves throughout the world.

ANDY MURRAY

It was a cold, grey Wednesday when Andy and his schoolmates turned up at school. There was fresh snow on the ground, and it was a bit slippery underfoot as the children played in the playground before lessons. The kids lined up and went into their classes just before 9 a.m. At 9.30 a.m., Thomas Hamilton entered the school with four handguns. He walked into the gym, and within a three-to-four-minute period, had fired one hundred and three times, shooting mostly at the three teachers and twenty-eight pupils in the gym before turning the gun on himself.

Murray and his classmates were heading towards the gym for PE just as the shooting started, but a teacher ushered them away when they were en route. Murray remembers fleeing to the headmaster's study with his other classmates. They were locked in there for two hours as all hell broke loose around them.

Murray and his family have always been reluctant to talk about the Dunblane massacre, mainly out of respect for the families of the dead. The only reason Andy has spoken about it in the past is because he felt that if he talked about it once or twice and made a short statement, the matter would be closed. To be fair to the world's media, his wishes have been, in general terms, granted, and although there were a few sensationalist tabloid headlines to begin with, the questions at his after-match press conferences have mainly concentrated on his tennis.

It was only when he broke through in America, by winning the US Open juniors in 2004, that he was questioned at length about Dunblane. When asked about the tragedy, he answered questions patiently but made it clear that he was not interested in discussing the matter further out of respect for the families of those who had died.

After he won the US Open juniors, he then dedicated his win to the people of Dunblane and the people of Beslan in Russia, where 344 civilians, 186 of them children, were killed after a terrorist attack on a local school in September 2004. 'I dedicated my win to the people and victims of Dunblane and also to the people of Beslan,' remembers Murray. 'I found it hard to watch those children coming out of the Russian school. I watched it on television and felt so much sorrow for them.'

Like many children in Dunblane, Murray knew Thomas Hamilton. The 43-year-old man had run youth groups in Dunblane which both Andy and Jamie attended. 'I knew the guy who did the shooting. We all went to his boys' clubs, and everybody knew him,' Murray said. 'It was a strange time, because some of my friends lost brothers and sisters. I couldn't understand it, because I knew the man. It didn't make sense to me. I was very young at the time and didn't really realise how it was a really difficult time for the town, but I think everyone has recovered really well from it, and the town has moved on. I remember hardly anything about the day itself. Only that we didn't go back to school for quite a few days, and we heard that children we knew had died. I was just conscious of this great sadness in the town.

'Because I was so young, I did not understand how big a world event it was. It was not until a few years later that I fully realised what had happened and how many people were affected. I really struggled to understand why it happened.

'Dunblane has coped really well with getting itself back on its feet, but it is still known around the world for the wrong reasons. I would like to think I am putting it in the headlines for the right reasons. Certainly, I hope I can do something for Dunblane. I hope I can make the town famous for something else, other than the tragedy.'

Judy Murray had to endure a heartbreaking wait along with every other parent at the gates of Dunblane Primary School on the day of the shootings. Out of respect for the families of the dead, she too has made it clear that she will not talk about the incident at length. 'Andy was too young to understand what happened that day, but his success is a very positive thing for the town,' she said. 'It's great that something positive like Andy's tennis can be associated with Dunblane. Our family have always lived there. It is a lovely little community.'

During Andy's schooldays, Leon Smith, a respected Scottish tennis coach who had been taken on by Judy to work with both her sons, became a growing influence. Andy had known Leon since he was five years old, and the pair got along well. Andy saw Leon as a cool guy, with his earring and fun-loving lifestyle, and the pair had a lot of laughs together.

'The teachers at Dunblane High School were helpful to Andy's tennis career and allowed him to miss certain subjects, like religious education, art and physical education, to allow him to have one-to-one day-time tennis tuition with Leon,' said Judy. 'Courts were easier to get and much cheaper during the day, and Leon was very much in demand and busy with national squad sessions and other coaching jobs in the evenings and at weekends. The school helped a lot and were very supportive.'

Judy's job as national coach took her all over Scotland, and she took training sessions in Stirling, Glasgow and Edinburgh, working many weekends. The constant work demands put her marriage under strain, and slowly she and Willie drifted apart. Both parents went out of their way to ensure that their separation and subsequent divorce would not affect their sons or their dreams to be tennis players.

Throughout it all, Judy's parents Roy and Shirley were a tower of strength, and Andy's and Jamie's tennis careers may not have progressed without their help. When Judy and Willie were working, the grandparents would pick the boys up from the airport, train station or school. Roy and Shirley fed the boys at short notice and would baby-sit for one if the other had to be ferried to a tennis match. Throughout it all, they were a great support for their grandchildren and played a big part in Andy's success.

THE EARLY YEARS

Both Andy and Jamie continued in the junior tennis world, and although their mum was Scottish national coach, neither of them was made to feel that they were any better or more special than the rest of the youngsters in the squad. They felt they were just one of the pack – the same as everybody else.

Andy's real hunger for the game soon became apparent, demonstrated by the way he played in tournaments up and down Britain. He has fond memories of winning the Under-10 West Midlands Championship in Solihull three years on the trot from the age of eight. He was really excited at the time, because the former British No. 1 Jeremy Bates had won it just the once.

There was a whole clutch of Scottish children who became good-quality tennis players around the same time as Andy. Part of the reason for that was they all had the opportunity to work with Judy. Most of the credit for the success of Andy and the other kids has to go to her, because she put in place expert individual training and competition programmes for all young Scottish players.

Tennis can sometimes be a lonely sport with one child travelling with one parent all the time. However, because there were a lot of good young players in Scotland, that wasn't the case, and there was excellent camaraderie between them all. Sometimes there would be four kids in a car, or ten in a minibus, heading to tournaments all over Britain. David Brewer and Frances Hendry from Edinburgh, who were 12-and-under British champions, were a couple of years older than Andy. Then there was Jamie Baker, Jamie Murray, Graeme Hood, Keith Meisner, David Culshaw, Mhairi Nish from Hawick, Nicola Allan, who played out of the Whitecraigs Club in Glasgow, and Andrew Milne from Aberdeen. The whole group, including Andy, used to go away to summer tournaments, where they would hook up with older Scottish kids like Elena Baltacha and Mhairi Brown, so there was always a feeling of togetherness.

When Andy and Jamie were deemed good enough to be invited to

Bisham Abbey, the prestigious sports training venue in the south-east of England, used by the British Judo Association, Amateur Rowing Association, Lawn Tennis Association (LTA) and the England football and rugby associations, they took their individual coaches with them as well. Such a move was vital for the Scottish players, who could tap into the expertise available at Bisham Abbey. Importantly, so could their coaches, which meant everybody learned together.

Andy received cash from sportscotland, the Scottish Executive's national agency for sport, to help him attend tournaments and work on his fitness. Up until the spring of 2005, the agency had committed over £5.8 million in lottery funds to tennis to cover every aspect of the game from grass roots to elite level. Tennis Scotland, the sport's governing body north of the border, also received over £750,000 in grants. From this funding, Andy received £60,000 over a nine-year period.

Murray was also a member of the Scottish Institute of Sport's individual athlete programme and benefited from a range of services, including medical support and strength and conditioning training at their base in Stirling. He also worked with physiotherapists Sue Warwick and Fiona Shanks, who helped keep him in shape.

In the early days, the sportscotland funding allowed the Scottish junior squad programme run by Judy Murray to travel down to England regularly, and at other times overseas, to take on top-quality opposition. This also allowed them to be helped by Olga Morozova and Andrew Lewandowski, both excellent tennis coaches, who worked long and hard with the top British junior players.

Young tennis players could only represent Great Britain, not their home nation, and, generally speaking, they had to be within the top four in their age group in the United Kingdom to be able to go on overseas trips. The sportscotland money was invaluable as it allowed Scottish players, including the Murray brothers, to gain much needed experience abroad.

At that time, Judy was travelling a lot with the LTA, which gave her an insight into the right tournaments for her to take her junior players to in the future. When Scottish players like Elena Baltacha, Frances Hendry and David Brewer were being selected for the Great Britain team, she was able to travel to even more events. This meant that the Scottish boys and girls got the experience of playing at a higher level abroad and had Judy, who they knew well, with them for support.

The training environment was just right in Scotland for players to blossom, and they kept getting better and better. However, some of them had to move down south, because there was no training base with a residential facility in Scotland, a situation Judy Murray and all those interested in tennis in Scotland believe should be rectified.

Once players like David Brewer, Frances Henry, Jamie Baker and Jamie Murray moved elsewhere – in Jamie's case to an LTA school in England, which Andy feels ruined his brother's game for a couple of years – it reduced the number of people Andy had to hit with on a regular basis. Murray's family, and Judy in particular, had known for a year that he would have to go abroad to improve his game but wanted the initiative to do so to come from him. He needed to be somewhere he could be stretched, and he could not do that in Scotland or England. It became clear to everyone that the time was right for him to move on, and a decision had to be made fast.

When he worked with Andy, Murray's former coach Mark Petchey recognised the importance of the work Judy did with her son during his early years: 'I think whenever you have the luxury of being able to go back to a player's earliest coach, which is what Judy was, it's a huge benefit, because you get information on where a certain stroke has come from or what their tendencies were in their strokes at a certain age. With Judy, I got a wealth of information, and that was a tremendous benefit to me. She understands tennis as well, so we had some good, solid conversations about strategy and things like that.

'Andy, like any other young tennis player, needs strong back-up.

There may be some parents who've been a little bit more in the public eye than others and there are some that are very much in the background, but they are always there, and they are very much behind that player, giving them their wholehearted support and being their back-up team. They just go about it in different ways.

'You do need that as a player – the encouragement and a place to go to without recriminations where you can have good, honest discussions about your career with people that you trust. Most children trust their parents implicitly. I think it is a really important part of any sportsman's career to have some strong parents to lean on, because there are going to be some difficult times.'

2

LIFE WITH LEON

Leon Smith is the manager of the Great Britain Under-14 team and one of the most respected tennis coaches in the UK. He was also one of the driving forces behind the rise of Andy Murray up the tennis rankings. Hand-picked by Judy Murray to travel with her son on the junior tour, Smith gives an insight into his life on the road with Andy Murray.

'TENNIS HAS ALWAYS BEEN IN MY BLOOD. I GREW UP ON THE SOUTH SIDE OF GLASGOW and lived across the road from Clarkston Tennis Club. I started playing with Toby, my older brother, and we used to play down at the courts every day after school. I loved every minute of it, and all our spare time was spent playing tennis. Both of us went on to represent Scotland, but I knew that I wasn't going to be good enough to make it at the top level.

'In saying that, I knew that I wanted a career in tennis, so immediately after I left Hutcheson's Grammar School, I decided to go straight into tennis coaching. I knew I wanted to be involved in the game for the rest of my life.

'I started my first job at Giffnock Tennis Club as assistant coach, where I worked for a year, and I really enjoyed it. I then worked at the Bridge of Allan Tennis Club and then at Troon Tennis Club before returning to the Bridge of Allan, where I started taking training sessions for Tennis Scotland.

'Through my work with them, I made my first contact with Judy Murray, Andy's mum, who was Scotland's national coach. I had known of her as she had been around at tennis tournaments when I was younger, usually coaching my opponents, like Graeme Darlington and Stephen McGuckin. It was at these tournaments that I first set eyes on Andy, although he won't remember much about it.

'He was around five years old, and, between matches, I used to play short tennis with him. I remember him at the side of the court hitting the ball around with his brother Jamie, and it was clear they loved playing the game, even at that young age. They weren't interested in winning points back then and played only for fun. That certainly didn't last for long, and soon Andy was showing his competitive edge and wanting to win every game.

'I started to get more and more involved in organising national squad tennis sessions for Judy and helped her at the Gannochy National Tennis Centre in Stirling and the Scotstoun Sports Centre in Glasgow, where we worked with the top players from all over the country. I loved the work and learned a lot. The sessions seemed to go pretty well, and around that time, I started coaching Nicola Allan, who was one of Scotland's up-and-coming young tennis stars. Nicola was a great girl to coach and won many national titles, which was thoroughly deserved as she worked incredibly hard.

'A few months after the national squad sessions in Stirling and

Glasgow which I had helped organise, Judy approached me to see if I could have a hit with Andy as she had been impressed, I assume, at the way I had handled myself.

'When I first started working with Andy, back in 1998, I was 22 years old and still playing pretty well, and he was just 11 years old. We got on very well from the start, and our first session was a lot of fun. Because Andy was so young, I had to strike the right balance between helping him improve his tennis and enjoying the sport he was involved in.

'That first session, like most of the ones we had early on, were held on the courts at Stirling University. I remember the occasion well: me and Andy on court hitting a few balls to each other. I tried to make a couple of jokes here and there to make him laugh and said to him that tennis at his age was all about having fun. He may come across as quite a serious guy, but his humour is very dry, and he is great at wind-ups.

'Despite the 11-year age difference between us, I got on with him straight away, and we remain friends to this day. What helped was the fact that we had similar personalities. We were quite fiery, and Andy, in particular, was very competitive, whatever he was playing.

'If I ever need reminding of that, I just have to think back to what happened at the end of our first training session. Even although he was just 11 and I was 22, we played a mini-game, and although I was older and better at tennis than him, he did not like it when I beat him by a few points.

'Both Andy and Judy must have been impressed with what I had done because, after a few sessions, I got a telephone call from Judy saying Andy had really enjoyed the sessions and would I consider taking him on as a player and working with him on a regular basis.

'I didn't have to think twice. From that first short hitting session I had with him when we just got to know each other, I knew he had something special. He had been winning tournaments in Britain aimed at the Under-11s when he was only nine. I could tell he had real talent and would go all the way to the top. Once it became clear that Andy and I got on and wanted to work together, I remember talking to Judy and she agreed she had faith in me to work with him without her being around. It was important I got her blessing to do that. I would not have taken the job if she had any doubts.

'Judy, as a mother who had been coaching Andy and Jamie from a young age, felt that he needed a change and a male influence in his coaching sessions. Somebody a bit more physically strong on the court to stretch him more. It is not easy to be a mother who is coaching your own son in any sport, so Judy always knew she was going to take a step back at some stage. It seemed a natural progression for me to get involved at that time.

'Judy had done a great job with him, and the work she did with Andy in the early years laid the groundwork for the rest of his tennis career. Everybody who worked with him in the future, like me or Mark Petchey, were just building on the great foundations which Judy had laid.

'From my point of view, having Judy around when I was working with Andy taught me a lot. As well as remaining a great influence on Andy's playing career, she also was a huge influence on my career, and I have learned more from Judy than I have from any other coach.

'After a few months getting to know him, I soon learned that he was obsessive about tennis. He also enjoyed football, following Hibernian, the team his grandfather Roy used to play for, and knew a lot about sport in general, but tennis was his real forte. He was and remains a real expert when it comes to the history of the game and has great knowledge of tennis facts and figures.

'It was really funny when I was coaching both him and Nicola Allan at the same time. I was pretty clued up on the players in the junior ranks at the time and knew many of their strengths and weaknesses. However, Andy was just as clued up as me, and if I told him the name of Nicola's next opponent, he would give me the run-down on the girl's tactics, every match she had played that season and how Nicola could beat her. He was obsessed by the sport. He was great at watching matches, studying matches, and within five minutes of watching somebody, he knew exactly how to play them. That attribute is one which has never left him, and he has used his speed of thought and ability to size up his opponent to his advantage on the main ATP tour.

'After I started coaching him, I also went to watch him play football, which was another sport he excelled at, and he was definitely good enough to go professional. On the football pitch, like the tennis court, it was apparent he had only one thing on his mind and that was to win. He was ultra-competitive and a really good player. He liked to play the glamour role behind the front two strikers, a position from which he scored a lot of goals, and he read the game superbly from that area of the field.

'Not surprisingly, in the early days of us hooking up together, he was quite quiet. There wasn't much conversation, but once we got to know each other, he started to open up a bit more. He was a bit introverted, as many kids at that age are, but he slowly came out of his shell.

'Although I was working with Andy on his training sessions, Judy was still doing a power of work behind the scenes. Being such a great coach with so much experience, she had a good feel for what was going on overseas in the junior ranks. For me to have her to call upon to discuss coaching techniques and keep me updated about other good players around Andy's age was great and a real bonus for both Andy and me.

'Although she was not on the court with me during Andy's training sessions, I asked her advice on matters like the overall running of his programme, the tournaments she thought he should play and many other things. For all her input, she never interfered in his on-court training schedules. She was very supportive of everything we were doing.

'When he was 11 years old, our first trip overseas together was to America, which saw him play in a few tournaments and culminated in the Orange Bowl tournament in Miami. We went to the Orange Bowl as part of a Lawn Tennis Association organised group, and it was a great experience for everybody.

'The Junior Orange Bowl International Tennis Championship is considered to be one of the most important junior tennis tournaments in the world. It is open to the very best 12 and under, 14 and under, 16 and under, and 18 and under players from all around the world. This prestigious tournament has seen participation from many tennis stars during their rise to fame, including Justine Henin-Hardenne, Kim Clijsters, Chris Evert, Andre Agassi, Jim Courier, Anna Kournikova and Monica Seles.

'Andy knew all about the famous players who had played in the tournament before him and was really up for the challenge, so we went out there four or five weeks early to prepare. It was just the two of us, and we started our preparation at the Harry Hopman Academy at the Saddlebrook Tennis Center in Florida.

'In addition to being one of America's largest tennis centres, the complex had 36 holes of Arnold Palmer-designed championship golf, a massive 500,000 gallon swimming pool, and a sports village with fitness centre and luxury spa. We didn't have too much time for enjoying ourselves, but it was an amazing place for us to visit.

'We both found out about Harry Hopman, the man the centre is named after. He was the most successful of all Davis Cup captains, leading Australia to 16 cups between 1939 and 1967. His main emphasis was on improving the fitness of his players, and he inspired some of the greatest Aussie men of the era, including Frank Sedgman, Lew Hoad, Ken Rosewall, Neale Fraser, Roy Emerson, Rod Laver, John Newcombe, Fred Stolle and Tony Roche.

'He emigrated to the US in 1969 and become a highly successful teaching pro, counselling such champions to be as Vitas Gerulaitis and John McEnroe at the Port Washington (NY) Tennis Academy.

'The facilities at the tennis academy were second to none, and Andy became very interested in Hopman and the players he had helped during his tennis career. I was also gaining lots of experience as we mixed with the coaches at the Hopman Academy and members of the Lawn Tennis Association who had come out with other players to try and qualify for the Orange Bowl.

'Some of the best help with Andy early on came from Olga Morozova. Olga is a retired Russian professional tennis player who was runner-up in the women's singles at Wimbledon and Roland Garros in 1974. On both occasions, she was defeated by Chris Evert, who was at the peak of her powers at the time.

'She was the first Russian tennis player to win a grand-slam title – doubles at Roland Garros in 1974 with Chris Evert – and to reach a grand-slam final – mixed doubles in Wimbledon in 1968. She has coached some fine players, such as Elena Dementieva. With that pedigree, it was no surprise she helped us a lot.

'Another guy who gave us invaluable help was Andrew Lewandowski, who was in charge of the Great Britain Under-12 national squad, and he was incredibly supportive.

'Andy was head and shoulders above everybody else in all of the tournaments he played in the Miami area, and he was one of the favourites going into the Orange Bowl, in December 1999. I remember the tournament and the way Andy played as if it were yesterday. He was magnificent and played great tennis throughout. When he hit the winning shot in the final, I jumped for joy.

'Now I know I said Andy had something special about him as a tennis player and was number one in his age group, but that is no guarantee to long-term success. Looking back at the Orange Bowl that he won, nobody in that Under-12 tournament apart from him made the breakthrough to the senior ranks, which is an indication of how hard it is to achieve what he has achieved.

'If you look through the record books, it is the players who come through at 14, 15 and 16 who usually manage to make the step up to the senior ranks. Andy, on the other hand, had been one of the best players in the world since he was nine years old. That is a young age to start being at the top of any sport. The fact he kept winning through every age group he played in showed his competitiveness. He never let things slip.

'As time progressed and we got into a routine and Andy continued to be successful, I was quite tough on him. There was no pussyfooting around just because he was the brightest young player in Britain. I like to think my attitude earned his respect as it was obvious I cared about his tennis and wanted him to do well.

'The trip to the Orange Bowl was one of many we made together, and whether it was because it was our first overseas trip or because Andy won it, it turned out to be one of the best. Another reason was the fact that there were other players from Britain in Florida at the time, so, at night, we could all go out together for a meal which meant we had other people to interact with. That wasn't always the case on the junior tour.

'As anybody will tell you, it's not an easy life being a coach to a teenage tennis player who is amongst the best in the world. Because he was so good, it meant he needed to travel a lot to find tougher opponents to keep his competitive edge, and he was playing in tournaments all over Europe. When he was eleven and twelve, it meant we were away ten to twelve weeks a year. When we were in Britain, we would be travelling down to England to national events every second weekend.

'At times, we were living in each other's pockets, and we spent a lot of time in railway stations, in cars and at airports. It was a tough time for Andy, being away from home, but I like to think I made things a bit easier for him. Throughout it all, I never once thought he would get disillusioned and stop playing tennis.

'A good example of his early dedication came when Glasgow Rangers were watching Andy's youth football team and wanted him to sign for them just before his 13th birthday. It must have been tempting for Andy as he loved the sport. As I said earlier, Andy was a great footballer and would have made it in the game. He never flinched in the tackle, and we were all worried he would injure himself and be unable to play tennis. Andy realised that himself and cut back on his time playing football but still enjoyed the game and usually played in a team which was made up of his school friends. Suffice to say, he turned down the offer to sign for Rangers.

'The final straw in terms of his football career came when he turned his ankle during a match after a bad tackle, the day before he was due to go to Florida for a four-week training camp at the Harry Hopman Academy in Saddlebrook, a place he had enjoyed so much when he went there to play in the Orange Bowl in 1999. He was hugely disappointed, because the injury meant he couldn't go. That incident affected him a lot, and he told us he was not going to play football seriously any more as he didn't want to risk any future injuries. Andy made that decision, nobody else, and his decision to play tennis rather than football has certainly paid dividends.

'What many people forget is that although Andy was doing well on the junior circuit, his brother Jamie was a better player than him around that time. He was a year older than Andy and almost won the Orange Bowl in Miami the year before Andy did, only losing in a tie-break in the final set.

'Jamie had won major European Under-12 and Under-13 events, but just after that, Andy improved beyond all recognition. When Andy won the British Under-14 title at age 13, he was moving ahead of his brother and most other players in the world, let alone Europe.

'It was around this time that Jamie moved down south to a LTA training school, and Andy believes that the coaching he got there ruined him for a couple of years. Andy felt that as a developing tennis player you need continuity throughout your work. You have so many areas to work on – the physical side of your game, your tactical plan, your shot selection – that you must be consistent and not get too many different messages from too many different people.

'Looking back, I think Andy believed that having one-to-one coaching from me and with Judy adding in her ideas, was just about right compared to Jamie, who got lots of different advice from different people at the LTA school. Jamie is still a great player and is fast becoming a doubles specialist.

'Despite the fact I was young and coaching one of the world's top junior players, I like to think there were no airs or graces about me. I had no ego, so I had no problems about calling on people who I respected in the game for their advice. I always had Andy's best interests at heart. There were a whole raft of people we contacted and places we went to visit to try and improve Andy's game through the years. I remember when he was 14 we went down and stayed at Peter McNamara's house in London. He had been a world top ten player in 1981–82, won the doubles title with Paul McNamee at Wimbledon twice and was a respected coach.

'When we went to see him, he was working with fellow Australian Mark Philippoussis. Philippoussis was injured at the time, and Peter was very accommodating. He spent a few days on court with Andy and myself, and that time was very beneficial for us.

'We also went to Paris to train with Bob Brett at his academy near Paris. He is one of the most respected coaches in the sport. We wanted to see if there was anything missing in Andy's development, and Bob gave us pointers on how to improve.

'At that time, the LTA was helping us, and, fortunately, I was a full-time salaried member of their staff through Tennis Scotland, which meant I could travel with Andy despite the fact it was still expensive and everybody had to be committed to the cause.

'Although Andy had great raw talent, we had to refine his play. At a young age, we identified what Andy's strengths were, and, to be fair, they were pretty obvious to anybody who knew tennis. His court craft was magnificent, he had excellent anticipation, great reaction skills and superb tactical awareness, which is the attribute that Andy will tell you is his best.

'He did not have any real, big weaknesses. When he was younger, his serve was probably the weakest part of his game but still wasn't too bad. Because he was so competitive and knew he could beat nearly anybody in his age group, he wanted to just roll the first serve in and make sure he could get into the point, knowing that he could win it. In other words, he was not taking any risks with his first serve.

'He was building a solid game and would not make any unforced errors. He was very solid from the back of the court, and his drop-shots were unbelievable, as they are now. I used to keep detailed records of his game, and I still have a chart at home which illustrates how he played 36 drop-shots in one match. He always had this variation and flair in his game.

'The year after he won the Orange Bowl, he went back and played in the Under-14 tournament. He won the warm-up competition called the Prince Cup, which was a big achievement as everybody plays in that before the Orange Bowl. It is almost like what Sydney is to the Australian Open or the Stella Artois tournament at Queen's Club is to Wimbledon. His win at the Prince Cup showed he was progressing along the right lines, but, unfortunately, he lost in the last 16 in the Orange Bowl. However, we saw enough to realise he was developing well, and the defeat was not the end of the world.

'Physically he was not huge when he was in his early teens. He is very tall now, around 6 ft 1 in., but he was average then. What made up for that was the fact that he was tactically a lot smarter than everybody else. Maybe the guys who were a year older were a little bit ahead of him physically and could beat him on power, but he could always hold his own on tactical awareness. He was smart.

'Around the age of fourteen, he was still winning every junior age group tournament going, mostly against players two years older than him. Nobody the same age as him could get close – he was that good. A year above him in the junior ranks you had people like his brother Jamie and Jamie Baker, and he was also competing with people two years above him, such as David Brewer. We were lucky in Scotland in that a lot of our older competitive players still played their tennis at home, and there was a competitive environment in place, so the juniors all had older players to take on, which is always good for their development.

'Our best home-based players trained at Stirling University, which meant we could tap into their expertise and get lots of practice with the guys on tennis scholarships. It was a big help for Andy taking on bigger, older and stronger players.

'Our next big test was at the world Under-14 championships at Tarbes near the Pyrenees. It is a big event which Matthew Smith, another British player, had won in the past. Eurosport, the television channel, covered the event, and the final was played in front of a capacity crowd of around 2,000 people. It was a big occasion, and playing there was a good experience for Andy. He made it all the way to the final, where he lost after having had a match point. I remember that point very clearly. His opponent hit a passing shot, it clipped the top of the tape and Andy just missed an open-court reaction volley. The guy he lost in the final to was the Russian Alexander Krasnorutsky, who has yet to make the breakthrough.

'People ask me why Andy, who is very single-minded, is such a good team player when it comes to Davis Cup. In answer to that I usually mention his time as a footballer and also take them back to the time when there was an Under-14 and Under-16 Summer and Winter Cup in place, which were international team competitions for juniors. Andy thrived in both competitions, and he took that team player attitude into the Davis Cup when he reached senior level.

'We tried to get Andy to peak for the key junior worldwide events, like the junior grand slams, but he also enjoyed playing domestic tournaments in Britain, which we encouraged him to do because he used to win them all. Winners like Andy like a challenge and always try to keep improving themselves, but they also like to win, and we wanted to keep him in that habit.

'Those who work with teenage tennis players will tell you that the crucial time is around 14 and 15 years of age, as that is when you try and help them make the transition from junior to men's tennis. With that in mind, we brought in some more adult players to play against Andy to push him harder whenever he was at home in the United Kingdom and travelled overseas a lot more when he was 14 to ensure he kept playing good opponents. Moving up the junior ladder, he played on the European Under-16 tour, where there were some tough events, and we seemed to be in Italy a lot around that time, where there were tournaments for three or four weeks.

'Throughout this period, Dunblane High School was excellent and we had a great relationship with the teachers who helped Andy a lot with his tennis career. I would sign a form to take him out and bring him back with a provision he kept up his school work.

'From the age of 11 to 15, I would pick him up every day from secondary school in the morning, maybe around 8.30 a.m. and take him back around 11 a.m. It was easier to get a court during the day, and we had some good practice sessions in the mornings.

'He was always on a bit of a downer on his way back to school, and I had to convince him to go in, but he was fine once he was back with his friends. He was on a downer not because he didn't like going to school but because he was passionate about tennis and focused on what he wanted to do with his life. I would also see him in the evening and take him to the courts at Stirling University for training.

'What Andy and I really enjoyed was travelling with other British players and their coaches to tour events, and we had a lot of fun on such trips. In 2002, just before Andy's 15th birthday, we went to Spain to check out the Sánchez-Casal Academy in Barcelona, which had just opened.

'I travelled there with Andy, Jamie and two other top Scottish players, Graeme Hood and David Culshaw. The guys loved the place with all the immaculate clay courts and the great weather. Players ranked from 200 to 800 trained there on a regular basis, and that was the perfect sort of opponent that top juniors like Andy were looking for. I knew that when the time came for Andy to move on and get more tuition to improve his game, the Sánchez-Casal Academy would be near the top of his list.

'He was running out of opponents to run him close, and it was no surprise to me that he chose the Sánchez-Casal Academy as his base. Judy agreed with the move, and Andy did his homework on the matter, talking to Spanish players he respected, such as Rafael Nadal, before making his decision. When he moved there, he was coached well as part of a group. He was put in with some older players for training, and his game came on a lot.

'He was very happy there, living with a family in Barcelona before moving into accommodation at the tennis academy. I used to go across for, say, a week at a time to help him with his coaching, as he didn't really get individual tuition there. That meant he benefited from group coaching from the academy staff and also my input as well. In other words, he was getting the best of both worlds.

'Things were going great for Andy in the summer of 2003, and he had got to the last 16 of the French Open juniors, beating Gael Monfils, another top junior, on the way. In the summer, he beat Wesley Moodie in a Challenger at Manchester, only a few weeks after the South African had reached the fourth round at Wimbledon. He then went on to win the Canadian Open junior title, which is the warm-up event for the US Open, where he also did well, losing in the quarter-finals.

'He was very pleased with his form, as we all were, but in the autumn of 2003, when he was playing in a Futures event on the island of Gran Canaria, he faced a major setback. I remember the day very well. He had been complaining for a while about a sore right knee, and during that tournament it got worse.

'We withdrew from the competition and flew straight back to Britain, as his knee was becoming more and more inflamed. He had a scan immediately when he got back. The news we were given wasn't what we expected but explained a lot.

'It turned out that Andy was born with a bipartite patella. That is a condition where the patella is composed of the main bone but has a second piece of bone connected to it by fibrous or cartilage tissue. Bipartite patella occurs in about 1 per cent of the population, and it affects men more than women. The most common symptom is discomfort or pain, especially when standing up from a sitting position or playing sports that require jumping. It is usually diagnosed when a patient goes into the physician's office to get an X-ray for a knee injury, which is what happened in Andy's case. Andy was told to rest the knee and given stretching and strengthening exercises for the quadriceps and hamstrings.

'Despite knowing exactly what was wrong with him, we were really worried about his future career, as he lost about seven months. That time was tough for both of us. They initially said it would take eight to twelve weeks to heal, but that timescale was extended.

'Andy was still growing, so we were never going to go down the surgical route. We wanted to let the injury heal naturally. We did a lot of strengthening exercises, and it was tough for him not being able to play tennis.

'During that time, we got into a routine, and I tried to keep him interested in his rehabilitation programme. We did a lot of gym work and based ourselves at Stirling University, which was good because Andy was able to work with a lot of different athletes, like top swimmers, runners and rowers. Some of them were coming back from injury as well, so he was not alone.

'We worked a lot on the bench press. To start with, he could do 50 kilos, but he got that up to 90 kilos, which helped with his serve in future years, as it built up his upper-body strength. Before that time in the gym, and Andy will admit this, he was not one for doing a lot of physical work. He was hugely talented on court and was winning anyway. He was naturally fast and his reaction skills were sharp. However, once he started in senior tennis, he realised that all the gym work he put in as a junior had paid dividends, because he was strong enough to deal with the sheer power of other players. That spell at Stirling University when he was recuperating helped him, and now he is a lot better in the gym and goes in and does his work.

'Throughout his time out, he was desperate to get back and play tennis. It got to the stage that we tried many, many different things on court to keep him interested and to get him back working on his tennis game. For instance, we even used a sports wheelchair so he would be mobile on the court, and he used to whiz around with a racket in his hand. When his right leg got a bit better, we did one leg tennis: he would put no pressure on his right leg and just hop on his left leg, hitting the ball when he could.

'You could see how much being out was hurting him, but such was his dedication, I knew he was never going to pack it in, even during the dark days when we used to go to the doctor and kept being told bad news in terms of the time it was taking the injury to heal.

'To fill out the time, we played a lot of snooker and used to eat in the same restaurant in the town of Bridge of Allan called Clive

Ramsay's. It got to the stage that we were the best customers in the place.

'We both put a brave face on things, but there were really some black moments. There were three or four times when we thought that it would be a case of going in to the doctors and simply getting the all clear. Unfortunately, we would go in and they would say they were sorry but it would be another month before he could play again. Andy would be absolutely gutted. I would take him away and try and cheer him up, and we would go back to playing snooker.

'With no tennis to be competitive about, he started to get pretty good at snooker. We were playing so much that we even went out one day and bought a couple of cues to make us look more professional.

'It was around that time, because he had so much time to kill, that Andy became really interested in boxing. I bought him some boxing gloves and a head set for his Christmas in 2004. He loves the sport and has got a couple of friends who are boxers, such as Alex Arthur and Amir Khan. His hero was always Muhammad Ali, and he also likes Ricky Hatton and used to watch a lot of his fights. Boxing gave him something away from tennis to keep his mind focused.

'When the doctors finally gave Andy the all-clear, we were both delighted. He had been magnificent throughout his injury, never giving up, and he had the self-belief to realise he was good enough to bounce back. I also realised that the good times would return.

'Looking back, spending each day with him during his injury was a test of character for us both. You have to give everything when you are the coach of an injured player, and it is a selfless job. Not getting the chance to watch him compete was difficult, but we got to know each other better and certainly improved our snooker game during that time, that's for sure.

'We didn't rush him back to action. Slowly it became clear things were getting better, and his right knee was strong enough for him to play again and give his all. He had such a good year before his injury, we thought he could maybe get a wildcard to Wimbledon in 2004. I was on the phone a lot to Mark Petchey at the Lawn Tennis Association, saying he was coming back and might have a chance of playing Wimbledon, and we tried to stay as positive as possible.

'We trained hard to get him ready for the grass-court season. Getting him back to peak fitness was our goal. We worked on strengthening his right leg and worked a lot at Stirling University before we moved to London to prepare for the grass-court tournaments.

'The summer of 2004, looking back, was a good laugh for both of us. We shared a room together in the Chelsea Village Hotel for sixty days straight, and then we got a week off before spending four weeks together on the Spanish Futures Circuit. It was a real case of us living in each other's pockets.

'We didn't have enough money to pay for two separate rooms at Chelsea Village, and we had two single beds in the most untidy room in the world. At least Andy's side was. He had his PlayStation with him, and the only time we argued was when he kept beating me on it all the time.

'It must be a world record: 60 days sharing a room with another bloke and not wanting to strangle each other at the end of it. The fact that spending that amount of time together didn't drive us mad means our friendship can survive anything.

'During our 60 days in the Chelsea Village Hotel, we had about 50 meals at Pizza Express, with Andy ordering the same food every night. I managed to persuade him to always have a salad and some protein, so he had the chicken pizza with a side salad and garlic bread. He also had to have two helpings of Pizza Express salad dressing. He was very fussy about his food, and the garlic bread couldn't come separately from his pizza and salad. Everything had to come all at once.

'The first tournament he played in after coming back from injury was a Challenger at Surbiton, but in his first round match, he pulled a muscle in his hip when 3–1 up. If he had managed to get through that match and stayed fit, he would have received a wildcard for Wimbledon, I'm sure of it. He could not play the following tournament, which was the Nottingham ATP event, because he had to rest, and the wildcard for Wimbledon did not materialise. We had to wait another two weeks to get back to full fitness and took up the option of wildcards to Challenger tournaments in Manchester and Nottingham. Andy did OK and made the second round in both tournaments. At least he was back on court.

'To be honest, both of us knew grass was not the best surface to work on after his serious injury. The change of direction is never very easy to cope with and players can get injured. In hindsight, maybe we should have left the grass-court season out altogether and just extended his rehabilitation period, but it was clear Andy was desperate to get back playing. I agreed with the decision to get him back to competitive tennis as soon as possible. Maybe other players would have had the patience to wait, but when you have someone like Andy, who lives for competing, it was always going to be difficult to stop him coming back.

'After a few games on grass and a bit more training, we went to Spain to get Andy more competitive matches on the Spanish Futures Circuit as the tournaments there are renowned for their high standard of play. Carlos Moya, Rafael Nadal and Juan Carlos Ferrero are just three of the Spanish players who have benefited from playing over there. Summer in Spain is unbelievably hot, and even in first round games, Andy would be on court for two and a half to three hours. The quality of the opposition was very high.

'Playing at the Spanish Futures events turned out to be a great learning experience. They were really tough events, but Andy did well. He played his first tournament in Xativa and won. To be back on clay and building up his game was great, and he had a fantastic week. He picked up 15 ATP points because of the win, and his confidence started to come back. It showed his strength of character that he could bounce back so well, and as well as winning in Xativa, he also won tournaments at Orense and Pontevedra.

'He loved Spain so much and our time there was such a success that when that he chose the Sánchez-Casal Academy in Barcelona to work from full time without me, you couldn't fault his thinking.

'I think the two of us had run our course, although we had lots of great times travelling together. As I look back over the six years we spent together, there were lots of highs and very few lows. For a coach to spend six or seven years with the one player is quite unheard of. We started working together when he was 11 and finished when he was 17. It was a very important period in Andy's tennis life, and I like to think I helped him.

'After me, he travelled with Pato Álvarez, the Colombian coach who he met at the Sánchez-Casal Academy. Álvarez was past retirement age when they started travelling together, and they didn't last too long. The age difference may have been a problem.

'Looking back, there is only one thing I would have done differently when I was travelling with Andy. Maybe it would have been better if we could have had one other player around his own age travelling with him for company instead of just me. That is because I think Andy enjoys a social environment and why he liked the Sánchez-Casal Academy so much. People from all over Europe attended the academy and not all of them were great tennis players like Andy. A lot of the students came from Britain, and Andy liked to socialise with them because they weren't so focused on tennis as he was. This meant that the chat varied, and he was able to take his mind off the game and unwind a bit.

'Going from me, who was relatively young, to Álvarez, who was old, was a big jump for Andy and a difficult move. He then went on to work with Mark Petchey, whom he had got to know when Petchey was manager of men's national training at the LTA, and seemed to strike up a good working relationship with him.

'Mark is a funny guy with a good sense of humour, and Andy would have appreciated that. He also played at the top level, which is something I didn't do. I could never tell Andy what it was like playing ATP tennis at the highest level, and Mark could at least pass on his experiences to him.

'Mark also does tennis commentary for Sky TV so was in touch with every player Andy came up against. All Andy needed to do was pick up the phone and ask Petchey about his opponent, although, in saying that, Andy's knowledge of tennis is so great, he wouldn't have needed much briefing.

'Some people may ask what I think I helped Andy achieve and how big a part I think I played in his tennis development. Now that is a difficult question, as his mum Judy is a brilliant coach and put everything in place before I came along. Also, you can't ignore Andy's natural talent. He was born to be a winner and a great tennis player and would have been a success whether I came along or not.

'He needed encouragement, guidance and direction, and I like to think I gave him that, along with Judy. Andy is a fiery character, and I had to work hard with him, otherwise he would not have practised enough or wanted to get on court, because his natural talent took him a long way. Despite his talent, he would not have got away with just practising for an hour on court – he needed to put in the extra hours. We had to find ways of getting him motivated and staying on court longer. He enjoyed doing things like speed work and sprints, and it was my job to identify what he enjoyed doing and how to make practice sessions effective and fun. Motivation is such a huge thing for somebody of Andy's age. He could easily have won at junior level without practising much, but he needed to put the hours in to help him at senior level, and all his hard work is now paying off.

'I have already mentioned the role Judy played in helping Andy, but his brother Jamie was also a huge help. He has been fantastic. A lot of people may have thought that there would be sibling rivalry, particularly as Jamie is a tennis player as well and was better than Andy early on, but they could not have been more wrong. Jamie has been the most supportive guy around for Andy. When Andy was injured, I took Jamie to tournaments, and I found him to be an intelligent young man with a bright future.

'As for Judy, what can you say? She has been a massive help to Andy, Jamie, me and countless tennis players in Scotland. She did all the groundwork for Andy's success and also paved the way for many other players.

'I am certainly not surprised by Andy's success. From that first coaching session in Stirling to our trip to the USA for the Orange Bowl, I could tell he was special.

'Andy does not like or know how to lose. He never puts in a sloppy performance and will hardly ever lose in the first round of a competition. He has come a long way, and it is a privilege for me to have been part of his success story.'

3

A PRODIGY AMONGST PRODIGIES

IN THE PRESS CONFERENCE AFTER WINNING THE US OPEN JUNIOR TITLE IN September 2004, Andy Murray was asked how determined he was to make a go of being a professional player. He gave an answer imbued with so much self-belief that it brooked no argument from anyone in the room. 'I hate losing,' he said. 'I don't play any tournaments to come second best. So I think for me, when I go into a tournament, I want to win every single match. I believe that I can go right to the top.'

He was right to be confident about his future, according to Luca Santilli, the International Tennis Federation's (ITF) Manager of Junior and Senior Tennis. 'Winning a junior grand slam is a very good platform, because if you look back at the roll of honour for the best junior players, you see lots of names that went on to succeed in the pros,' says Santilli. 'What was good about Murray is that he won the

US Open when he was 17, which is so much more difficult. The girls mature early, but for boys it's a very big thing, and it creates a lot of opportunities. I think the confidence that it gives to an individual from winning a junior grand slam, especially before they are expected to, is definitely going to help with the daily challenges of international tennis.'

Success in tennis never comes overnight, though – even to teenagers – and by the time the world began to take notice of Murray, he was already a veteran of the ITF's junior circuit, a facsimile of the pro-tour designed to prepare players mentally, physically and emotionally for life as a professional tennis player. It's where the likes of Roger Federer, Stefan Edberg, Andy Roddick, Ivan Lendl, Martina Hingis and Amelie Mauresmo learned their trade, as well as countless others who found it too tough and thus saw their dreams wither and die before most of their contemporaries had even graduated from high school.

'It mirrors the pro-tour in nearly every way,' says Santilli. 'We have a world ranking, a code of conduct, big events – including the junior grand slams – and smaller events which attract good crowds and a lot of media attention. At junior events, players know that they are going to be visible. They know that there are going to be agents and sponsors around, and for many of the players, being a top junior in their country leads to wildcards from their national association. It's a way of showing their talent and creating an opportunity for themselves. It's a safe environment to compete and grow and learn. In Andy's case, ITF junior tennis was very important, because it gave him lots of opportunities, and the fact that when he won the US Open he had already played three years of junior grand slams meant that he was already quite used to the big arenas and being around the professional players.'

Murray's first opportunity to shine came in December 1999 when he was 12 years old at the Orange Bowl tournament in Florida, a prestigious event renowned for unearthing future stars. A pugnacious youngster named Andy Roddick won the prestigious 18-and-under trophy that year, joining an honour roll that reads like a roster of tennis greats past and present, including the likes of Guy Forget, Jim Courier, Roger Federer, and the man the Swiss maestro beat in the 2006 Australian Open final, Marcos Baghdatis.

While one Andy was winning the Orange Bowl at 18-and-under level, another one – raised in a small town on the southern edge of Perthshire, Scotland, rather than in Boca Raton, Florida, like Roddick – was winning the 12-and-under boys' title. Murray, whose brother Jamie had reached the final the previous year, beat Tomas Piskacek of the Czech Republic 6–4, 6–1, making him only the second Briton ever to win an Orange Bowl title. The first was Jamie Delgado, who won the 14-and-under title, in 1991.

Winning an Orange Bowl title, even in the youngest age group, gets you noticed, and while it would be two years before he would begin travelling and playing regularly on the ITF's junior circuit, it got his tennis career off to an auspicious start.

Murray played his first ITF junior circuit event in Bergheim, Austria, as a shy and callow 14 year old in January 2002. Although Bergheim marked his junior debut, he had already dipped his toes into the choppy waters of the professional game by playing in qualifying competitions at UK tournaments on the ITF's Futures circuit, the first rung of the professional game where the total prize money for the whole tournament is never more than $15,000 (prize money in tennis is usually counted in US dollars to avoid confusion between currencies) – a hundred dollars less than you get for losing in the first round of Wimbledon.

British tournaments, be they at junior or senior level, are partly financed by the LTA in the hope of giving its developing players a chance to leave the practice court and learn to play competitive matches. The junior circuit, because it's supported by the ITF, is also far cheaper to play on than the pro-tour. Hotel rooms are subsidised by the tournaments and meals are provided on-site, which can make a big difference to families struggling to afford to finance the burgeoning careers of their talented offspring. There might not be any prize money in junior tennis, but given that it costs, on average, £1,000 to fund one player for a week at a Futures event, a free hotel room can go a long way.

Having lost his first match against Matthew Smith in Glasgow, Murray did well to win a match at his second attempt and earn his first ranking points on the pro-tour by beating a then 19 year old from Taunton called Chris Lister, 7–5, 6–1, in the second round of a Futures tournament in Edinburgh. Like most juniors, Murray would go on to sprinkle pro-events into his schedule to test himself against older, more experienced players, but for three years from the start of 2002, he would spend most of his time travelling with his coach Leon Smith, his older brother and his mum, pitching himself against his peers and learning his trade alongside hundreds of other teenage hopefuls from around the world.

Jamie's presence alongside Andy in the juniors and Futures was undoubtedly a help both on and off the court. For one thing, it allowed Judy to travel with both her sons and keep the family together, albeit in an increasingly nomadic existence, and the brothers' close relationship also helped combat the loneliness that many fledgling players suffer from as they trawl from airport to airport and tournament to tournament. However, it wasn't an easy or luxurious life for any of them, and they ended up staying in a variety of digs in hospitals, nurses' quarters, boarding schools as well as in an array of dodgy hotels around the world.

One insider, who was around the junior circuit when the Murrays first began to travel, remembers Andy as the quieter, more reticent of the two brothers: 'Jamie is just naturally more open and outgoing, whereas Andy always seemed a bit shyer, especially at that age. It really helped him to have Jamie to hide behind a little bit. They were always together, and it was Jamie who made friends and spoke to everyone, while Andy often hung back and let his brother do the talking. He was definitely the quiet one, at least until he got to know people. He made friends OK, but it would have been interesting to have seen how he would have managed without Jamie around because he might have had to become a lot more extrovert. I think Jamie was the one who chatted up the girls for the both of them.'

The ITF places great emphasis on helping players develop the peculiar social skills needed to travel with strangers, most of whom don't speak English as a first language. For this reason, almost all junior tournaments have at least one social function where they can get to know each other, albeit in a chaperoned environment to limit the high jinks that inevitably arise when you place teenage boys and girls together away from home.

'It's not just about what's happening on court, it's about the whole lifestyle of a tennis player. It's not easy to travel on the professional circuit – often they have to learn other languages, stay in hotels a long way from home – and the juniors is a good way to see if they like it or not,' says Luca Santilli.

'For me, success in juniors was as much about developing friendships as it was about developing my game,' says Roddick, who was junior World No. 1 in 2000 and won both the junior Australian Open and US Open titles that year. 'I enjoyed being around kids from around the world who understood and shared the commitment to becoming great at something. It helped that every tournament had a party for us; it was like having a homecoming dance or prom a dozen times a year.'

As well as his big brother, Murray could also rely on the company of older Britons, such as fellow Scot David Brewer, who was two years older, and Derbyshire-born Tom Rushby, who was in his early days on the junior circuit. Rushby was born a year earlier than Murray and made it to 22 in the junior rankings, largely as a result of his success in doubles. (The ITF junior rankings are combined to reflect singles and doubles success as it encourages players to play both forms of the game; this is especially important because doubles is viewed by many coaches as the perfect way to develop net play and tactical awareness.)

Success in junior tennis, particularly amongst the boys, is often dictated by who grows fastest and furthest, and for a skinny 14 year old (as Murray was when he first began playing in the juniors), having a bigger, stronger doubles partner and hitting opponent is an advantage. While he would form a successful partnership on the court with his brother, it was with Rushby that Andy enjoyed his first triumph on the circuit and, impressively, in the very first junior event he played.

Murray lost in the singles in Bergheim in the second round, having notched his first match victory in juniors against Austrian Philipp Hammerle, but he and Rushby cut a swathe through the doubles draw, not dropping a set until they got to the final against the 18-year-old Czechs Jiri Linha and Vaclav Vana, whom they beat 4–6, 6–3, 6–2.

There was another significant moment for Murray later that year, when he was given a wildcard into the pre-qualifying rounds of Wimbledon. Pre-qualifying, as the name suggests, is a play-off to decide which players enter the qualifying competition for a place in the main draw of the Championships themselves and is held in the unprepossessing surroundings of halls of residence of the Roehampton Institute in south-west London, a good couple of miles from the All England Club itself. A few weeks past his fifteenth birthday, Murray managed to win his first pre-qualifying match against Englishman Tom Pocock to get his Wimbledon career under way, before losing to another Englishman, Jonathan Marray, all without going anywhere near the All England Club itself.

His first-ever competitive outing at the hallowed ground in SW19 came in July 2002, which also marked Murray's first junior grand slam match, an edgy 6–7, 6–4, 4–6 defeat to Belarussian Alexander Skrypko.

'I was actually very excited,' Murray remembered later, 'but after the match, I couldn't remember one point I'd played, I was so nervous. I didn't think what I was doing on court at all.'

Murray reached another milestone in juniors a month later when he won his first title, a grade five event in Nottingham (the lowest rung of the junior circuit, which has Grades one to five, then Grade C for teams, Grade B for individuals and Grade A, which is composed of the four junior grand slams). Murray didn't drop a set all week, and his run included victory over Andrew Kennaugh, with whom he had won the doubles title at the Scottish Junior International Championships on clay a few weeks earlier. Murray also won the doubles in Nottingham, this time partnering another Scot and friend, Jamie Baker.

Murray's second junior singles title – and his first overseas – came in October of that year in Andorra, where he also won the doubles, this time with an Armenian partner, Ara Harutyunyan. In January 2003, he won his first Grade One junior singles title in Colombia, while he was becoming increasingly accomplished in doubles, winning titles in Peru and Bolivia with Rushby before joining up with Venezuelan Daniel Vallverdu to win four tournaments back to back in Italy in April and May, during a purple patch in which Murray also won the singles title in Citta de Prato. The more rigorous training regime and increasingly intense competition he was getting during his punishing practice sessions at the Sánchez-Casal Academy, where, by now, he was largely based, were beginning to pay off.

In between training periods in Spain, Andy spent time in Scotland as part of a group of young Scots put together by Judy, who at that time was national coach for Scotland. The group, which included

Andy and his brother Jamie, Jamie Baker and Keith Meisner, would often train at the Scottish National Training Centre in Stirling, a facility which hardly appeared to offer fertile ground for future champions. Stuart Bathgate, Chief Sports Writer for *The Scotsman*, visited the centre and reported that one of the group's morning training sessions had been cancelled because the Scottish Rugby Union had booked the courts. Bathgate quoted Judy extensively, in remarks which must have made uncomfortable reading for her paymasters at the LTA in London: 'We have no designated court of our own, and the national centre doesn't belong to us in any shape or form. At the moment, we are beholden to the LTA, with a little bit of money from sportscotland. There's me and two other coaches for the whole of Scotland – that's from the Under-10s right through to the seniors. Once kids get to a certain level, we're losing them all the time. What I really need is more people to help me and more people to believe.'

That said, it didn't appear to be holding her youngest son back, and by the time the Wimbledon junior tournament came around again in June, Murray was seeded tenth and already starting to attract the attention of a press room hungry for British interest to augment the annual diet of Henmania. It was Murray's first tiny taste of the pressure that Henman had endured for a decade, and the 16 year old struggled to cope with being expected to win every match he played at his home grand slam, even in the juniors, despite the fact that he trained on clay and hardcourts and was still learning to move and read the ball on grass. (Incidentally, those with an eye on the minutiae of British tennis history will record that Henman was, by his own admission, a mediocre junior and never actually won a singles match in the only year he played in the boys' singles competition at Wimbledon in 1992.)

Murray lost meekly in the first round to unheralded German Peter Steinberger, and Judy confided to friends afterwards that she felt he had succumbed to the pressure of the circumstances. He erased the disappointment of Wimbledon by returning home to Scotland to join up with Jamie Baker to win another doubles title at the clay-court Scottish Junior Championships, then won two rounds of the Manchester Challenger on grass, a men's event a rung up from the Futures tournaments he had previously played.

Three attempts to get matches at similarly testing men's events followed, before a successful return to the juniors followed at the Canadian Open. Murray won the title after a run which included notable wins over Jo-Wilfried Tsonga, who went on to win the US Open junior title later that month, and, in the final, Florin Mergea, who had just won Junior Wimbledon. Mergea got his revenge in the junior competition at Flushing Meadows, beating Murray 6–1, 7–5 to knock him out in the quarter-finals. Murray's time there would come.

In September, he enjoyed what was at that stage a career high when he won his first fully fledged men's event, a Futures tournament at the Scotstoun Leisure Centre in Glasgow. He became the youngest ever Briton to win a $10,000 event when he came through five matches against opponents aged between sixteen and twenty-eight, including the nineteen-year-old Belgian Steve Darcis, whom Murray outlasted 6–3, 3–6, 6–3 in the final. That range of ages is common on the lowest tier of men's tournaments, where those on their way up are frequently pitched against those on their way down – it's a place where boys, which is what Murray was at that stage, are expected to compete against men.

There are between 300 and 400 Futures events on the ITF Men's Circuit, which acts as a feeder for the ATP Challenger Circuit, which, in turn, acts as a feeder for the main ATP Tour. According to the ITF, as of the end of 2005, 98 of the world's top 100 men had previously participated in Futures or Satellites (tournaments in a league structure which are of a similar level of ability to Futures). Success at this, the least glamorous of all the layers of professional tennis, is as good a barometer as any of who is going to make it.

Murray played out the rest of autumn 2003 without matching his success in Glasgow, but he must have headed towards 2004 – his 17th year – full of hope for what lay ahead. Little did he realise that he would have to cope with an injury serious enough to threaten not just his ability to match his contemporaries but his entire future in tennis.

Knee problems are a familiar hindrance to anyone who plays the sport, be it the hobbling club player or pros like Steffi Graf, Serena Williams and Mark Philippoussis, the last of whom endured three knee operations and lost a third of the cartilage in the joint, at one stage contemplating life in a wheelchair. The bending, twisting and sudden changes of direction that tennis puts the body through are often felt first in the knees, so when Murray began to experience pain and inflammation in his right knee during the 2003 US Open, he must have put it down to little more than the usual aches and pains of a growing body.

He was due to head to Melbourne to compete in the Australian Open juniors in January 2004 – ironically, the same week when he reached his highest-ever world-junior ranking of No. 2 – but his knee had worsened, and over the Christmas break, an MRI scan at the Scottish Institute of Sport had revealed that he had a bipartite patella. In layman's terms, Murray was born with a kneecap in two parts, a relatively common condition which requires weeks of rest and, crucially, no tennis.

'I couldn't play at all. I wasn't allowed on the court,' Murray later recalled. 'It was quite difficult for me because I knew I'd been playing through it, and the physio told me it was OK to keep playing, and I'd done that for three months. Then I went to get my scan, and he said my kneecap was in tatters. I couldn't do anything for four or five months. It wasn't actually their fault because they told me what the problem was, and it was actually right what they said the first time. It's just I kept growing. I was playing on hard surfaces, so that was the real problem.'

Murray was initially told to rest for eight weeks and undergo an extensive rehabilitation programme, but the knee proved stubborn, and he was forced to sit out month after frustrating month – hell on earth for any active teenager, let alone one who lives and breathes tennis. It must have seemed like the end of the world, but such injuries are common to young tennis players whose growing bodies sometimes fail to cope with the strain being placed upon them. Tim Henman, for example, was diagnosed with a congenital problem which meant bits of bone floated in his elbow, keeping him out of tennis for almost a year – contemporaries recall a teenage Henman standing by the side of the court in tears as he watched his fellow players train.

As he nursed his wounded knee, Murray would have empathised, though there were some blessings, albeit heavily disguised, in being sidelined for so long. For one thing, the teenage tennis obsessive indulged his addiction by watching hours of matches on television, many of them with commentary by a certain Mark Petchey – a man whose opinions he came to value. As Petchey later said, with a smile, 'He listened to my commentary and thought I was talking at least half sense.'

A few weeks after coming back, Murray said, 'The injury helped a little bit because it made me a bit sharper mentally and physically stronger, especially in my upper body. I think when I was out injured, it made me mentally stronger, because before that, everything had been given to me – everything was really easy. But after that, obviously, it was really difficult to come back.'

The knee and the fact that he was still growing also affected his training regime. At times, he couldn't bend his right knee at all, and his use of weights was restricted to work on his upper body, but he also did some sessions with a sports psychologist who gave him breathing and positive-thinking techniques, both of which he was to employ to useful effect in later matches.

Murray was also allowed to travel with the Great Britain Davis Cup team for the first time, accompanying Tim Henman and company to Luxembourg, where he watched them defeat a Luxembourg squad spearheaded by Gilles Muller, another Sánchez-Casal Academy alumnus.

It proved to be a high point in a period which was both physically and mentally agonising. As the months dragged on, the knee would appear to get better only to flare up again, in an infuriating and increasingly worrying cycle. It seemed, at the time, to be a frightening portent for the rest of his career. Murray later said that he learned a lot from the experience, though it can't have been pleasant for him or those around him, especially those charged with the unenviable task of keeping his spirits up at a time when it appeared everything he had worked and dreamed of was being threatened by chronic injury.

By the time winter and spring 2004 were beginning to turn to summer, the knee had healed enough to allow him to test it on grass. He attempted a comeback at the Surbiton Challenger, the traditional grass-season appetiser, held in the first week of June but, as so often happens to athletes returning from a long lay-off, a subsidiary injury – a mild pain in his hip – struck to frustrate him further.

The hip problem healed enough for him to play the traditional junior Wimbledon warm-up event at Roehampton, where he exceeded even his own expectations by reaching the final and finishing runner-up to the then seemingly omnipotent Gael Monfils. 'We hoped he would get through a couple of rounds as it was his first tournament back, and I'm delighted at what he has done this week – he is still very competitive,' Judy told Henry Wancke from the LTA's official website.

A PRODIGY AMONGST PRODIGIES

In the season of 2004, Monfils was to the juniors what Roger Federer is to the men's tour today, and by the time he and Murray were seeded one and two respectively for junior Wimbledon, the French teenager had already won the first two junior grand slams of the year and all but sewn up the year-end junior world No. 1 ranking, even though it was only July. His presence in a junior draw was enough to wash away the self-belief of all but the most robustly confident players. Clearly, Murray, even at that pre-grand slam winning stage of his junior career, wasn't easily awed. Asked, while sitting in one of Wimbledon's interview rooms for the first time, whether Monfils was ahead of everyone else in the juniors, he struck a typically bullish note: 'I don't think so. I think, obviously, he's done really well, winning in Australia and the French. But last week I had a tight match with him, and he struggled through his match today. I beat him last year at the French Open 6–4, 6–1. So he is beatable. I just think it's a confidence thing – just him winning his matches.'

Murray went on to reach the third round that Wimbledon, a result which would ordinarily have irritated him but which he took in good heart, reasoning, rightly, that it was the most he could have expected after so long on the sidelines. He lost 7–5, 6–3 to Woong-Sun Jun of Korea to end his hopes of winning a first junior grand slam title on home soil. As it turned out, he would have to wait only a matter of weeks before the ultimate ambition of every junior player was to become a reality for him.

Monfils went on to win the junior Wimbledon title, beating surprise British finalist Miles Kasiri in the final.

After trying his hand, unsuccessfully, on grass again at post-Wimbledon Challenger events in Nottingham and Manchester, Murray returned to Spain in search of matches, anxious to practise the Sánchez-Casal mantra of spending hours on court until every movement and shot becomes automatic. No surface offers as many chances to strike the ball as clay, and after months of being unable to play, it was all the stir-crazy Murray wanted to do – anywhere, anytime.

One of the benefits of being based in mainland Europe was the number of Futures tournaments available to play in, and Murray duly entered four consecutive clay-court Futures events – three in Spain and one in Italy – going on something of a tear. He won the first in Xativa, made the semi-finals of the next in Vigo, went out in the second round in Irun, but atoned for that in Rome the following week by winning another title there. In total, 2004 was to see him bring home four Futures trophies – not a bad haul for a 17 year old still in the juniors.

Incidentally, during that run, Murray found himself playing 11 Spaniards in succession – a string only broken by Italian Marco Meneschincheri in the first round in Rome. It's a statistic which, if nothing else, offers an indication of the veritable production line of players that the Spanish system produces.

The clay-court odyssey proved to be the perfect antidote to all those months of frustration and worry over the painful knee. It also ensured that he was match sharp and full of confidence as he headed across the Atlantic to New York to play in the US Open juniors.

By the time Murray arrived at Flushing Meadows, the main event was nearly a week old, and Tim Henman was already busy turning it into a memorable event for British tennis. Henman had arrived in New York initially believing that he was free of the back pain which had plagued him all summer, only to be disabused of that notion when he went out to dinner and found himself suddenly unable to get up from the table because of back spasms. Henman had somehow hobbled through to the second week at Flushing Meadows for the first time in his career, with the help of a Long Island-based chiropractor, a spray of luck with the draw and a lot of determination.

As their respective tournaments wore on, Murray and Henman (who had met when Murray travelled with the Davis Cup team to Luxembourg the previous April) bonded as the last two Britons in the players' lounge. At the start of what was to become something of an unofficial mentoring programme, Henman provided advice and support before and after Murray's matches, partly because Henman's old friend and colleague Colin Beecher was travelling with the British juniors, thus providing an easy introduction. Murray, who is thirteen years Henman's junior, repaid his elder's friendliness in typically cheeky style by beating him on the electronic putting machine in the players' lounge – a galling loss for a proud three-handicap golfer like Henman.

'When it comes to the junior grand slams, being around the second week of a grand slam is a big thing for these players because they really do feel and live the atmosphere of a major event,' says Luca Santilli. 'They also often spend time on court with big players, and both Roger Federer and David Nalbandian regularly hit with juniors or use them to warm up with before big matches. There aren't many other players around to hit with during the second week of a grand slam, and because they've been juniors themselves and have played junior events, they feel comfortable with them.'

Federer agrees: 'I remember when I was on the junior circuit being really nervous of the older players, and it's a good way to break down the barriers.'

Juniors are apt to say that one of the best things about playing the junior grand-slam tournaments is the chance to be around the biggest names in the sport in the locker-room and players' lounge, and there is many a teenager who has tried to look nonchalant while Andy Roddick or Serena Williams sauntered past them. Murray certainly appreciated having Henman, one of the biggest names in the sport, treating him as a friend and even teaching him how to play backgammon. At the time, Murray said, 'It's been good to have Tim around to look up to, and he's really gone out of his way this week to be nice to me.'

Early on, Murray, who was seeded third, had more than Henman for company. Jamie Murray lost in the second round of the junior singles (as did Tom Rushby) but remained to play doubles, while Miles Kasiri (fresh from his run to the Wimbledon final a few weeks earlier) and Murray's good friend Jamie Baker made the third round.

Buoyed by his success amongst the grown-ups in Spain and Italy, Murray whipped through his first three rounds, polishing off, in succession, Juan-Martin Del Potro of Argentina, Vahid Mirzadeh of the USA and notoriously bumptious New Zealander William Ward – and all for the loss of just seven games in three matches. Even the hours of dismal, humid rain which fell on Wednesday and Thursday, which necessitated much sitting around before all the junior matches were moved to indoor courts nearby, failed to put him off his stride. History records that the first British junior US Open singles champion took his second and third steps towards history not at Flushing Meadows itself but in the inauspicious surroundings of the South Shore Indoor Tennis Center in the down-at-heel New York suburb of Queens.

In any other era of junior tennis, Murray's pre-season form and the way he ripped through his first three opponents would have made him favourite for the title, but there was only one teenager who bore that label – his good friend Monfils. Having won the first three grand slams of the year, the 18 year old was bidding to finish off his junior career in typically flamboyant style, by becoming the first boy since Stefan Edberg in 1983 to complete the grand slam by winning all four majors at that level.

'I'm not going to put pressure on myself to do what Edberg did,' said Monfils, speaking in his native French, after his first match in the junior US Open competition. 'Edberg is Edberg, I am Monfils.' He had good reason to be circumspect, because, in a peculiar quirk of fate given Murray's injury problems earlier that year, he had twisted his kneecap while practising after winning Wimbledon and had been out for six weeks. He only started hitting balls a week before the junior US Open began and was fortunate to start the tournament at all.

Like Murray, Monfils — a cheerful, extrovert character — found some hidden benefits in an enforced period of being a tennis spectator rather than a player. 'I couldn't play, but I spent a lot of time watching tennis on television, and it made me realise a lot,' he said. 'I learned a lot about what I need to do on the court to make myself a better player. I may not have had the match practice, but I was still improving my game.'

However, it was only a matter of time before Monfils paid for his lack of playing time, and he succumbed in the third round to little-known Serbian Viktor Troicki, indoors at the South Shore club. A few minutes after walking off court, Monfils was seen smashing his racket into pieces, and such was his fury and disappointment that it was a long time before anyone from his camp or Faye Andrews, the ITF Administrator then in charge of the juniors on-site, could go near him. His reaction was a reminder that the junior circuit replicates every aspect of the professional game, even down to the cloying pain of defeat.

In the wake of Monfils' defeat, Andreas Beck, the second seed from Germany, became nominal favourite, a position which was strengthened when Murray, who'd been largely flawless up to that point, suddenly began to look vulnerable. As one by one the other British players lost and went home, Murray's ability to win the title came under the closest scrutiny.

Against the tall Californian Sam Querry in the quarter-finals, Murray, by now back outdoors at Flushing Meadows, lost the first set 6–2 and was in severe danger of slumping out of the tournament before he found a way to get himself out of trouble. Afterwards, he was typically forthright in his assessment of what had gone wrong: 'I started off pretty poorly, and I was a bit sluggish and probably underestimated my opponent. I hadn't really seen him, and I didn't expect him to play as well as he did.' The dark edge of confidence is arrogance and Murray had allowed one to blur into the other. It nearly cost him. How different Murray's life and career might have turned out had Querry managed to make good on his lead. As it was, a break at the start of the second set was enough to keep the Scot on track. Sitting at one of the round tables in the players' lounge, taking not a blind bit of notice of Roger Federer and his team who were at an adjacent table, Murray continued, 'In the second set, I got into it a bit more, and I found his weakness and kept the ball high. Once I won the second set, I think mentally he was a bit gone, and he also got a bit tired, I think.

'It's important for me to have a tough match because I'd been winning pretty easily up until that point, and it's not always a good thing to have too many of those. Now I know what it's like to be in a tricky position. That could be useful going into the semis.'

As it was, Murray's 6–3, 6–2 win over the tall, left-handed German Mihail Zverev was a far easier match to handle, especially as Murray had beaten him soundly on a hardcourt a year earlier in what had been their only previous meeting. In fact, the small press conference afterwards proved to be a far more difficult proposition than Zverev had been. Sitting in one of the windowless, airless interview rooms in the bowels of the Arthur Ashe Stadium, Murray had to face not just a small smattering of British journalists, only some of whom he had met before, but also a well-respected American journalist intent on drawing parallels between Murray's links with Dunblane and the fact that that particular Saturday was the third anniversary of the 9/11 terrorist attacks on New York.

The anniversary had dominated television coverage in New York that morning, with hour upon hour of sombre remembrance, and it had been inescapable, even for a 17 year old trying to maintain the right mindset to play a big match in the Louis Armstrong Stadium, by far the biggest stage he had ever played on at that time. As ever, mention of

Dunblane provoked much shifting in seats, though the majority of the awkwardness came from the British hacks in the room rather than the teenager himself, who handled the American's somewhat insensitive line of questioning with eloquence and poise. Realising that their connection to Dunblane would always provoke questions about the tragedy, and acutely conscious of the fact that many of those who lost children are still living in the town and might be offended by discussion of it at something as frivolous as a tennis tournament, the Murrays had long formed a strategy of dealing with questions about it with a straight bat. Andy followed this strategy perfectly.

'I didn't realise what day it was until I switched on the TV this morning,' Murray told his inquisitor. 'I watched some of the coverage and the marches and when they read out the names of the people who died, and it was really sad, but when I saw people crying, I turned it off. I didn't want to feel like that when I walked on court. I don't remember much about what happened in Dunblane that day. What shook me the most was that I knew the guy who did the shooting. A lot of people at the school went to his boys' clubs, and then he came to the school and started shooting people . . .'

The less polished side of Andy's fledgling interview skills was also apparent in the same conversation when he had the Brits chuckling into their notebooks by blithely – and rightly – criticising the All England Club for the way it isolates the juniors and accommodates them in student digs in Roehampton instead of at a hotel like the other three grand slams. It was one of the first indicators to those present that here was a young player who wasn't inclined to toe the party line when he felt strongly about something.

'The US Open is my favourite grand slam just because of the way Wimbledon treats juniors – you all get put up at Roehampton, which is just a room with a bed and a desk in it and is nowhere near Wimbledon itself,' he said, in words that must have gone down a storm at SW19. 'Here you get to sit in the players' lounge and stay in a free hotel and see the players. The atmosphere is better here too, and the crowds support the underdog, not just their own player. At Wimbledon they are a bit boring.'

After winning his singles semi-final, Andy then joined Jamie to play their doubles semi-final against American top seeds Brendan Evans and Scott Oudsema. They lost, albeit narrowly, and it was up to Andy to keep up the family pride in the singles, where he was to face 18-year-old Ukrainian Sergiy Stakhovsky, seeded seventh for the tournament. Stakhovsky was a surprise winner over Andreas Beck in the other semi-final.

Meanwhile, that same Saturday afternoon, Henman's run was coming to an end in the semi-finals of the men's event, when he took on Federer in the Arthur Ashe Stadium and lost – as most players do. 'I'd like to have played out there a bit longer but my Swiss friend had other ideas,' said Henman afterwards, with a wry smile.

He had words of encouragement for Murray, too: 'It's great to be in the final here. I think more importantly, so are his results away from that. I knew that his knee hadn't been great and around Wimbledon time was his sort of comeback, then after that he went and played the Futures, and he was in a semi and won two events and got his ranking up. I like the way that he's playing some big matches here in the junior events, but I think he knows where the bread and butter of his career is going to be, and he's already taking some big strides, and that's very important. We've had plenty of examples of kids that have done well in the juniors but haven't made that transition. Not only his game but between the ears, he knows what he's doing. He works hard, and I think that's a good combination.'

Murray refused to get ahead of himself, echoing Henman's words. 'Getting to a junior grand slam final is a great achievement, but it's not the most important thing,' he said. 'I want to go on and achieve other things. Even if I win, I don't think it will affect me like it has some other British players.'

A PRODIGY AMONGST PRODIGIES

There are several of Murray's fellow Britons whose careers peaked in juniors and who proved unable to build on their teenage accomplishments. Delgado was an outstanding junior but never got past 121 in the professional rankings, while James Baily won the Australian Open junior title in 1993 and yet drifted away from tennis altogether. In fact, when Henman, who was a contemporary of Baily's, first broke through by making the quarter-finals of Wimbledon in 1996, intrepid journalists tracked Baily down in Sydney, where the one-time hope for British tennis was waiting tables in a restaurant.

So far, Miles Kasiri seems, unfortunately, to be following that model. At the time of the 2004 US Open, he had just made the final in Wimbledon, ensuring that British players featured in consecutive junior grand-slam finals. Like Murray, Kasiri trained predominantly abroad, having just returned from Nick Bollettieri's academy in Florida to train under the LTA's supervision. It was a relationship which was to go sour very quickly. It began when Kasiri criticised the LTA at Wimbledon by saying that he was surprised at how soft his new training was compared to that at the Bollettieri school, though, confusingly, he later found himself kicked out of the LTA programme for, allegedly, not working hard enough. Whatever the reason, Kasiri has yet to build on the success he enjoyed in the juniors, though he did serve to provide some healthy competition for Murray.

'I think all of us push each other to do well,' said Murray. 'I was really happy for Kasiri when he made the final, but it really made me want to do better.' Sunday, 12 September 2004, offered him the chance to do just that.

Court 10 at the US Open is one of the larger of the outside courts at the United Sates Tennis Association (USTA) National Tennis Centre. Sitting in the shadow of the large silver 'Unisphere', an instantly recognisable landmark of the US Open for tennis fans everywhere, the court is just in front of the entrance to the vast Arthur Ashe Stadium, with a bank of seats on one side and two rows of seats on the other, leaving it open on one side for the spectators milling about as they waited for the men's final between Federer and Lleyton Hewitt to begin at 4.15 p.m.

Plenty of those courtside at 12 noon, when Murray and Stakhovsky walked out to start the final, probably had no idea who or what they were watching, though Judy, Jamie and the rest of Murray's supporters, positioned in a corner in the narrow stand behind the baseline, certainly did. The sound of his mother's voice, shouting 'come on Andy', punctuated almost every point – Andy had complained, not entirely seriously, before the match that 'she gets too excited'. Judy was about to come into her own.

The LTA deemed it necessary for 30-year-old Henman, a veteran of thousands of press conferences down the years, to have a member of the LTA communications staff with him in addition to the large and hugely experienced ITF communications team, whose job it is to look after all male players at the grand slams. Yet no one from the LTA's communications department helped Murray, a 17-year-old relative press rookie, through the hours of print, radio and TV interviews he undertook after the final. Instead, not for the first time, it was left to Judy.

Such matters were probably a million miles from Murray's mind as he knocked up against Stakhovsky. As the match got under way, there were nerves from both boys, an inevitable product of the occasion. The same feelings were probably coursing through the veins of 15-year-old Michaela Krajicek and 16-year-old Jessica Kirkland, who were playing the girls' final at the same time on the adjacent Court 11.

Murray, perhaps because of the preceding weeks of match hardness honed at those clay-court Futures events, played the far more composed tennis of the two. While Murray had been racking up matches in Spain and Italy, Stakhovsky had been playing higher level Challengers without much success and couldn't, therefore, boast the same bedrock of confidence. Murray fashioned a break point on the Ukrainian's serve in the opening game but Stakhovsky served himself out of trouble. Murray then held to love to score a palpable hit in the mini-psychological war that always marks the opening few games of a tennis match while opponents assess each other with wary, vigilant eyes. Stakhovsky buckled in the next game, when two errant forehands were punished by Murray sending through a skidding sliced backhand on break point. Stakhovsky attempted to wrestle back the advantage in the next game, but Murray survived two break points to take a 3–1 lead. He then broke again to find himself with a two-handed grip on the first set. Stakhovsky retrieved one of the breaks, but it scarcely mattered: he was having such trouble holding his own serve that resistance seemed futile. When Murray's chance came to serve out the first set, he did so without ceremony, forcing three errors from his opponent before befuddling him with a neatly carved backhand sliced drop-shot. After 45 minutes, he was a set to the good and bouncing back to his chair with his mum's shouts of encouragement ringing in his ears.

It's often said that a player is never more vulnerable than after he has just won a set – rather like a football team that has just scored – but that is truer of lesser players than those with an instinctive understanding of how to ram their point home. When Murray watched a Stakhovsky backhand sail long in the opening game of the second set to give him the break of serve, his throaty cry of 'C'mon' spoke volumes about the significance of the advantage he had taken in the contest. In a best-of-three set match, a set and a break down is a large hole to climb out of, and once Stakhovsky had missed his chance to break back in Murray's next service game, the Scot was romping towards the title. Another break gave him a 3–0 lead, and though Stakhovsky at least had the gumption to hold serve thereafter and make him work for the win, the only thing likely to stop Murray from securing the title was a sudden bout of nerves.

'I thought I played a pretty clever match,' said Murray afterwards. 'I was solid; I used my sliced backhand well. I was expecting him to come forward a bit more because, well, everyone had told me that he was a serve–volleyer. But I think I started off really well, returned his serve and passed him a few times and then he backed off a bit.'

The nerves did come, though not until Murray was serving at 5–2 up. After one hour and thirteen minutes, he fashioned his first match point at 40–30 with a thumping smash – a tension-easing shot which elicited another shout of 'C'mon' – but he missed a makeable backhand as he tried to snatch at victory. A missed forehand suddenly saw him facing a break point, and the spectre of losing his lead briefly appeared before a huge serve and a forehand winner put him at match point again. After one hour and seventeen minutes, another serve found its mark, and Stakhovsky could only flail at it. Murray was a grand-slam champion.

He raised both his arms above his head, then grabbed his hat and threw it on the ground, and hoisted a ball up to Judy in the stands. He was to claim later, with his usual dry humour, that he was aiming straight for her: 'I was trying to throw it at her, actually, just to shut her up because she was making so much noise the whole match, but I just overcooked it a bit.' Judy, whose immediate reaction to her son's winning shot was to drum her hands hard on her lap, probably wouldn't have minded him taking pot-shots at her – at that moment, as she hugged Jamie, her youngest son could do no wrong.

Meanwhile, back at home, his grandfather Roy Erskine, who had been glued to the US Open's website and the tiny live scoreboard on his computer, could finally relax. 'I watched the game by looking at the score point by point on the internet,' Roy later revealed. 'I had a large whisky watching the updates on the screen. It was amusing but not a good thing to do. It is believable because he has been knocking at the door for a while now. But we are thrilled to bits with the whole thing, and we are so happy for his mum, who has worked so hard for this too. We went down to Dunblane New Golf Club after the game where people were anxious to see how Andrew had got on. So there were about 60 of us having champagne at the club. It was a lovely night.'

There was a brief presentation ceremony with speeches after the match, but both he and Krajicek, as junior champions, were later invited to step onto the court at Arthur Ashe Stadium ahead of the men's final – as is customary at the US Open – to receive their trophies in front of the 23,000 packed in there.

'I'd just like to say thanks to all the fans for coming to watch, you've helped me through,' said Murray in his on-court speech after his match. 'I'd like to thank my mum and everyone in my corner from Scotland.'

Stakhovsky was gracious in defeat. 'Andy was much better than me – much better,' he said.

'I just couldn't believe I had won,' Andy explained to the press as he sat behind a large and imposing desk in the main interview room 45 minutes after coming off court with the scribes hanging on his every word. 'To win a junior grand slam after being out of tennis for seven, eight months is a big thing for me. I'd only been playing again for two and a half, three months. I don't know, when I won, it just felt unbelievable. I'm a little bit surprised to win, but not too much. I played four warm-up tournaments in Spain and Italy before – senior tournaments – and I'd won two of them playing really well. I think the competition in those tournaments was stronger than what it was here. I felt like I could win the tournament, but I wasn't really expecting to.'

The room was largely full of the British press contingent, but there were also a smattering of local journalists, anxious to get some colour on this auburn-haired boy from Scotland. Murray obliged: yes, he liked haggis but not paella; yes, the weather in Scotland was usually bad; no, he didn't mind being compared to Henman – he considered it a compliment. He also said all the right things about their home grand slam, which is always a good way to ingratiate yourself with your hosts. 'This is my favourite tournament,' he said. 'I just think the atmosphere in all of the matches that I played here was really good. You know, the fans are great. I think the night matches here are just really good for the supporters. I'd love to come back and hopefully play a night match one day. But to play here, I think it's the biggest tournament in the world.'

He was to find out just how big a tournament it was over the course of the next 24 hours, when he went from being just another 17 year old to the next big thing in British tennis. The journalists on-site, who were just getting over the effort of covering Henman exhaustively on gruelling US deadlines, where the sports desks are forever five hours ahead and thus unusually impatient for copy, suddenly found themselves writing reams on Murray, bombarding Faye Andrews and the rest of the ever-helpful ITF communications team for statistics on Britons winning junior grand slams.

Judy's mobile phone, meanwhile, went into meltdown as she fielded call after call, not just from well-wishers and relatives back home but also from television programmes like GMTV and BBC Breakfast news and what seemed like every sports and news desk in London and Glasgow. She wasn't the only one. The LTA press office was also getting its share of calls and put out a quote from performance director David Felgate, praising the young player's efforts. 'He fully deserves his victory after a week of fantastic tennis,' said Felgate. 'It is testament to the hard work and determination he has shown all year.'

Murray even received a congratulatory email from Scotland's first minister Jack McConnell, who praised his 'tremendous achievement'.

He wrote, 'Since my visit to Wimbledon last year, when your talents were the main topic of conversation, I have followed your progress with interest. You are a great credit to Scotland, and I wish you continued success.'

With all the hullabaloo going on around him, not to mention the fact that he was keen to watch Federer and Hewitt play in the final, Andy and Judy decided that the family would stay in New York an extra night to complete their newly drawn-up roster of media commitments. It also gave Murray an extra day's grace before he returned to London and on to La Manga in Spain, where he was due to join the Davis Cup squad as it prepared for a promotion/relegation tie away to Austria.

As one of the perks for winning the junior title, Murray was invited to watch the men's final from the President's Box, which is usually only open to high-ranking USTA officials, celebrities and dignitaries. Murray asked if he could bring Jamie and Tom Rushby, whom he had arranged to sit with during the match, but was told the invitation only applied to him. So Murray politely turned down the offer, opting instead to sit high up in the stands (in seats known to aficionados as 'the nosebleeds') with Jamie and Tom rather than hobnob courtside with the rich and famous.

A celebratory dinner that evening marked the fact that Murray had joined the likes of Andy Roddick, Pat Cash, Stefan Edberg, David Nalbandian and Richard Gasquet as a US Open junior champion.

The next morning was spent on the kind of relentless media junket that would have seasoned Hollywood superstars calling their union rep. Murray left the Hyatt Hotel near Grand Central Station and was taken from floor to floor at the Reuters building, doing live television links back to the UK. Tennis players are apt to become jaded by the relentless appetite for interviews with them – after winning the Australian Open in January 2006, Federer didn't complete his media commitments until 2.30 a.m. – but early on, there is a novelty value in being the centre of attention. There were also sound economic reasons for Murray capitalising as much as possible on his moment – not only did it repay the investment of his existing sponsors (which at that time included Adidas and Robinsons), it also brought him to the attention of other potential investors. Murray might have a replica trophy, but that wasn't going to pay the next lot of fees for the Sánchez-Casal Academy, nor provide a budget to allow him to travel to Futures events around Europe in the autumn.

By midday, Judy decreed that her 17-year-old son needed a break from being a superstar and dispatched him off to go shopping. She wanted him to spend the few hours he had before his flight enjoying the city that had just played host to one of the most important moments of his young life.

It didn't take long for reality to bite. After a sobering experience watching Tim Henman and Greg Rusedski lose to Austria in Portsach, which turned out to be Henman's Davis Cup swansong, Murray returned to the men's tour. October and November proved to be a relatively thin time, partly because his young body was rebelling after a gruelling second half of the season. He entered the last month of the year with only a quarter-final at a Futures event in Glasgow – where he lost to his future Davis Cup teammate David Sherwood – and a first-round defeat at a Challenger in Bolton to show for his efforts.

His outing at the Superset exhibition event, where he was mauled in a one-set match against John McEnroe, was fun but can hardly have filled him with confidence.

December, though, proved to be far more fruitful. A return to Spain saw him resume his habit of winning consecutive events, and he showed his versatility, this time by taking titles at Futures in Orense on a hardcourt and in Pontevedra on clay. As Christmas approached, he was also named the BBC Young Sports Personality of the Year for 2004. It necessitated a trip to London, a new suit and the making of a rather awkward speech straight to camera, in the grand tradition of the programme, which has long been a must-see for sports fans wanting to relive the year's highlights as chosen by the BBC.

The previous December, Murray had been contemplating his injured knee and wondering what the future held for him. Twelve months on and that future was suddenly looking very promising indeed.

4

HOME AWAY FROM HOME

THE HARDEST THING ABOUT GETTING INTO THE SÁNCHEZ-CASAL ACADEMY IS FINDING it. Set back from the tangle of *autovías* that lead in and out of Barcelona and snake around the nearby airport, it's an easy place to miss. A small sign is all that alerts you to the entrance, which is down a long, scruffy lane with a smelly open drain running alongside it. There is certainly nothing to suggest that you are entering a hothouse for international sporting talent.

The dull institutional buildings are unlikely to inspire awe in those who come to visit, nor are they intended to. All that matters is what happens on the twenty-nine tennis courts spread out over 100,000 m², where the attendees spend up to eight hours a day doing drills, playing practice matches, attending coaching sessions and undertaking fitness work, all designed to turn them from promising pupils into fully fledged professional tennis players.

Of course, some of those who use the facility already deserve that label, not least 2004 US Open champion Svetlana Kuznetsova, who these days has an apartment in Barcelona itself but uses the academy as her training base in between tournaments. Her name features heavily on the academy's promotional material, as does that of Gilles Muller, who knocked Andy Roddick out of the same tournament in 2005. There is also mention of a certain Andy Murray, who went there at the age of 15 and has never looked back.

'Barcelona was fantastic for Andy and one of the reasons why he is where he is right now, there's no doubt about that,' says Mark Petchey, Murray's former coach. 'It's definitely helped Andy's ability to play tennis in terms of building points and staying out there and constructing a rally. Andy is unique in how he does it, but it's still built on the foundations of being in Spain.'

Petchey advocates the building of a similar facility in Spain or Portugal – financed by the LTA – specifically for British players, so that the Murrays of the future can go abroad in numbers and flourish as he did. 'Safin did it by going to Valencia; Sharapova did it by going to the States. The list of people that have gone somewhere else is endless,' he says. 'How many times do you have to look at that and say "that's the way it worked" before you actually make something happen. The system we've got hasn't worked, and I think if you look around the world, it isn't just the LTA. There aren't too many players who've come through their national federations: most of them have gone away from home and done it in their own way.'

It was Rafael Nadal, his elder by a year, who was among the first to recommend the Sánchez-Casal Academy to Murray when they met at a junior racquetball tournament. It was February 2002 and Spain had just defeated Great Britain in the final of the European Under-16 team championships in Andorra, Spain. At that time, 14-year-old Murray was finding it difficult to juggle school, travel to and from training facilities near Dunblane and finding hitting partners of a high enough standard. Plus, like most British players, he was limited by the climate he lived in to playing indoors most of the time in windless, unchallenging conditions. He was worried about falling behind the rest of his age group, many of whom trained at academies where practice, training and schoolwork were weaved into a lifestyle designed to maximise their chances of making it to the pros.

'Down in London, I think the young players tend to get a little bit spoilt,' Murray said of his desire to go abroad. 'I chose to go to Spain because I thought it would mean harder work and be better for my tennis.'

Judy later wrote in *The Guardian*:

> Anyone who has ever watched their child go off to boarding school knows how difficult it can be to watch them leave their family, friends, home and school when they are very young. My sons Jamie and Andy left home to train in Spain at the ages of 12 and 15 respectively, and they reacted in different ways to the move. Jamie returned home after six months, while it was difficult to persuade Andy to come home at all, even for Christmas.

With her experience of being Scotland's National Coach, Judy had first-hand knowledge of the facilities available in the UK and was therefore well placed to judge what would suit the talents and personality of her younger son. She also knew full well that what was then on offer in Scotland was unlikely to be enough for Andy once he reached the age of 15. Tennis in Scotland was badly underfunded, a situation which was no better by the time she resigned her post as National Coach in 2004. Falling lottery sales had meant that the funding the sport received from sportscotland's Talented Athlete Programme had been cut from £76,000 in 2002–03 to £30,000 in 2004. Those figures make it all the more remarkable that the region has punched so far above its weight in recent years – three members of the Great Britain Davis Cup team for the September 2005 tie against Switzerland were Scottish – and are, perhaps, a tribute to Judy's energy and drive.

When it came to sending her younger son to Barcelona, her first task was to get together enough funding from sponsors and various governing bodies. Given the scant funds available in her own organisation and the fact that the minimum cost of sending a player to live and train abroad is around £30,000 a year, that was no easy task. The LTA committed £10,000 of what was required, with the rest coming from sportscotland, Tennis Scotland, some private sponsors and the Murray family.

They could have opted for Nick Bollettieri's famous academy in Florida, which has nurtured the likes of Andre Agassi, Maria Sharapova and countless others, but the Murrays felt it was simply too far away from home – Andy could hardly come home for weekends. With the family having settled on Europe so that he would only be a couple of hours' flight away, Andy expressed a preference for Barcelona, with Sánchez-Casal – founded by Spanish tennis legends Emilio Sánchez and Sergio Casal – proving to be the most appealing of the three academies they looked at there. He knew a handful of players who already trained there and felt so comfortable on his first three-day visit that he beat one of the academy's founders (and a five-time grand-slam champion in doubles to boot) Emilio Sánchez 6–1, 6–3 in a practice match.

Once you've come off Autovía C31 and managed to find the place, the first impression of the Sánchez-Casal Academy is a sort of boarding school with balls. The main building houses the pro-shop, stringer, gym and sports medicine facilities, and also contains the secretariat, which functions like a school secretary's office. It has a noticeboard which offers forthcoming trips to the supermarket, cinema (Murray sought out the only English language one in the city) and the nearby seaside resort of Castelldefels. It also provides an internal bank, looking after the students' spending money. A café-cum-tuck shop tends to be the centre of social life, as does the outdoor ping-pong table, which is a magnet for the academy's ultra-competitive residents in the evenings. There is also a lounge with internet facilities and satellite TV. True to the obsessive natures of the people who watch it, it is tuned to tennis most days.

'Most of the time they are too tired to do anything,' says the academy's Arantxa Gallastegui, who runs the commercial department but also appears to function as something of a den mother to the teenagers in her care. She speaks fondly of Murray and the way that he, like many of his fellow pupils, used to hang on the arrival of his mother and the comforts of home which she brought with her, usually in the form of digestive biscuits and milky bar buttons. 'The British kids always seem to like those strange boxes of soup and pot noodles,' says Gallastegui, with a mild air of suspicion. 'Soup doesn't come in a box in Spain.'

Apart from the odd fix of junk food, most of the meals on offer at the academy are, like everything else, designed to help performance, with meals conceived to provide the correct nutritional balance for growing athletes. Murray became good friends with the football-mad chef during his time there, using his limited Spanish and the chef's smattering of English to discuss the merits of Barcelona's defence and other weighty matters. 'He would try with his Spanish, and he definitely understands more than he speaks, but his accent wasn't very good,' remembers Gallastegui, with a laugh. 'Even when he spoke English that Scottish accent made him hard to understand sometimes. I kept saying to him, "Andy, you have to open your mouth when you speak!"'

With so many nationalities represented at the academy, English – in whatever accent – appears to be the common language. There is a large Spanish contingent, but Germany, France, the USA, the UK and

Asia are all represented in its demographic, a mix which provides good training in how to get along in the international muddle of players on the pro-circuit. It's the perfect place to merge into the crowd, too, and somewhere to avoid the pressure that was ever-present for Murray but which intensified after he won the US Open junior title. His friends at the Sánchez-Casal were pleased for him, but he relished the lack of fuss they made compared to what he called the 'over-the-top' attention which he was getting back home.

When Murray first arrived at the academy, he was still of school age and therefore required to attend the classes at the small on-site school. All students are obliged to spend three hours a day studying – in Murray's case French, English, maths and colloquial Spanish – and they graduate with the equivalent of an American high school diploma. When he was still studying (he stopped at 16), his days would begin with three hours of hitting on court, be followed by an hour in the gym, an hour for lunch, two hours of school work, an hour and a half of practice matches and would then finish with another hour of school. Once he had dispensed with the books – something he was only too delighted to do – Murray joined the older players in spending, on average, six hours a day on court and the rest of his time in the gym.

Evenings were, more often than not, spent in his room, lying on his bunk in one of the small bedrooms he shared in the boys dormitory (which are on the floor above the schoolrooms), either emailing on his laptop or chatting to the friends he had made at the academy, both male and female. With the girls' dormitory just next door, one of Gallastegui's tasks is to limit the amount of room swapping that goes on when adolescent hormones inevitably kick in – 'Typical teenagers,' she sighs.

Once Murray began travelling to more and more tournaments as he made his way from the juniors into the pro-ranks, he moved from the dormitory to the relative luxury of one of the academy's short-stay bungalows – he was still sharing a room, but it afforded a little more space for the dirty clothes and general mess. The *Daily Telegraph*'s Mark Hodgkinson visited Murray in Barcelona in December 2004 and painted a picture familiar to anyone accustomed to the living habits of teenage boys.

'The floor is smothered with a week's worth of discarded rackets, clay-stained shorts, used tennis balls, empty food packets,' wrote Hodgkinson, before noting, wryly, that this was *after* Judy had tidied up. 'With all the chaos, this could be your average 17-year-old's bedroom. Only smaller. And with a Ukrainian stranger as a room-mate. At least Murray got the top bunk.'

He also received other privileges during his time at Sánchez-Casal, not least because Sánchez recognised his talent, even at 15. This included being placed on a squad of touring players, aged from 19 to 26 and ranked as high as 200 in the world. As even any mediocre club player will attest, practising against players of a higher standard is the quickest way to improve, and thus Murray found he was making progress within weeks of arriving in Barcelona.

While Murray's time at Sánchez-Casal is often cited as a reason for his clay-court prowess, only ten of the twenty-nine courts are clay – the rest are made up of six hardcourts, three Rebound Ace courts, eight DecoTurf (the surface the US Open is played on) and two artificial grass courts. Murray was encouraged to switch frequently between the different surfaces to get used to the different movements required on each. Crucially, all of the tennis at Sánchez-Casal is played outdoors, something no British academy, including the LTA's new £40 million national training centre in Roehampton, would ever be able to boast.

'Let's face it, 80 per cent of tennis is played outdoors. If you play indoors where conditions are always perfect, it's unrealistic. It's just not the way that tennis is played these days,' says Petchey. 'You look at players like Mario Ancic, or you look at Ivan Ljubicic, and you look at how big their serves are. They are still serving and staying back, then they construct 15 shot rallies. OK, it's aggressive, it's hit hard, it's hit safe, but it's ten or fifteen shots every single time. You don't do that indoors. It doesn't matter how slow it is, it will still be a different style of tennis. It's fine when you get older and you can adjust and you start learning how to play on different surfaces, but at a young age, you need the fundamentals of your game to be so strong. I feel that you can only get that by playing outdoors on clay or on hard. I don't think you get that indoors.'

Alan Jones, who coaches British women's No. 1, and Murray's fellow Scot, Elena Baltacha, concurs: 'The best answer when you ask what's wrong with British tennis is to look at all the clubs and look at the surface they are playing on. For most clubs it's economically sensible to have carpet courts with sand in them, but that means that most of our kids are growing up on a surface that bears no relation to the tour. That's why our competitive base is so poor.'

Murray got a far higher calibre of practice partner in Barcelona than he ever would have got in the UK and regularly played in local Spanish events, where the competition was tougher than it would have been in the equivalent British tournaments. He was also well placed to play plenty of Futures events without having to travel too far, since Spain boasts a thriving tournament circuit with many competitions almost on his doorstep.

Sánchez-Casal also attracted ATP Tour players for him to hit against, including former French Open champion Carlos Moya and Guillermo Coria, who was one of Murray's favourite players at that time. He split sets with Moya and beat Coria, then ranked in the world's top five, two days running in practice. 'What I did against those two just shows what I am capable of,' Murray said afterwards.

Moya later sung Murray's praises while speaking to BBC Radio. 'I had never heard about him before, but he looked a very complete player,' Moya said. 'He can serve, he can volley and is strong from the baseline. I think he can go on to be a great player. He is in a great academy with Emilio Sánchez and Sergio Casal, because they have great experience, and he can develop his game not just on hardcourts but also on clay, which is important. He is strong and very determined, and that is a good sign.'

It seems certain that Murray's days of living in a dormitory in Barcelona and waiting for chocolate digestives to arrive are now long gone, although Arantxa Gallastegui points out that he was seldom there for the full ten months that most annual boarders are booked in for anyway: 'Andy would stay for three or four months, then we wouldn't see him for a bit, then he'd come back. He seemed to get bored of staying in one place.'

Whether or not he ever returns for any length of time, the three years Murray spent in the Catalan capital were fruitful for both him and Sánchez-Casal, which has seen its reputation enhanced by the success he has enjoyed. After Murray won his first ATP Tour title in San José, Emilio Sánchez pointed out that his former charge's success was an example to all those budding players still toiling away on the academy's courts back in Barcelona. 'We were very glad to have him here for three years,' said Sánchez. 'Andy's a role model for our students.'

5

MURRAY VERSUS McENROE: MAN AGAINST BOY

WALKING OUT IN FRONT OF A HUGE CROWD AT WEMBLEY ARENA IS MORE THE STUFF of dreams for budding pop stars than tennis players, yet for a few brief moments in October 2004, Murray got a taste of what hundreds of boy-band singers and soul divas must have previously experienced when he got to do just that. The fact that he was about to take on the great John McEnroe made it even more extraordinary. Add to the occasion the lights, noise, loud music and the presence of a leggy, semi-clad model on each side of him, and Murray must have thought he was in some bizarre parallel universe.

Superset tennis was the brainchild of fast-talking Australian Stephen Duval and was an attempt to take a staid sport and inject a huge dose of entertainment into it. It involved a night of quick-fire one-set matches played in a raucous atmosphere, where players and coaches were mic'd up and encouraged to question calls, waiting to see if they were right when the findings of line-calling gizmo Hawkeye were shown on the big screen. All manner of gimmicks were planned for its debut (following a pilot tournament in Portland, Oregon), including heart rate monitors for the players, but the biggest gimmick of all was that the only player who took home prize money – all £250,000 of it – was the overall winner.

'When they walk into Wembley Arena, they are going to have far more of a sensory overload than at a normal tennis match,' Duval said excitedly, some months before the event. 'We want them to go crazy, and we want it to be dripping with excitement. There will be lots and lots of theatre, with an MC, music playing and stuff happening on the big screens, and that's before they've even started playing. When the place is full, all that is going on – and you're going to have someone serving for a quarter of a million pounds – there's going to be a lot of energy in there. We want to try and make tennis sexy again.

'We are not trying to be in competition with the grand slams or with the tennis tours; we truly believe that we are healthy for them because we are going after an entertainment demographic as well as sports fans. We're going to reinvigorate interest, which is good for tennis as a whole.

'We looked at a whole load of different sports and entertainments, like WWE wrestling, rock concerts, theatre, and blended the whole thing with traditional tennis. It's a blend of everything. We've also modelled it on a world-title fight. If you watch any world-title fight, [what] it's basically about is undercards and then a world-title fight itself, and that builds up excitement. In Superset, every match is knockout, building towards a crescendo.'

Tim Henman was initially asked to join Greg Rusedski, Mario Ancic (who was a replacement for Murray's friend Rafael Nadal), Tommy Robredo, Robby Ginepri, Boris Becker, Goran Ivanisevic and John McEnroe but was forced to pull out with shoulder and back problems, leaving the way clear for the organisers to approach Murray. What more appropriate player to ask to play an event which bills itself as the future of tennis than a 17 year old? Given that part of Superset's selling point was to pitch popular players of the past, present and future against each other, Murray's presence created an opportunity to set up a battle of the tennis generations. 'All I know is I was supposed to play Tim and clearly he got scared,' said 45-year-old McEnroe, with a cheeky grin.

Murray's first opportunity to rub shoulders with McEnroe and the rest came at a pre-event press conference in Chelsea, where he and his fellow players were crammed side by side behind a large table, with a news crew from Sky Sports and a handful of written journalists present. Murray didn't say much at first – he could hardly get a word in edgeways in that company – but it wasn't long before he and McEnroe were bantering like old buddies. One funny moment came when Murray was asked who his on-court coach would be (another of Superset's innovations was to have a coach beside them at the change of ends) and whether he would consider asking Judy to do it. He reacted with the horror of a teenage boy faced with the prospect of his mum embarrassing him in front of audiences watching Sky TV and *Grandstand*, which were televising the event live.

'There's no chance that she'd be out there as my coach. She'd be far too excited,' said Murray. 'She always loved John, so . . .' At this point, McEnroe raised his eyebrows saucily, much to everyone's amusement and Murray's embarrassment.

Instead of his mother, in a portent of the future, he chose Mark Petchey to sit with him on court. Few who watched Petchey in action that night assumed that they were getting a glimpse of what was to come. Indeed, one veteran tennis writer watching on a TV monitor listened to a mic'd up Petchey speaking to Murray at the change of ends and said, with a snort, 'Well, it looks like Petch has blown any chance of a coaching job there then.'

In the press conference, Murray was asked his thoughts on playing McEnroe and was suitably respectful of the seven-time grand-slam champion and former world No. 1: 'I'm going to try and go on court and play my own game against him. Obviously, he's one of the greatest players. To be on the same court as him is an honour, but I've got to play my own game.'

'And what is your game?' came the quick retort from McEnroe.

Afterwards, Murray confided, 'I'm starting to get used to doing press conferences, because I did one after I won the US Open and two at Davis Cup against Austria. But it's pretty nerve-racking having to do it in front of seven players like them, especially when it's people like John McEnroe and Boris Becker, two of the greatest players ever. I think I did OK though. Having done it at Davis Cup helped a lot, because I had to speak in front of Tim and Greg and Jeremy, so that was good.'

To be involved in such a starry, high-profile event at such a young age would be enough to turn any young player's head, but even as the prospect of a glitzy, noisy showdown with McEnroe approached, he refused to get carried away: 'I think I realise that just now I'm nowhere near where I want to be. These tournaments are a great experience for me and a good learning curve whatever happens. I practised with Tommy Robredo and Robby Ginepri yesterday, and I'm practising with Greg today. Just to hit with players like that is good for my game. I saw a lot of John's matches on tape, and he was someone who I loved watching because of his character and the fact that you never knew what he was going to do next. So, to go on the court with him is going to be amazing. It's an honour to be on the court with him, because, in my eyes, he's one of the greatest players ever. That's the thing that I've got to get out of my mind, because if I go out there thinking about it, then obviously I'm going to be a bit nervous and intimidated, and I won't play well. I think I'm just going to go out there and play my game and not worry too much about him.'

The knowledge that he had a run of unglamorous Futures and Challenger events – in places like Bolton – to look forward to certainly helped keep his feet on the ground, as did the knowledge that his CV only showed one junior grand-slam victory and was a good deal less full than McEnroe's. 'I've got a quite busy few weeks coming up. I'm sure next week going back to playing guys who are ranked 600 in the world will help me keep my feet on the ground, because, obviously, this for me is going to be huge. The US Open was important for my confidence, because people like Andy Roddick, Stefan Edberg [and] Pat Cash had all won it, and they obviously went on to be great players, and it's good to know that I could do that too, but, at the same time, I've still got a lot of improving to do. Hopefully, if I keep getting practice like I'm getting this weekend, it will help.'

Coming so soon after the trip to Austria for the Davis Cup, Superset also offered another opportunity for Murray to bond with Rusedski, who, like Henman, had consistently gone out of his way to be a source of advice and support. He was fulsome in his praise when asked about Murray ahead of the match with McEnroe: 'I think he's got a strong enough mind, and he knows what he's got to do out there; that's the most important thing. Physically he's very good, and mentally he's very strong, too. I think he knows what he's got to do and what he wants to get out of this game, and I haven't seen that in a British player in a long time, so that's the biggest plus. Every time he gets himself in situations like this, it's a positive, whether he wins or whether he loses. I think he should be confident about playing McEnroe, and he's got a good chance to win. The more you put yourself out there, the better you're going to do. I think he's got the right attitude to do very, very well.'

The day after his press conference, Murray arrived at the ageing Wembley Arena to play McEnroe. With heavy promotion on BBC TV and Sky, as well as in the written press, Superset appeared at first glance to be a success; the full stands and buzzing, noisy, atmosphere must have been exactly what Stephen Duval and the rest of the organisers were hoping for. Henman came to watch, spoke to the crowd and then took a turn behind the microphone for the evening, as did most of the players in action.

However, the event certainly suffered from the weight of its ambitions. Some of the technology – including the heart monitors – malfunctioned on the night, while other gizmos and gadgets got stuck in transit. As a result, it was simply a series of short tennis matches with a noisier-than-usual atmosphere, a big screen and loud music, and, as such, had plenty in common with existing tennis events like the US Open and livelier Davis Cup ties. The excitement over Hawkeye – now commonplace at events the world over – was dampened somewhat by players' reluctance to call on it.

Some players, that is, save for a certain 17 year old, who had the audacity to question a call on McEnroe's serve in the very first point of the match. McEnroe's face was a picture of smugness when the replay rejected Murray's challenge – smug as only an inveterate line-call challenger like him can be.

Murray may have done it simply to prove that he wasn't intimidated by the situation, which was a wise move given that McEnroe was trying every trick in the book to milk his greater experience of the big stage. When Murray walked on court flanked by two blondes, he smiled and looked slightly embarrassed. When McEnroe did it, he was jogging, jabbing an imaginary boxing foe and raising his hands like an old warrior.

As a regular on the senior circuit, McEnroe's tennis wasn't too shabby either, and while the part-time TV commentator talks a better game than he plays these days, he was still too canny for Murray. Taking advantage of the unusually quick indoor court, on which the ball skidded low like the old-fashioned grass courts he used to love, McEnroe soon made a mockery of the 28-year age gap between them. The American reeled off five straight games, and the set was over in a blizzard of clever angled volleys and sharp serving – neither Murray, nor Mark Petchey, could do anything to stop an embarrassing rout. McEnroe took the set 6–1 and looked rather pleased with himself afterwards.

'It's nice to come back here to Wembley. I've got some good memories of when I used to play here,' said McEnroe. 'I wasn't going to go easy on him because you risk losing the match if you do that. I feel like I smothered him before he got a chance to get into it. That was my plan. He looks like he's got the potential to be a good player, he says the right things and I'd love to help him out with his game, but a guy like him needs to get used to situations like this.'

Afterwards, Murray said, 'I enjoyed myself. I wasn't nervous, and I tried to get the crowd involved. The surface was just far too quick for me, and I'm not used to playing someone who plays like him. He may not be as good as he used to be, but he's still pretty good.'

For the record, Mario Ancic won the event, sneaking the £250,000 winner-takes-all prize money from under Rusedski's nose in the final, earning the Croatian the biggest pay day for three sets in the history of the sport. It had been an interesting experience for all concerned, and Murray, for one, gleaned plenty from his evening's work: 'I learned a lot, and I got to play one of the greatest players of all time.'

6

UP FOR THE CUP

THE DAVIS CUP, WITH ALL ITS ATTENDANT PRESSURES AND EMOTIONS, CAN BE THE making of some players and the breaking of others. For every national hero in team tennis, there are plenty who have cracked when confronted by a stadium full of flags, banners and noisy, frantic support, and the knowledge that they are letting their teammates down with every missed forehand.

The players who thrive when playing for their country are usually the ones who have the happy knack of finding genius at the moment when it is needed most and circumstances are at their most demanding. The way Andy Murray took to his debut Davis Cup match, a vital doubles rubber with David Sherwood against Israel in the intimidating surroundings of the Canada Stadium in Ramat Hasharon, suggests that he and the competition are made for each other.

The win that Murray and Sherwood fashioned over Israel's Jonathan Erlich and Andy Ram in the third of the tie's five rubbers had everything that makes Davis Cup such a gloriously thrilling and unpredictable business. Here was a 17-year-old junior – the youngest ever Briton to play in the competition's history – and a journeyman from Sheffield taking on one of the best doubles pairs in the world on their home turf and winning, giving their team a lead in the tie and going a huge way to saving Great Britain from relegation to Davis Cup obscurity.

It wasn't just that Murray and Sherwood were underdogs; it was that their win came at a time when Great Britain's Davis Cup squad was at its lowest point for a decade and badly needed some good news. Tim Henman, having been a faithful servant to his country for 11 years, had just announced his retirement from the competition, and though Greg Rusedski had opted to stay on, being the determined Davis Cup stalwart that he is, he couldn't win ties on his own.

The ideal Davis Cup team is one which boasts two good singles players – usually one marginally better than the other – and a separate, settled doubles pairing, all of whom face competition for their places. At the beginning of 2005, British team captain Jeremy Bates had nothing of the sort. He had a 31 year old who was prone to injury, a 17 year old who had travelled with the squad on Davis Cup trips to Luxembourg and Austria but had never played a match, one reportedly handy doubles player who was also untested, and a couple of other players who had never shown the slightest hint of being up to the demands of playing for their country.

When Henman decided that his chronic back and shoulder problems meant his body was no longer up to playing team tennis in January 2005, even the most optimistic of British supporters would have conceded that Bates's team would do well to stay in Europe/Africa Zone Group I, effectively the second division of the competition, and would certainly have no chance if Rusedski chose to follow Henman's example.

Rusedski gave Bates a worrying fortnight or so when, irritated at the timing of Henman's announcement, which came on the eve of the Australian Open, he said that he would only make a decision in his own time as to whether to keep playing or not. One can only imagine Bates's relief when he opted to carry on and attempt to help his captain nurture some cover for the sizeable hole left behind by Henman.

'Jeremy's very happy,' said Rusedski, with a large slice of understatement. 'I realised that I still enjoy Davis Cup, and it's something I've always been passionate about. I like playing in a team. I've got many fond memories, and many times when I've played well in Davis Cup, it's really helped my game. I've been working with a lot of the youngsters, and it made me think that I still want to be part of this team and still want to help out as much as I can. In the end, it was an easy decision.'

The days when Rusedski and Henman, playing in their pomp, led Great Britain into the Davis Cup World Group, and entertained ambitions of getting within touching distance of the Cup itself, were long gone. The first priority was to not get relegated and the second was to try to build a squad good enough to attempt, eventually, to get promoted back into the World Group.

On the plus side, the circumstances afforded Murray, Sherwood and 20-year-old Alex Bogdanovic an opportunity they would not have had if Henman had still been playing. Bates had no choice but to blood young new players in Israel, even if Murray, in the week leading up the team announcement, was sounding a strangely downbeat note about his chances of being included. 'I would love to play in the Davis Cup, but I don't expect to get picked,' he told the *Daily Telegraph*. His confidence had been hit by a poor run of form in the early months of 2005, when he had struggled with a painful back, brought on by a growth spurt that saw him grow as much as a centimetre in one week. 'It's possible that I may go as a hitting partner, but I'm going out to Portugal at the end of this week to play in qualifying for a tournament, and I may enter another tournament in Portugal the same week as the Davis Cup.'

Bates, fortunately for Murray, didn't take a blind bit of notice. 'I am sure that he is desperate to be in the team and is fighting for a place,' he said. 'In fact, I have seen myself that he is fighting for a place. He probably didn't want to second-guess anything.'

Rusedski, meanwhile, sent the message out loud and clear to Murray, Bogdanovic and Sherwood that he could not win the tie without their help. 'I still think we have a chance to get through the match in Israel, but one of those players is going to have to step up and come through for us,' he said. 'The Davis Cup is where they get to test whether they actually believe they are good enough. They can then take that confidence with them on to the tour. I feel the responsibility of helping them out with their transition, and if I can get them through this tie, that would be a great accomplishment in itself.'

Winning an away tie in the Davis Cup is never easy but going to a city like Tel Aviv, which is regularly scarred by terrorism, adds another dimension of concern for the travelling team. The Friday before the tie, a suicide bomber had hit a karaoke bar close to the team hotel in Tel Aviv, killing four, and while the LTA issued a statement following the attacks confirming its confidence in the security measures for the British team, there was an unspoken unease about the trip.

'We have had, and continue to have, ongoing discussions with the Israeli and British authorities, the team, and the International Tennis Federation,' said the LTA release. 'We have every confidence in the organisation and security of this tie. We will, of course, be continuing to monitor the situation carefully.'

They weren't the only ones. Journalists covering the tie were given stark warnings about where and where not to go in the evenings, and they were ferried to and from the venue, which was just outside the city, under guard.

'We spoke about the bomb, and we were told that we must not leave the hotel on our own,' Murray told the *Daily Telegraph*. 'Jeremy told us to be careful when we go out of the hotel and not to do anything stupid. The bomb went off just a few miles from where we are staying. I will try not to think about what happened, but I don't think it will have any effect on the British team's concentration. We will be safe if we stay in the hotel and the tennis centre.'

Before the draw was announced on the Thursday, there was some discussion about how Bates would shuffle the deck and whether there was a chance that Murray might play singles. British No. 3 Arvind Parmar was out of the tie with a knee injury, so either Bogdanovic or Murray was almost certain to be given a singles berth alongside Rusedski. In the end, Bates opted for Bogdanovic, who had played a live Davis Cup rubber against Lleyton Hewitt in Sydney in January 2003 and had at least some relevant experience.

Murray was to be blooded in the doubles, alongside David Sherwood, although Bates could have substituted his doubles team right up until the last minute for any other combination of players under Davis Cup rules. Yet it seemed inevitable that, after two ties as a non-playing member of the team, Murray was about to make his Davis Cup debut.

Bates, who is in charge of men's tennis for the LTA, had been aware of Murray long before he won the US Open junior title and had asked him to come to Luxembourg with Henman and Rusedski (for what was Bates's first tie as captain) and the rest of the British squad in April 2004, when the teenager was still hobbling with a knee problem. 'Obviously, at the time, he hadn't played in a long time, but he was the best young player we had by a long way, and I've always been a big believer in giving young guys experience,' explains Bates. 'It was very interesting to watch him around Tim and Greg, because he wasn't overawed at all, and I know that they were both very impressed with the way he carried himself, given that he was only 16 at the time. It was as if he was quite prepared for the situation. I wanted to give him a boost by bringing him along, but I also thought all the signs were there that he would be a good Davis Cup player in the future. His presence was significant. I'm not saying I knew for sure, but the signs were definitely there.'

The relationship he forged with both of his elder teammates was to be important for Murray, and to this day, he relies on both men for advice and support, while they, in turn, have spoken of their pride at being mentors to him. 'I'm delighted for Andy,' said Henman. 'I really, genuinely get on great with him. I really have a good relationship with him, and I've known Petch [Mark Petchey] for so long, it's fantastic.'

After coming along as what is known in Davis Cup parlance as an 'orange boy' in Luxembourg, Murray was a fully fledged member of the team for the tie against Austria in Portsach. He was considered for selection alongside Henman and Rusedski, even though he was still in the juniors, having just returned from his triumph at the US Open in New York.

In an interview with the *Sunday Times*, given during the British team's training camp at La Manga, Henman was effusive in his praise of Murray with whom, by now, he had spent plenty of time. 'It's important that he learns for himself, but I will definitely be there to offer help if he wants to ask,' Henman said. 'There's a whole load of learning processes Andy has to go through, and there's going to be lots of comparisons and criticism. But the bottom line is: all that means absolutely nothing. The only thing that should be important to him is that when he steps onto the court, he believes if you play well, work hard and act as a dedicated professional, the results will happen. That way you are going to compete in the biggest and best tournaments and aspire to a certain lifestyle that goes alongside. You have to say first and foremost that Andy has the ability and a good understanding of the game. He looks the part and is a player already. He's got a good head screwed on tightly to his shoulders, and, looking at his temperament, he's determined to succeed.'

As his country's only genuine home-grown prospect, Murray has always had to bear comparisons with Henman and has repeatedly said that, while he has nothing but respect for the Englishman, he wishes to be regarded as his own man. Henman agrees: 'Who knows if he is "the one", but we all hope he goes from strength to strength. We have all been guilty of identifying promising youngsters in the past, and they've fallen by the wayside. One thing is for certain – he is far ahead of me at an equivalent age. It's wrong to make comparisons between Andy and myself. As a 17 or even 18 year old, I simply wasn't good enough to play the junior US Open, let alone win it. I'd somehow managed to get into the Australian and French Opens, losing in the first round of both. Then, in my only Wimbledon as a junior, I lost 6–2, 6–1 to a Mexican called Enrique Abaroa, who has hardly set the world on fire since. It's fair to say there weren't too many people who held much hope for me.'

Bates also sees the importance of the relationship: 'I think Andy has been very appreciative of both Tim and Greg, but having people like that around can only be influential if you want to learn. Andy is one of those people who takes everything in.'

In the end, Bates went for his tried and tested duo of Henman and Rusedski in Portsach, where their chances were not helped by cold, damp conditions. The pair of veterans proved unable to cope with the Austrians on a slow, damp clay court and lost the tie 3–2, with Stefan Koubek clinching Austria's promotion to the World Group by beating Rusedski (who was struggling with a badly blistered hand) in the fifth rubber. Two vital factors contributed to Great Britain losing the tie and remaining in the Europe/Africa Zone Group I for another year: one was Henman's painful back, which is what ensured it would be his last match for his country; the other was that Henman and Rusedski lost in the doubles, the first time the pair had ever been beaten in eight ties and eight years of playing together.

If those grim, dank days in Portsach had culminated in a thoroughly miserable weekend for Great Britain and proved to be the tipping point for Henman to stop playing a competition he had loved for years, then the trip to Israel at least represented a fresh start. Rusedski led the team into action, taking on World No. 256 Harel Levy, Israel's No. 2 player, who had previously been ranked as high as 30 in the world. The Israeli succumbed fairly meekly – 6–4, 6–3, 6–0 – which quietened the 5,000-strong home crowd in the ironically named Canada Stadium.

'The conditions were tough with the wind swirling around the stadium, but I think experience saw me through,' said Rusedski, who had taken just one hour and twenty-nine minutes to put his team one point ahead. 'We got the draw we were looking for with me playing the first match, and I don't think we could ask for any more. I don't know if any match is easy, but I want to play at a high level throughout, and since getting my consistency back, that is what I was able to do.'

Rusedski was then asked if he was likely to play doubles and gave a rather disingenuous answer, designed to muddy the waters and leave the Israelis guessing as to who would play on Saturday. 'In Davis Cup, you never really know what to expect, but to win in straight sets and do it so easily is obviously very good for me,' he said.

Having led from the front, Rusedski then joined Murray and Sherwood on the British team bench to cheer on Bogdanovic and see if he could respond to the veteran's rallying call by beating Noam Okun, Israel's No. 1 singles player, who was ranked 148 in the world.

Bogdanovic, known as Boggo to his teammates, was ranked 173 and therefore expected to give Okun a close match, especially since the young Brit already had the experience of playing a live Davis Cup rubber away from home to fall back on.

It didn't help. Bogdanovic slumped disappointingly, undoing Rusedski's good work and the momentum his teammate's win had given the British. Unable to capitalise on a bright start and the four set points he had in the first set, Bogdanovic's challenge melted away, and he ended up losing 7–6, 6–2, 6–2. It was a disappointing end to the first day and gave Saturday's doubles an extra frisson of pressure.

That evening, Bogdanovic was in a fog of disappointment at the opportunity he'd missed and was bracing himself for the next day's headlines about him freezing under pressure and not having the necessary heart for the Davis Cup. Rusedski sought him out, speaking to the 20 year old for 45 minutes in his hotel room about the match, how he could recover and where he would go from there.

'I'm not going to go into details because that's between the two of us. I think everybody was pretty tough on him in the press. Now he's just got to go out there, and it's either going to make him or break him,' Rusedski said. 'It's his decision which way it goes for him. He's man enough that he realised that after the match and now, hopefully, he does the right things, and he will be back with us in September. But he's got to go out and prove it to everybody else now.'

Bogdanovic wasn't asked back in September, largely because his teammate Murray, together with David Sherwood, upstaged him in spectacular style.

The doubles was always going to be the vital point in Tel Aviv. With two singles players ranked outside the World's Top 150, Israel's strength appeared to be in the doubles, with Erlich and Ram an established pairing on the men's circuit and ranked fifth in the world as a duo at the time of the tie. As a team, they had reached the Wimbledon semi-finals in 2003 and had played 27 tour events together the previous season. Beating them was always going to be the most difficult task of the tie, whichever doubles pairing Bates opted to field.

In Friday's press conferences, much was made of whether Rusedski would play doubles with either Murray or Sherwood. Davis Cup rules allow for late substitutions in doubles, and every effort was made to keep the Israelis guessing as to who they would be up against, even though, as Rusedski later revealed, the British line-up had been settled since the beginning of the week.

'I was just going to play two singles matches, and the doubles was going to be Andrew and David, which had already been decided earlier, [while] Alex was told on Tuesday that he was going to be playing singles,' explained Rusedski. 'So, everybody knew what their role was, which made it really, really good. In the press, I was still playing the game – "well maybe I'll sneak in for the doubles" – and it made the other guys think. So, the morning of the doubles match, all four of us walked on court, and they were thinking, "OK, Rusedski is going to play with Sherwood", because we were the first two to step on the court. And then Andrew and Alex came in later – so we had a little bit of gamesmanship in there. But we knew what the team was.'

Mind games like those are always a part of the intrigue of Davis Cup, but they tend to mean very little once the first ball is struck. On 5 March 2005, that ball was a serve from Erlich. The second that Murray pelted it back past the Israeli for a clean backhand winner, he got his name in the history books.

'I had faith in Andy and David,' said Bates. 'You can see who wants to play. You can see the sparkle in their eyes.'

Murray had walked on court for the opening ceremony with his iPod earphones belting out 'I'm Gonna Be (500 Miles)' by the Scottish duo The Proclaimers to get him gee'd up. 'It's what they play when Hibs, my team, score a goal,' he later explained.

'About once every season they play it,' Sherwood quipped in response.

The banter between the two was a sign of how comfortable they were feeling in each other's company even before the match. 'At the start of the week, for both of us it was a slight concern that we didn't know each other so well, but each day, we started to play better and better,' said Sherwood. 'We got more friendly, and we were having a bit of fun on the court. We understand each other's humour.'

With Bates sitting on the edge of his chair at the side of the court, and the British team yelping on their support from the bench, Murray and Sherwood broke Erlich's serve to give themselves a lead, which they converted into a one-set advantage after 42 minutes. Slapping hands after every point and playing tennis that was as passionate, animated and committed as their body language between points, the two players, who'd barely exchanged more than a sentence before they met up for Davis Cup duty, seemed to be working in symbiosis.

'I knew I had two players who could perform, but the thing that surprised me was how well they coped with the situation,' said Bates. 'A lot of thought went into selecting them, but I was really pleased, because you never know until they get out there. You can't buy that quality. I wasn't surprised to see Andy play as well as he did, because I'd seen it in his practices, but it was a question of whether he could produce it on the day.'

He did. Rusedski, who cheered himself hoarse from his courtside seat, couldn't have been more impressed with what he saw. 'I thought the boys really came through, and we found out a lot about the new generation, especially Andrew. I thought that he had a great performance. It's quite nice to see the exuberance, because I remember when I was his age – 17, 18 – and I had as much energy as him. I'm 32 – I can't be getting that pumped up for four sets like he did any more. I'd be flat out on the court in about a set and a half!

'David played really, really well as well. It was really encouraging because we won the point out of the three that I didn't think we were going to get – that was the doubles match. That was a great thing. All we asked was the boys to believe, give 100 per cent and have good body language. Andrew from the first point was really pumped up. He won the first point with a backhand down the line, and he was already pumped up. So we had the combination of one who was extremely aggressive, showing his emotion, and David, [who] was really stable throughout. They made a really lovely combination.'

While Murray was the more animated on court, Sherwood's contribution that day should not be underestimated. The then 24-year-old redhead from Sheffield is an outstanding sportsman – he is the son of two Olympic silver medallists in athletics, was a sprint champion at county level and was an apprentice at Sheffield Wednesday – but he had not always been in the LTA's good books. His selection in the tie marked something of a redemption for him after his funding was taken away in 2004 under Mark Petchey, who was the LTA manager of men's national training at that time. Petchey didn't feel that Sherwood was pulling his weight; the Yorkshireman responded by working harder and rewards were reaped all around in Tel Aviv.

Having got the first set in the bag, Sherwood and Murray set about trying to secure the second and were twice a break up as the momentum shifted to and fro. By the time the set had reached a tie-breaker, the Britons were 1–4 down, but they hit back to take a two-set lead. This prompted a worried murmur to go around the crowd, which had booed and whistled every time either one of them went to serve.

The adrenalin which had been coursing through the British pair drained away in the third set as a lull in their play allowed Erlich and Ram to hit back and bring the scoreline to 2–1. Having allowed the Israelis to get their challenge going, Sherwood and Murray then struggled to contain them in a fourth set. Sherwood lost his serve to put them 1–2 down, but Murray secured the break back with a forehand lob as Erlich served at 5–4 to level the match. The Britons had to fight back again to force the tie-breaker after Sherwood's serve cracked once more at 5–5. They somehow managed it, despite the Israelis having three set points to take it into a deciding set.

In the tie-breaker, the match took another turn when Murray and Sherwood suddenly and thrillingly regained the form of the first and second sets by whipping up a 5–1 lead. An unreturnable serve from Murray gave them three match points, and Sherwood took the last of them with a second serve. The tension of the moment was heightened by jeering from the crowd as he tossed the ball up, an unsporting interjection of noise which prompted the umpire to belatedly warn the crowd that if they did not behave, he could dock their team a point.

After nearly three and a half hours of nerve-racking, pulsating drama, Sherwood fired his second serve down, and Ram thumped it into the net to give the Britons a 6–4, 7–6, 2–6, 7–6 win. Murray hurled his racket into the air, and the British team erupted in joy and relief. The two players enveloped each other, and then Bates as well, in a bear hug. They were soon joined by Rusedski and the rest of the British team, all of whom understood the significance of taking that doubles point. They hadn't won the tie, but with Rusedski heavily favoured to beat Okun in Sunday's first singles match, they knew they had dealt the Israeli team a body blow from which it was unlikely to recover.

In the locker-room afterwards, it was Rusedski who pointed out to his elated younger teammates that there was still work to be done, though even he found it hard to contain his excitement. 'After the doubles, it was like they had won the tie,' he said. 'I was like, "Guys, that was an unbelievable win, and you'll probably never forget that match for the rest of your life, but we've got to find that third point.

Then we can have a bigger celebration and enjoy it." But, at the time, everybody was so excited, because we never expected to get that doubles win.

'You can't replace hard work, and it's also belief: the belief of walking on the court and standing up tall. Even if you don't have that, you have to find a way to fake it. Then the other opponent doesn't get an easy ride, because at the top of the game, it comes down to one or two points, and that's what the kids have to learn. I think with Andrew, he played for a set and a half and didn't miss a ball, and David, in the fourth set, he just raised the level. They just competed so well, and they never dropped.'

Even the normally poker-faced Bates admitted afterwards that he had struggled to contain his emotions during the match. 'It was one of the best performances I've ever seen, no question about it, if not the best I've ever seen,' he said. 'I was just in shock by the side of the court during the tie-breaker. I had no idea what I was doing; I was probably complaining like a complete prat. I was shaking like a leaf, it was just so exciting.'

It was then up to Rusedski to wrap the tie up in Sunday's first singles match against Okun, though there was a contingency plan in place for the fifth rubber which would, in all likelihood, have meant Murray making his singles debut. Brimming with confidence after his performance in the doubles, he proclaimed himself ready for more. 'If it goes down to the wire, I'd love to play, as would any of the guys,' he said. In the end, he wasn't needed.

Rusedski, the anchor of the team and its unofficial leader, polished off Okun with efficient professionalism, beating him 6–3, 6–4, 6–2 to cue more British celebrations and ensure that the heroics of Murray and Sherwood hadn't been in vain.

'That weekend, I think we found, in Andrew and David, two players who really showed us a lot. That was something I was very, very proud of,' said Rusedski. 'I was proud of the way they played, the way they gelled, the way that everybody got on. I was really proud because it was one of those ties which everybody didn't think we were going to find a way to get the third point. But we did. So that was the most satisfying and one of my best moments in Davis Cup.'

Murray might say the same.

7

FUTURE IMPERFECT

TWO THOUSAND AND FIVE WILL BE REMEMBERED AS A TUMULTUOUS YEAR IN THE life of Andy Murray, but for the first six months, it must have seemed like anything but. Having finished 2004 on a high with victories in two Futures events and accolades like the BBC Young Sports Personality of the Year, the new year began in low-key style and was to get a good deal worse before it got better.

At the end of 2004, Murray and his coach, William 'Pato' Álvarez, a 69-year-old Colombian based at the Sánchez-Casal Academy and key member of their coaching staff, had formed a plan designed to get Murray into the world's top 50. It was an ambitious goal considering he ended the season ranked 411 after steady but unspectacular progress up the rankings. Yet Álvarez, who had coached more than 40 top 50 players during a long and distinguished career (including tennis legend Ilie Nastase, and the Academy's owners, Emilio Sánchez and Sergio Casal), glories in the nickname 'El Guru del Tenis'. He had every confidence in his charge, telling the *Daily Telegraph* that he had 'never seen a better talent than Andy'.

Álvarez's plan for the start of 2005 was to get Murray to South America in the hope of picking up enough points to qualify for the string of ATP tournaments out there, including the Viña Del Mar Movistar Open, in the first couple of months of the season. However, to do that, he would have to play a lot of matches and win most of them. The season began with back-to-back weeks spent trying to qualify for Challenger events in Chile: phase one of the plan. In the first tournament, in La Serena, he got through two rounds of qualifying only to lose in the final one – the most frustrating outcome possible. In the second, in Santiago, he lost in the first round of the 'quallies'. That was the end of that idea.

For all the glamour and glitz associated with being a professional tennis player, life as a touring pro, at least early on, is full of fruitless, grim trips to far-flung places, sometimes in venues and hotels where the only thing more suspect than the food is the plumbing. Almost all players who reach the top do so by fighting their way, at least for a time, through the difficult, gritty layers of first the Futures and Satellites, then Challengers before eventually reaching the Holy Grail of the ATP Tour.

It's an environment where linespeople and ball kids are considered the height of luxury and where keen 17 year olds are regarded with a weary eye by the older, more seasoned pros. In such a tough and testing environment, the four Futures titles Murray had won by January 2005 earned him a lot more respect than his junior US Open win.

Marcos Baghdatis, the Cypriot who was runner-up to Roger Federer in the 2006 Australian Open final, is two years older than Murray and, like him, a junior grand-slam champion (he won the Australian Open title in 2003), but he spent three years in the lower tiers of men's tennis before he made his mark on the ATP Tour. Baghdatis says, 'I think people don't realise what players go through. It's not easy. I'm not talking about me; I mean everybody. Even guys who get wildcards, it's not easy, because we work our butts off. There are millions of players working the same way, doing the same thing, and it's tough. There are only like 50 that are really in there.

'Winning a junior grand slam title gives you some confidence, and it gives you some hope. It meant something for me to be a good junior — for my family, for my country, for sure — but I knew that I had to go on and the way would be long and tough. I played Futures and Challengers in India, in Uzbekistan, and that's not fun. Maybe some people think it's easy, but I can tell you it's not. You have to go through a lot of sacrifices. But that's life I think, and you have to be strong in life and not give up and one day it will be easier.'

It would get easier for Murray but not for a while. To make matters even more trying, he went through a growth spurt during the early months of 2005 which gave him an aching back. As a result, he sat out most of February, playing only one Futures event (in Portugal), which, due to his being a late entry, he had to qualify for. During the last round of qualifying, his back played up again, and he was forced to retire from the match. After all the problems he had been through with his knee the previous season and just when he was trying to regain some momentum, back trouble was the last thing Murray needed.

At least his trip to Israel with the Davis Cup squad provided a massive highlight. The win in doubles with David Sherwood and the nature of their tie-winning performance in beating the world-class team of Jonathan Erlich and Andy Ram was a timely confidence boost for Murray and a reminder to him and the doubting world that he had the potential to be a world beater.

He got another lift in March by qualifying for a Challenger in Barletta, Italy, and scoring a first-round win in the main draw over

Arnaud Di Pasquale, who had been ranked as high as 39 in the world. It was Murray's biggest win to date. Two more unsuccessful qualifying weeks followed in Naples and Valencia, where he failed to win a match in either, before he put in one of his better performances of the season by reaching the semi-finals of a Futures event in Cremona.

But there was better news to come: thanks to his relationship with the Sánchez-Casal Academy, Murray had been granted a wildcard into the ATP event in Barcelona, which began on 18 April. Wildcards into tournaments are like gold dust for players in the lower leagues, for they offer an instant free pass over the difficult Challenger level and straight to the ranking points and prize money on offer in tennis's equivalent of the Premier League. There had been talk, in March, of Murray getting a wildcard into the prestigious Nasdaq-100 Open in Miami, an event which likes to call itself 'the fifth grand slam', but it never materialised. This time, however, he had been gifted a chance in his adopted city and on clay, a surface which, on Álvarez's advice, he found himself playing on more and more.

To make the prospect even more tantalising, Murray was drawn to play 25-year-old Czech journeyman Jan Hernych, then ranked 79 in the world, in the first round. Beating Hernych wasn't impossible, and Murray went into his first-ever match on the ATP Tour expecting to do just that, despite the fact that his own ranking was barely inside the top 400, more than 300 places below Hernych. The night before his match, his mother sent him a scouting report, of sorts, which might have buoyed his confidence, telling him that his granny was a better volleyer than the Czech was.

It may have been the big league, but the circumstances weren't exactly dripping with glamour. The Real Club de Tenis might be accurately described as Barcelona's equivalent of Queen's Club in that it has a long tradition of being a sporting and social hub for the more well-to-do residents of the city and occasionally puts its wealthy members out by hosting professional tennis events. It has two show courts of reasonable size, but, since it is a tennis club more often than it is a tournament venue, most of the outer courts are not designed for spectators. It was for this reason that Judy found herself, according to a report by the *Daily Telegraph*'s Mark Hodgkinson, watching her younger son's first ATP Tour match while sitting on a dustbin lid.

Hodgkinson was the only British reporter sent to Barcelona to cover Murray, whose lacklustre start to the season had dissipated some of the hype which had built up around him the previous year. Hodgkinson himself watched the match on Court Four – which was played in searing heat – through a hedge, peering through the gaps in the bushes to see Murray give Hernych a severe test: one which the Scot could, and perhaps should, have won. Instead, he lost 3–6, 6–4, 6–4.

Also watching and cheering him on – presumably from another part of the hedge – was Murray's friend, and fellow Sánchez-Casal alumna, Svetlana Kuznetsova. A video analyst from the Sánchez-Casal Academy was perched on a nearby stepladder.

Most 17 year olds who had just pushed an experienced, seasoned pro so close on their main tour debut might reasonably have been a little disappointed but heartened by having avoided a humbling defeat, but Murray was in no mood to tell anyone he was just happy to be there. Instead, he railed at his failure to win, telling Hodgkinson, 'That was a terrible, terrible performance from me.' Much of his fury stemmed from having let Hernych off the hook. Having recovered from a bout of cramp early in the third set to go 3–1 up, Murray was twice within a point of a 4–1 lead before Hernych dragged the match level. Even after that, the young Scot had break point opportunities.

'I probably played well for about six or seven points of the entire match,' said Murray. 'I had plenty of chances in that match and just didn't take them. That was probably down to inexperience from me. I was too defensive and played some stupid shots on the big points. I relaxed too much. I thought I had won and started to think about my next match, possibly playing against one of the Spaniards on the centre court. I had expected to win. Hernych is nothing special.'

It may be Murray's good fortune that the 6 ft 4 in. Hernych, who lost in the next round to David Ferrer, is not a *Daily Telegraph* reader, given the young tyke's rather disparaging remarks about a player seven years older and more than three hundred places higher up the professional standings than him. At the time, the teenager seemed to be getting ahead of himself, yet Murray had no qualms about taking consolation from his belief that he was just as good a player as Hernych, if not a better one.

'The only positive thing to come out of this match is that I now know that I can definitely get up there into the top 100,' said Murray. 'Hernych is a pretty average player. If he can get that high in the world, then I don't see why I can't either. There isn't anything that he can do that I can't.' Murray, of course, went on to be vindicated by his performances later in the year – Hernych finished the year at 76 in the rankings, 11 places lower than Murray.

The following week, Murray remained in Spain. It was back to the weekly grind of the Futures circuit, though his experience in Barcelona had given him a dose of confidence which helped propel him to the semi-finals in Lleida and the quarter-finals in Vic in successive weeks.

However, behind the scenes, large and irreparable cracks were starting to appear in his relationship with Álvarez. Ostensibly, their dispute was about match tactics – Álvarez wanted Murray to hone his defensive game by playing most of his matches on clay, while Murray wanted to stay true to his instincts to be more aggressive and play more on hardcourts – but the breakdown of their partnership had as much to do with the generation gap as anything else.

The relationship between coach and tennis player can be a suffocating one, forcing teacher and pupil to share rooms, meals, and hours of practice and down-time together. Any such arrangement between a 69-year-old Spaniard and a 17-year-old Scottish lad was always going to be difficult, but when they began to clash over the fundamentals of Murray's tennis, the die was cast.

'I just wasn't enjoying things on or off the court. He was trying to get me to play in a way I didn't like, and it just wasn't working,' said Murray. 'He wanted me to be less aggressive and play more like the Spanish players. That's not the way I play. I like to play hard.'

The antipathy between them, which was fast turning to acrimony, was not helping Murray's results either. He lost in the second round of the Dresden Challenger, and his last match under Álvarez was a dismal 6–4, 6–1 loss to Spain's Marcel Granollers-Pujol in the second round of qualifying for a Challenger in Ettlingen, Germany.

'I think it was personal because off the court we were arguing a lot. We weren't having so much fun. There were a lot of problems,' said Murray, who turned 18 the week he and Álvarez parted. 'The last week we were together, it got a bit nasty. He was saying bad things about my tennis and bad things about me. I don't really need somebody that negative in my corner just now. So I thought the best thing for me to do was to stop with him. He just said if I continue like I have been the last two months, I'm not going to be any good. If I have the same mentality as I do now, there's no chance of me doing well. But the reason for me being like that is because I wasn't happy off the court, and I wasn't enjoying being at the tournaments alone with him. So that's why I had to stop.'

He arrived at Roland Garros, for what would turn out to be his last junior tournament, with a familiar coach – his mum Judy, whose most important task for the week was to ensure a steady and unstinting supply of baguettes slathered with chocolate spread for her still-growing boy. Making the transition back to the juniors after

115

playing so many Futures and Challenger events is never easy, and young players often complain about how difficult it is to motivate themselves after tasting life amongst the grown-ups, but Murray had reasons to be excited about coming to Paris. It was his first junior event since winning the US Open title, and he was top seed, both facts which made trying to win the junior title a matter of personal pride. Also, having missed the event the previous year because of knee trouble, he wanted to make his mark.

'I didn't get the chance to play last year because I was injured,' he said. 'It's a junior grand slam and a lot of good players have won the junior title here. I wanted to come here and prove that I can play on clay and not just on fast surfaces. I don't think the seeding makes a big difference, because you still have to win all your matches. In a junior grand slam, you get a lot of experience playing on the big courts, like today. I'm not going to get to play on courts like that if I'm playing some of the smaller senior tournaments. You get a lot of experience. If you do well in the tournament, it's good for your confidence, because you can see a lot of the great players have done well here as well.'

It probably wasn't the baguettes or the chocolate spread, but something upset his stomach before his first match against Piero Luisi of Venezuela, which very nearly ended his tournament before it had really begun. 'I ate something last night and since 9 o'clock this morning I've been going to the toilet every 20 minutes. At the end of the first set, I felt really bad,' he explained, after coming through 6–4, 2–6, 6–3. 'When I was playing, I had no energy. I didn't feel like moving, and the other guy played OK. In the third set, I knew I had to go for it, because I knew if I carried on like I was in the second set, then I probably would have lost.'

He felt a little better against accomplished French teenager Jonathan Dasnieres de Veigy in the second round, beating him 6–3, 7–6 to move through to the third round, where he was joined by his friend and doubles partner for the week, Andrew Kennaugh.

'I wasn't feeling bad at all, and from the first set, I was pumped up. I knew the guy was good and that I would have to play well, and I did,' said Murray, as he sat in one of the tiniest of Roland Garros's four interview rooms and spoke to the handful of British tennis writers keeping tabs on his progress. 'It was still quite a tough match, and I really had to concentrate – he really didn't play well at the crucial times. Playing in the seniors teaches you that sometimes it can be the best thing to play tougher opponents earlier in the tournament, because they aren't quite at their best yet. I feel good about how I played. There were times when I was nervous because it's Roland Garros and it's so important. It's very good for getting attention from sponsors and people like that to do well here, but it would also be good for my confidence.'

Another morale-boosting win followed in the third round, this time a 6–2, 6–2 rout of Italian Gianluca Naso. His quarter-final opponent looked like being arguably the toughest prospect in the draw, the extremely talented Argentine Juan-Martin Del Potro, who is widely being tipped as the next high achiever from his country's seemingly unending supply of world-class players. Murray beat him 6–4, 6–2, and it was clear from his genial, chatty press conference afterwards (in a nearly full main interview room, no less) that he regarded it as tantamount to a final.

'I'm seeded to get to the final, and I'm expecting to do well, but today was by far my toughest match,' he said. 'Definitely he's the highest ranked player, and he's been playing really well the last couple of months. The other guys I think can play well but not the same as him. I knew it was going to be really difficult. The guy is like 440 in the world. He's won three senior tournaments this year and a couple of semi-finals. I played very well, so I'm pretty happy.'

His jovial post-victory mood was catching, and he charmed his audience, which included a smattering of other nationalities –

including veteran American tennis writer Bud Collins – anxious to see what the Brits were making such a fuss about. He regaled them with the gory details of his fall in the first set when he had scraped his knuckles along the clay, noting, with a grin, that, 'There was blood on the court. I like that.'

The question of his nationality was raised by one of the British journalists, to which Murray replied in typically feisty style: 'It's just a lot of people, like from abroad, see *Britain* as just *England*. I can accept maybe foreigners making that mistake, but when it's like *English* people calling me English . . .'

Collins, whose questions are often far sharper than his avuncular manner would suggest, decided to play devil's advocate and followed up by pointing out that he was a foreigner and couldn't really understand what the difference was between being Scottish and English. It had the desired effect. Murray's reaction was polite but impassioned, a fiery young Scot standing up for his heritage. 'I was born in *Scotland*,' he said, enunciating every word as if speaking to the hard of understanding. 'If somebody says to me I'm *English*, I correct them because it's not true. And I don't mind when people call me *British*, but it really annoys me when I get called *English*.'

'Really. Why?'

'Because I'm not from there. It's like calling someone from *France German*.'

Having firmly established his ancestry, Murray then went on to assess his next opponent, Croatia's Marin Cilic, and, in the process, make the mistake of underestimating a player who would turn out to not only ruin Murray's chances of winning back-to-back junior grand-slam titles but would also go on to win Roland Garros and come within a handful of ranking points of ending the season as junior world No. 1 and world junior champion. The Zagreb-based 16 year old was unseeded and, at that point, had not made his mark in junior or senior tennis, so perhaps Murray should be forgiven for talking up his chances, even if, with hindsight, it was unwise. 'I practised with him the day before the tournament started, and that was the first time I saw him, but I think he plays quite similar to Del Potro. He's maybe 6 ft 4 in. He serves pretty well. He's a bit erratic from the baseline. I think if I play like I did today, I should win pretty comfortably.'

He didn't do either and lost 7–5, 6–3 after putting in a performance which was as uneven as it was bad tempered. He was furious with himself for blowing a lead to lose the first set, and though Judy moved from her seat in the bleachers to be closer to the court halfway through the match, there was nothing she could do to stop her son losing in a blur of frustration, missed chances and smashed rackets. At one point, Murray screamed out to the half-full, windy Court No. 1, which is known as the 'bullring', 'What are you *doing* Andy?' When he walked off court and said to his mum, 'That was rubbish, wasn't it?' she could hardly disagree.

It didn't help that Murray and Kennaugh had still been on court late into the previous evening playing their doubles quarter-final against Russians Pavel Chekov and Valeri Rudnev, before losing 8–6 in the third set.

'It wasn't good today. I didn't play well the whole match. I didn't have any energy. Yesterday was a long day, and this morning I didn't feel great – I just couldn't get myself going,' he said. 'Obviously, the older you get, the better you learn to cope with things like that, but I do think playing doubles means you can end up playing a lot of matches and getting tired. That's not an excuse, because I should be fit enough to play two matches in one day, but I don't like playing doubles for that reason.'

He tried to find an upside, though, and with the start of the grass-court season now just 48 hours away, he didn't need to look too far for one. 'If I'd won here, then all that would have happened is that I would have had ten times as much pressure on me, so when I look at it like that, maybe it's a good thing,' he said. 'Everyone will have slightly lower expectations of me over the next few weeks. It's going to be an important time for me. I've only played one ATP tournament before, and now I get the chance to play three of them in three weeks at Queen's, Nottingham and Wimbledon.'

He then made a prediction. It sounded rather hollow as he sat and contemplated losing a junior match that only a handful of journalists and his mum had watched, but his words would come true within a few days: 'I'm looking forward to the next few weeks on grass. I like playing in big tournaments and in good atmospheres, so I think I'll lift my game.'

8

QUEEN'S CLUB

ANDY MURRAY PRACTISED WITH TIM HENMAN AT QUEEN'S CLUB, THE UPMARKET tennis centre in London, the day before the Stella Artois tournament due to be staged there started. Murray was still disappointed about losing in the French Open junior semi-final to Marin Cilic in Paris the day before returning to London, although he was happy about moving into a rented flat with his mum Judy, where he would stay for the duration of the grass-court season. Henman could detect the young Scot was on a bit of a downer. 'Who cares what happens in the juniors?' said Henman. 'The main tour is what it's all about.'

The words would have made Murray realise that all the titles and the adulation that had come his way during his time on the junior circuit counted for nothing now. It was year zero, and his first test would be on home soil in the Stella Artois Championships, the traditional curtain-raiser for Wimbledon.

Emilio Sánchez was delighted that the young Scot had been given a wildcard into the Stella Artois tournament. 'What he needs is to get used to the top level of tennis,' said Sánchez, speaking from his tennis academy in Spain. 'Andrew is a great talent, and he has a promising future in front of him, but there is still a long way for him to go. It's not the same to win in the juniors as it is to win on the main tour.

'He still needs to build some strength and to put some more order in his game to make the next step, but he has a very smooth and easy game, plays very good ground strokes, and he can mix it up with nice angles. He needs to come forward and volley more, but with his height, that is something that he can learn. This wildcard will help him gain much needed experience.'

The tournament had an impressive history, and among its previous winners were Pete Sampras in 1995 and 1999, Boris Becker in 1996, Lleyton Hewitt in 2000, 2001 and 2002, and Andy Roddick, who had won the title in 2003 and 2004 and was going for his hat-trick.

Greg Rusedski, Mark Philippoussis and Richard Gasquet, the young French star, were also competing, along with the Wimbledon semi-finalist from 2004, Mario Ancic, and Sébastien Grosjean, a two-time Stella Artois finalist. Other established players in the draw included three-time winner Lleyton Hewitt and British No. 1 Tim Henman.

Murray was not the only young, up-and-coming tennis player given a wildcard. He may have won the 2004 US Open junior title, but it was Gael Monfils who was the real star of the year lifting the Wimbledon, Australian and French Open junior crowns and finishing the year as the top junior in the world. For Monfils, the Stella Artois Championships marked another point in his tennis education. He had made the step up from junior to senior level reasonably well, and the way he had made the transition gave confidence to Murray that he could do the same. Monfils had already beaten 2004 French Open champion Gaston Gaudio in Doha, Qatar, in January 2005 (6–4, 7–6), and the top-ten player Nikolay Davydenko was beaten 4–6, 6–1, 6–4 in Miami in March, so it was clear that the Frenchman could compete with the best.

Also scheduled was a special challenge match between John McEnroe and Goran Ivanisevic. Murray was keen to watch them play, but such was the impact that he had on the competition, it was Ivanisevic and McEnroe who were talking about him and wanting to watch him play by the end of the tournament and not the other way round.

'It's a sparkling field,' said tournament director Ian Wight. 'Lleyton, Andy [Roddick] and Tim are joined by an outstanding crop of young European players headed by Mario Ancic and Richard Gasquet, and we also have Andy Murray in the draw who is an up-and-coming player.'

Murray only had a day and a half to make the transition from the clay of Paris to the grass of London, and he prepared as best he could. As well as practising with Tim Henman, he also played a match on grass at Surbiton against Mario Ancic. 'That was my first proper match practice on grass,' said Murray. 'It was good to play against someone as good as him and who serves well. We played first to eight games. I lost 8–5 and was broken once, but it was well worth it.

'Remember, Mario made the semis at Wimbledon in 2004, and he beat Tim Henman on the way, so he's one of the best grass-court players in the world, and I played quite well against him.'

Murray talked about how he wanted to play better than he had done in his first and only ATP tour event in Barcelona in April. 'I was very disappointed, as I didn't play well against Jan Hernych,' said Murray. 'I had lots of chances and lost my concentration in the third set when I was 3–1 up. I want to play better at Queen's Club than I did then.'

His first round opponent was Santiago Ventura of Spain, who had not played much on grass and was clearly not comfortable on the surface. The Spanish player had come to Queen's Club on a bad run of form after first-round defeats to Christophe Rochus of Belgium (6–3, 6–2) in Hamburg in May and to Chris Guccione of Australia in the French Open later that same month (6–3, 2–6, 6–1, 3–6, 6–2).

Murray was excited about the prospect of playing his first match in front of a large home crowd and was confident he could cope with the pressure of being the bright new hope of British tennis. However, he made it clear that grass was not his favourite surface and there was more chance of him winning the French or US Open in the future than Wimbledon.

Because Murray's best wins had been abroad, he was a player whom the British tennis public had heard a lot about but had not seen play live at the top level. Such was the anticipation, thousands flocked to Court 1 at Queen's Club to watch him play. His game was third on court on Monday, 5 June 2005, and Murray looked confident as he strolled out waving to the gallery. It was the first time the British public had had a close look at the youngster, who came on listening to the Black Eyed Peas song 'Let's Get It Started' on his iPod. The temporary stands of Queen's Club's Court 1 were full of supporters wearing anoraks because of the unseasonably cold weather, many of whom did not quite know what to expect from the young man on court.

It became evident that Murray was totally focused on his match, and he did not look nervous. He served well, which was a real bonus as he had been struggling with his deliveries during the French Open juniors. He had been throwing his ball-toss too far to the left, causing him to drag the shot down towards the net. This meant he was off balance when he landed after his serve, and it took him time to recover to play his next shot.

Against Ventura he rectified the problem, and although he stayed back for most of the match, it was clear from the first point that

Murray was too strong for the Spaniard and won 6–1, 6–2 in just 44 minutes. During the match, he served five aces, made just one double fault and won 85 per cent of his points on serve. He played consistently, was exciting to watch and his first time on British soil in a major event was a huge success.

Mark Petchey, who was helping to coach him after the split with Pato Álvarez, had made an immediate impact, helping Murray to restructure his serve slightly, which gave it more pep and offered him a weapon to complement the ground strokes he had honed with the hours of pounding practice on the clay courts at his training base outside Barcelona.

'You couldn't fault him at all, and he played really well in his first game in his first big tournament,' Petchey said. 'There was a lot of pressure and expectation on him, and to go out and play the way he did tells me a lot about him as a person. It would not have been easy for him. He served beautifully and coped with the pressure superbly.'

Afterwards, the talk in his press conference was about how well he could do in future, bearing in mind Tim Henman and Greg Rusedski were reaching the twilight of their careers. As the hype increased, Murray called on the British public not to get too carried away: 'A lot of people will expect a lot of me during this summer, but it's always the same for British players playing at home during the grass-court season. With Tim and Greg, everybody expects them to win tournaments at home, but it doesn't really work like that.

'If I get some good draws, I've got a chance of winning some matches. However, if I play against one of the good players in the coming weeks, I don't have a chance, because I've got no real experience on grass or of playing in big tournaments.

'I am fine with all the interest in me, and I have played in big matches before, but, to be honest, the crowds have never really been with me. I played in the Davis Cup in Israel, and there was a really big crowd there, but pretty much 5,000 of them were against me.

Then I played the US Open junior final, which was a big match, and the crowd was kind of half and half. Now to play at home in front of a lot of people who are on my side is good motivation for me. It really helps you. You feel like you've got a lot of people there helping you and wanting you to win. It really makes you play better.'

The quick transition from the clay courts of Paris to the grass at Queen's Club was something Murray had taken in his stride. 'The match against Ventura was my first real competitive one on grass. I only had a day and a half practice after my French Open semi and I didn't play so well there,' he said. 'I felt I played a pretty good match against Ventura. The guy wasn't so good on grass, but, still, it was tough for me, because I hadn't really got any practice in before.

'In fact, playing on grass was actually OK and better than I thought. On the courts at Queen's Club the ball comes quite fast on the serves, and it takes spin quite well. If you play a top spin, it sits up quite a lot. If you play a slice, it stays down quite low. It played more like a slow hardcourt, and it suited me quite well.'

On the Tuesday, Murray practised on an outside court with Petchey, preparing for his second-round match against the number nine seed Taylor Dent, who had beaten Tomas Behrend of Germany in the first round 6–4, 6–3. On paper, Dent, the big-serving American with bags of experience, should have beaten Murray comfortably. However, Murray's fighting qualities could not be underestimated, and the momentum was with the young Scot, who was relishing being in the spotlight in Britain for the first time. In saying that, Dent was the world No. 30, had won an ATP Tour title at Newport on grass in 2002 and had been ranked as high as No. 21 in the world.

Once again, Murray walked out onto court listening to 'Let's Get It Started', and the British fans were with him from the off. However, the 7,000 crowd were still getting used to having a new local hero, and the sounds of both 'C'mon Andy' and 'C'mon Andrew' could be heard as nobody was quite sure how to address him.

In the first set, Murray was in complete control, easily winning it 6–3 in just 28 minutes. He never let the American settle, and Murray's passing shots were sublime, as was his return of serve. Although Dent served reasonably well, Murray hit back fierce returns to the feet of his opponent, which left the big American powerless.

Murray's battling qualities were also evident early on. At 2–2 in the second set, he was 15–40 down, but he pulled out a backhand winner and a magnificent first serve to save the game and make it 3–2. The decisive break was then forced in the next game with the help of a piercing service return to make it 4–2, and there were no dramas from then on in with Murray easily winning the set 6–3 to take the match. At the end, he rushed off court to celebrate with Mark Petchey and Judy, and then had to battle his way through the adoring crowds to get back to the locker-room. The win over Dent had propelled Murray into the public consciousness.

Afterwards, he admitted he had enjoyed playing in front of a big crowd and had raised his game as a result. 'I don't understand why people would get nervous playing in front of their home crowd,' he said. 'I like playing tennis in front of crowds like that, and anybody who doesn't shouldn't really be playing. If you want to be one of the best, you're going to have to play in some big arenas. Queen's Club isn't half as big as some of the places I have played, like New York. I just enjoy it when I play in front of these big crowds. When they are with you, it makes it much easier to play well.'

Murray also paid tribute to Mark Petchey, who seemed to have had an instant effect on his charge. 'I got beat in the semi-finals of the French Open juniors last week,' he said, 'but Mark has picked me up since I arrived here at the Stella Artois. He has a lot of confidence in me, and we can chat about anything. He has been a big help. If I keep playing like this, there is no way I'm stopping working with Mark. He works for the LTA and does Sky Sports, so maybe it's not going to happen. I'm not going to rush into making any decisions, because the next couple of months and the next couple of years are important for me.'

Petchey sounded pleased with the work he was doing with Murray: 'He has just beaten Taylor Dent, a man ranked 327 places above him, and he played some shots most people can only dream about. I have watched a lot of guys through the years, and I remember playing against Lleyton Hewitt when he was 15 years old, and he was brilliant. Andy is every bit as good as he was. We don't want to rush him as there is a lot of expectation on his shoulders. People want him to be the next Tim Henman, but that is not easy as Tim was very consistent and did not get the credit he deserved.

'Andy is a great prospect, and I would like our other young players to learn from the desire he shows on court. He wants to compete and win, and that is healthy.'

Andy's next opponent was Thomas Johansson, the world No. 20 who had become Australian Open champion in 2002, beating Marat Safin in the final.

'I returned well against Dent but my match against Johansson will be completely different,' said Murray. 'Johansson plays much better from the back. He still serves well, and he returns better.'

The match was played on the Thursday and proved to be one of the pivotal moments in Murray's fledgling career. It also turned out to be one of the most exciting and dramatic matches that Queen's had seen in years and so nearly had the perfect ending.

The charismatic teenager kept the centre-court crowd captivated for nearly three hours. The match was finely poised throughout, and the first set went to a tie-break, but the Swede easily won it 7–1. In the second set, Murray kept his cool superbly as the pressure mounted and battled from 4–1 down in the second-set tie-break to win it 7–5.

It was in the deciding set that the drama unfolded. Murray was fast becoming a real tennis showman, and with the scores tied at 3–3 in the deciding set, and after a remarkable eight deuces on his serve, Murray turned to the crowd and urged them for more support. They responded, and from then on, Johansson hardly got a cheer, while every shot Murray hit was lauded by the capacity crowd who, as usual at Queen's, were in good voice after a day of sampling the products of the tournament's sponsor, Stella Artois.

With Murray 30–15 up on the Johansson serve and 5–4 to the good in games, the young Scot suddenly fell, straining his left ankle in the process. After lengthy treatment, Murray tried to soldier on but Johansson made it 5–5 before the teenager ran into more fitness problems. In the 11th game of the deciding set, he fell at the back of the court as if a sniper had taken him out. The way he went down was so shocking that Johansson ran to check on his opponent and recognising the signs of cramp, raised Murray's leg against his shoulder to ease the tension in the teenager's muscles. The crowd held their breath as the young Scot lay face down, not moving for at least three minutes. After extensive treatment, he decided to play on, but it was in vain, and Johansson won the final set 7–5, without Murray winning another point. It was a sad end to a great display by the young player.

'I'm very disappointed, because I played a pretty good match, and I'm a bit annoyed that I wasn't able to finish it,' said Murray. 'I was 5–4 and 30–15 up when I went over on my ankle, and I couldn't really continue. I was getting a lot of cramps, and I couldn't really move.

'I played the point, and I hit a lob before I went over on my ankle. I could have got up, because I was able to walk on it. I'm annoyed that I didn't, because I think he let the ball bounce and then just popped it over the net. I think if I'd got up, I could have gone on to maybe win the point and the match.

'The second time, I heard something crack, though, and that's why

I didn't get up. I thought it could have been pretty bad. I've done that ankle three or four times before – not lately, but maybe back in 2004 or even earlier – so I didn't want to take any risks. I put ice on it afterwards, so I can't feel it so much, but I did manage to walk into my press conference, which can only be good.

'What can't be forgotten is that I was playing against one of the best players on the tour. The rallies were very long, so, obviously, there was quite a lot of pressure on me, and I was trying to gee myself up physically. The other disappointment for me was that I would have played Tim Henman in the quarter-finals, and I am sorry to miss out on that.'

Johansson was full of praise for the way Murray had played against him. 'He is very, very tough,' said the Swede. 'He is already very, very good, but he's going to be even better. He can certainly be a top 50 player. He serves very fast, and to do that at 18 is very impressive. The only thing he can improve is his second serve return.

'It was very hard for him during our match because of all the interest in him, but he handled it well. I was lucky, because I saw his game against Taylor Dent on television and saw how capable he was.'

Murray was pleased that a grand-slam champion, who had beaten some of the best players in the world, thought he had potential. 'It's good for the confidence, and it shows that maybe I got a bit of respect off him,' said Murray. 'I like what he said, and although top fifty would be good, I would like to be top ten, but it's going to take a long time, and I'm going to have to work very hard until I get there.'

After his exit, Murray simply didn't care who was doing well in the tournament. All he wanted was to make sure that his ankle was OK so that he could play in the following week's event at Nottingham and if not that competition, most definitely at Wimbledon.

On the Friday afternoon, heads turned as Murray walked into the manicured grounds of Queen's Club for a final time. It was striking to compare the interest in him then to that on the Sunday before the tournament began, when he walked into the grounds with nobody giving him a second look. After just two fine grass-court performances, he was now fêted by the mix of 'Sloane Rangers' and well-heeled tennis fans who frequented the club and by the wider public, who'd watched his matches on the BBC.

Murray made his way through the adoring crowd with his agent Sian Masterton of the sports agency Octagon. The pair then took up residence on a plush red sofa in the players' lounge as Boris Becker and Tim Henman walked by. Despite being in the company of superstars, the teenage Scot looked as though he was the most laid-back person in the place.

As he started his lunch of pasta and a chocolate bar, the only thing that seemed to surprise and excite him was the fact that John McEnroe had offered to help him with his training. 'He is one of my heroes – one of the greatest players around – and I would definitely take him up on that offer if it was possible,' said Murray. 'I always liked him. He was different from everybody else, and the fans loved him. For him to help me would be an honour.'

Behind him on the wall were pictures of past winners of the Stella Artois tournament, such as Becker, McEnroe and Jimmy Connors. Murray allowed himself a little smile when he was asked when his picture would be joining them on that wall: 'Grass isn't my favourite surface, and, to be honest, although I would love to win Wimbledon, I think I maybe have a better chance at the French Open. I've always thought winning the French was a better achievement, because so many different players tend to win it, and it is more competitive. Pete Sampras won Wimbledon seven times but never won the French. Don't get me wrong, I would love to win my home tournament, but the French is a bigger test. Having said that, I have been happy with the way I have played on grass this week.'

That, as anybody who had been around Murray those past few days would have realised, was a massive understatement. He easily defeated the Spaniard Santiago Ventura in the first round, overpowered Taylor Dent of America in the second and only an injury, when he was two points from victory against Thomas Johansson, denied him a quarter-final clash with Tim Henman.

He had gone from zero to hero and was being hailed as the hottest British player of his generation. The public saw him as the new Henman and the perfect young man to replace the Englishman in their affections. Murray, though, was a very different type of player. Events at the Stella Artois Championships had showed that he had attitude. He was a player who pumped his fists as if he meant it – a charismatic showman who could whip up the crowd and get angry with himself. He was petulant, even.

He bounced his racket off the ground when things weren't going well and celebrated like a footballer when they were. Henman may have had that English reserve, but Murray wore his heart on his sleeve, and the Queen's Club tennis fans knew it.

The Scot had also taken all the media interest and adulation in his stride. The fact that he had been in Dunblane Primary School on the day Thomas Hamilton had shot dead 16 children and a teacher in 1996 had been mentioned once again, but Murray made it clear that he had spoken about that once and would not do so again.

On court, his passionate behaviour had endeared him to the tennis public. The number of prim and proper English men and women trying to put on fake Scottish accents in celebration of his efforts would have shamed a 'See You Jimmy' convention.

Interviewed by Sue Barker, cheered on by Cilla Black, chased by autograph hunters of all ages, it was the week that Murray came of age as a tennis player. The ultimate accolade had come on the Thursday when he had been practising two courts away from Lleyton Hewitt, the former Wimbledon champion. At the end of the practice session, more young autograph hunters, the best barometer of who is hot and who is not, had been waiting for Murray than for the Australian.

'I've enjoyed the whole experience of playing the Stella Artois,' said Murray. 'I came into the tournament with low expectations, and despite that, I felt I played very well.'

Off the court, it was clear that Murray was well looked after. Mark Petchey was becoming a bigger and bigger influence, and Judy was ensuring that her son was handling the media exposure and pressures of top-class tennis. Lisa Eyre, the former international rower, was his fitness coach, and 'Team Murray' had come through its first tennis test superbly well.

But what was next for Murray? He was realistic enough to understand that two good matches at Queen's Club was just the first step on his way up the tennis ladder. 'I am very level-headed and realise just because I won two matches this week I'm not a superstar and will not be in the top one hundred in the next couple of weeks,' he said. 'I did well but have a lot to work on and have to go back to playing in some of the smaller tournaments to get my ranking up. Hopefully, I will get a few more chances, and if I take them, I can get into the top 100, but it's all down to me.'

After the grass-court season, Murray envisaged having to step down to the Futures Tour, which is far removed from the grandeur of Queen's Club. 'It is difficult to play in the Futures tournaments as you don't usually get more than ten people watching your matches,' he said. 'For me, playing in a tournament like this at Queen's then having to play in front of just ten people at a tournament in a different country is pretty tough.

'If I do well in the next couple of weeks, I may be able to play in the Challenger Tour, which isn't quite as bad as the Futures, but that will only happen if I get my ranking inside 300. I have to realise that to get to the top I have to win most of the games I play in, because I'm not going to get wildcards into championships, like the one at Queen's Club, all the time.'

Boris Becker, who won Wimbledon at the tender age of 17, also had positive comments to make about the rising British star. 'Andrew is talented and a very exciting player,' said the German. 'He has a good personality and seems to speak his mind as well. I would not wrap him in cotton wool as he looks comfortable in his own skin. He is clearly the best young player Britain has.'

A few days later, Andy Roddick won his third Stella Artois title after he beat the 6 ft 10 in. Croat Ivo Karlovic 7–6, 7–6. It was a great achievement by the American, but the Stella Artois championship of 2005 would be remembered for the emergence of Andy Murray more than anything else.

9

MURRAY AT WIMBLEDON: EIGHT TUMULTUOUS SUMMER DAYS

MURRAY'S PERFORMANCES AT QUEEN'S CLUB HAD INCREASED THE HYPE surrounding him as Wimbledon loomed. He was one of three Scots given a wildcard into the grand-slam event, the others going to Alan Mackin and Elena Baltacha. He had hoped that Jamie would also make the tournament, but on Tuesday, 7 June 2005, his brother lost in the first round of the Wimbledon wildcard play-offs to Neil Bamford (6–4, 7–6) at Raynes Park.

After picking up his ankle injury at Queen's Club, Murray's preparations going into the Championships fortnight were far from ideal. As he sat in his flat in Wimbledon, he reflected on whether he should withdraw from the ATP tournament in Nottingham, the last British tennis event before Wimbledon. The enticement for him to play in Nottingham was the chance to improve his world ranking, which he had upped from 357 to around the 315 mark by winning two matches at Queen's. If his ankle could stand the pressure, he would have found himself unable to turn down a chance to rake in the kind of ranking points that it would take him months to earn at the lower-level events he was used to playing in up to that point.

'I spoke to my physiotherapist, and he told me that around 15 June, which was two days after Nottingham started, I could start practising,' said Murray. 'But I really wanted to try and be fit before that for Nottingham, because it was a chance to get a few more matches. I thought if I go into Wimbledon after a week off and I have to play five sets, then I don't think I'd be fit enough.'

On Saturday, 11 June, Murray had an idea that his ankle would not stand up to the rigours of Nottingham but gave it every chance to improve as he really wanted to play. The next day, though, there was no marked improvement, and he realised that he would have to work hard on his fitness to be ready for Wimbledon, let alone play at Nottingham. By the same token, he did not want to tell tournament organisers he was going to withdraw just yet, in case his ankle healed quicker than he expected.

He realised he had to improve his physique to have a chance of matching the success of fellow teenager Rafael Nadal, who had broken through on the world stage in 2005 by winning the French Open. 'Nadal is physically better than everyone else in the world, and maybe I have got two or three more years to catch up with him on that score,' said Murray. 'My body's not developed like his. I have still got some growing to do and some filling out, and I have got to get stronger. It is going to be difficult to do what he has done, but I've got to aim for the top. Out of all the young players, he is the best prospect just now.'

On the Sunday, the day Andy Roddick was winning the Stella Artois tournament at Queen's Club, Murray was a few miles down the road, lying on his sofa. As he lay there watching the final, he continually applied ice to his injured ankle. He was also keeping a close eye on events across in Germany, where Roger Federer, the world No. 1, warmed up for Wimbledon with a 6–4, 6–7 (6), 6–4 victory over the 2005 Australian Open champion Marat Safin to win his third consecutive Gerry Weber Open title at Halle.

Murray had long been an admirer of Federer, and one of his ambitions was to play the man from Switzerland. The Scot, being a great student of the game, realised he would learn a lot taking on the best player of his generation. At Halle, Federer showed he was in great form going into Wimbledon. The 23-year-old Swiss player produced a masterly performance on the grass courts, his finesse proving too much for the powerful but erratic Russian. On the way to the title, Federer defeated Robin Soderling, Florian Mayer, Philipp Kohlschreiber and the No. 7 seed Tommy Haas.

The four-time grand-slam winner had not lost in twenty singles finals since 2003 and extended his impressive three-year winning streak on grass to twenty-nine games after his win in Germany. He was still some way short of Björn Borg's record of forty-one grass-court victories over five years from 1976 to 1980, but he was clearly head and shoulders above everybody else in the world.

It was apparent to Murray that Federer was the man to beat at Wimbledon, and the man from Switzerland was talking a good game as he prepared for the tournament: 'I feel confident going into Wimbledon, but there can always be a tough draw which will make things very difficult. There can always be a shock loss in the first round. My performances in Halle were good, and that is exactly the way I want to feel heading into Wimbledon.'

At that stage of Murray's career, facing Federer or Roddick was still a dream. He was a great admirer of both men and was frustrated at having to watch their matches on television rather than face them over the net.

On Monday, 13 June, Murray officially withdrew from the

Nottingham Open in a bid to safeguard his place in the main draw at Wimbledon the following week. It was a good decision. Having been diagnosed with slight ligament damage, Murray realised that his senior debut at Wimbledon may have been placed in doubt if he had pushed ahead and played at Nottingham.

A statement from Murray's representatives read, 'Andrew's ankle has not healed as quickly as he had hoped. The ligament in the ankle is still slightly inflamed, and he has had to withdraw from the 10tele.com Open in Nottingham. He will be fit for Wimbledon.'

Later, he issued his own statement which made it clear how keen he had been to keep his good run of form going by playing in the final tournament before Wimbledon. 'I was very disappointed to miss the opportunity to play at Nottingham,' he said. 'It was a close call, but as there is a slight inflammation still in the ankle, I was advised to limit my time on court and that I need two full rest days going into Wimbledon.'

The news represented a huge blow for the tournament organisers and also for Thomas Johansson, who had been relishing the prospect of a rematch with Murray after their showdown at the Stella Artois Championships. Johansson, who faced Russian Dmitry Tursunov in the first round at Nottingham, said, 'Murray is a good player and a talented guy, and I was looking forward to playing him again. Last week was tough for him, and he hurt his ankle. I think resting the injury is a good thing for his game so he can concentrate on making Wimbledon.'

Taylor Dent, the big-serving American who had been beaten by Murray at Queen's Club, also played at Nottingham. He recovered from his defeat by Murray with a comfortable 6–3, 6–3 win over German grass-court expert Alexander Popp in his first-round match. The American echoed Johansson in tipping Murray to make a big impression on his senior Wimbledon debut. 'Murray proved that he could turn out to be one hell of a player,' said Dent. 'He has room to grow, and hopefully he will have the support of all the fans.'

In the run-up to Wimbledon, Murray was really under the spotlight with even John McEnroe getting in on the act. Murray was not old enough to have seen the American in his prime but realised the place the charismatic New Yorker has in tennis history. McEnroe, in Britain to commentate on the Championships, said Murray had been 'born to be a tennis player'. The former Wimbledon champion had watched him at the Stella Artois Championships and was impressed with the teenager's performance. He once again reiterated his desire to help coach Murray, but because of McEnroe's television and family commitments, it could clearly never be on a regular basis. 'Me coaching him has been talked about a bit, and I think Andrew is a real talent,' said the tennis legend. 'I'd like to work with him. I'm not going to travel the circuit with him, but there's plenty of people he should turn to in my opinion.

'I would like to work with him on a part-time basis, and I have already offered to do that. I think I could help Andrew. I think he is a great kid. I have six kids of my own and I've got a couple of kids older than Andy, so I'm not looking to travel all the time. I'd like to be part of trying to help him. I think whether he gets help from me or not, he's going to be a very good player.'

McEnroe warned Murray would have to work on his fitness after he suffered cramp and twisted his ankle against Johansson at Queen's Club: 'He's still evolving. He has some issues as it's unusual to cramp in the third set of a two-out-of-three grass-court match, but he is talented and headed the right way.'

After his open shows of emotion on court at Queen's Club, there was also much talk in the media about whether Murray's conduct was becoming of a British tennis player. Up until then, Tim Henman had always kept his emotions in check, apart from the odd fist-pumping, and the restrained way the Englishman played was what was expected at Wimbledon.

On the eve of the tournament, Graham Spiers, chief sports writer of *The Herald* newspaper and a respected television pundit in Scotland, made mention as to why Murray's rebellious nature on court should be encouraged rather than criticised. Spiers wrote:

> I must say, I like the cut of this young bloke's jib. I read a comment last week which made me think even more highly of our tennis prodigy from Dunblane. One of Blighty's distinguished tennis commentators, having witnessed some of Murray's spikier attitudes while tumbling from the junior French Open, said, 'If this is the future of British tennis, then God help us.'
>
> In journalism, I find it an almost unfailing rule that anyone who irks or riles the sports media is usually a good person. So, I take my hat off to Andy Murray. I also savour the experience of seeing how many – if any – early Wimbledon men's singles hurdles he can survive.

Murray's draw was much anticipated but proved to be an anticlimax. He was to meet a qualifier in the first round, which meant waiting for the qualification tournament to be completed before finding out the name of his opponent.

In the days leading up to Wimbledon, Murray-mania, a phrase coined by the tabloids, reached fever pitch, especially in his native Scotland. Shocked by the fact that there was a Scottish tennis player who was making headlines, everybody wanted 'a piece' of the great new talent.

Murray was more interested in sticking to talking about how his tennis game was progressing. 'I'm not fazed by expectations,' he said. 'I set myself quite high standards, and I've set goals for myself. It's up to me and nobody else whether I take my chances and how hard I work. I think I can do it. Some British players just do well in the grass-court season and then fade away, and I don't want to do that.

'I'm not going to comment on what others have done, but I like to think I have a level-headed approach. I don't think that just because I've won two matches at the Stella Artois tournament I'm going to be in the top 100 in the next couple of weeks. I've still got a lot of things to work on, and I know I'm going to have to go back to playing smaller tournaments to lift my ranking. Hopefully, if I get a few more chances like this, and if I keep taking those chances, I'll get to the top 100.'

On the Friday, Murray made his first public comments about McEnroe's offer to occasionally work with him. The Scot conceded that the offer was flattering but the best he could hope for were occasional hitting sessions with the former Wimbledon champion. 'It's a great honour for someone like McEnroe to say he would coach or help me, but it is never going to happen on a full-time basis,' he admitted. 'He has his family and a lot of television commitments in the USA and is only in Great Britain for four or five weeks a year, so there is no chance of him coaching me on a regular basis. In saying that, it is nice to have great former players like McEnroe saying nice things about me.'

During the weekend before Wimbledon, he tested his injured ankle, put the finishing touches to the preparations for his debut and purchased what turned out to be a vital piece of equipment – a new mobile phone. He had received such a high number of phone calls since his remarkable performance at the Stella Artois Championships, he had no option but to bin the old phone and buy a new one with a private number just given out to family and friends.

A constantly ringing phone, a slew of interview requests, and the presence of TV crews and photographers stalking his practice sessions are routine for Tim Henman at Wimbledon, but it was a new and a rather unsettling experience for Murray. 'There are some positives and some negatives about all the interest in me,' he said. 'Everybody is being very supportive of me, and I'm going to get good backing in my matches, but the negative is the fact that I know the press are being really nice just now, but if I don't do so well, then a lot of them are going to start saying things about me that perhaps aren't true.

'I think I've always been able to focus, and I've come across well in the press, so that helps. Also, people around me, my agents and my mum, are very good at sorting things out so that I don't have to worry about things. It's not as easy to concentrate on your tennis when you've got so many other things going on.'

The maelstrom of pressure and excitement swirling around Murray increased with the news that he had been handed a first-round match against George Bastl, an opponent he could beat. The man from Switzerland was ranked 141 in the world, and his only claim to fame was that he beat Pete Sampras in the second round at Wimbledon in 2002 in what turned out to be the seven-time champion's last-ever match at the All England Club.

'I think it's good that people expect a lot of you,' said Murray when he heard the draw. 'Always when I've had pressure put on me, I've played my best tennis. I don't think about it too much, but I suppose if I do start to do quite well, that side of things may get more difficult.

'Obviously, it's one of the better draws I could have got, but he has won three matches on grass to qualify. He will have a good feel for the grass, and it won't be easy.'

There was plenty that Murray liked about being among the big boys at Wimbledon, despite the pressure it placed him under. For one thing, the hefty ranking points on offer at the tournament offered him a chance to give his position of 317 a considerable hike upwards, which, in turn, would get him closer to breathing the rarefied atmosphere of top-level tennis more often. 'This is a lot different from the juniors,' he said. 'It feels like I'm part of the big tour, and I've had a chance to meet some of the top players. It's also good to have been put in the top men's locker-room, because you don't get that as a junior. I'm really looking forward to being at Wimbledon.'

The ankle he twisted at Queen's appeared to be recovering well, albeit slowly, and he was being sensibly cautious about the number of times he practised in the run-up to the Championships to give himself the maximum chance of recovery. He also had to overcome the mental scars left by being injured so cruelly when two points away from victory over Johansson at Queen's Club, which would also take time to heal.

He tried to lessen the weight of expectation on his shoulders by explaining that he had spent some of his formative years training in Barcelona and was far more comfortable on clay and hardcourts than grass. He was never going to be a player who rushed into the net, although he proved himself more than capable of adapting his game to the surface.

The one thing he did take into the Wimbledon fortnight was the ability to cope with the intensity of high-profile matches in front of noisy crowds, something he had encountered at the Stella Artois tournament when he was the centre of attention. 'I knew I could play very well, but there's a big difference between doing it in practice and doing it in matches. When I went out there for my first match at Queen's Club, I felt very comfortable. When I won matches there, there wasn't really any pressure on me, and I played two good matches after that. I just treat every tournament like that.'

To that end, and in the hope of calming some of the more hysterically optimistic of his new-found supporters, Murray was anxious to remind everyone that he was a teenager playing his first professional grand-slam event and that they should adjust their expectations accordingly: 'It's going to be a very good experience for me. It is my first Wimbledon and my first grand slam and first five-set singles match, and, obviously, it hasn't helped that I've not been able to practise this week, because of my ankle, but I'm still really looking forward to it. It's going to be a good tournament.'

Murray's success at Queen's Club and his raised profile going into Wimbledon helped him financially, and it also put pressure on the LTA to increase his funding. In particular, LTA performance director David Felgate was taking notice of Murray's progress. Of course, he had good reason: Tim Henman and Greg Rusedski were in the twilight of their careers, and Felgate and the LTA needed someone to take over the baton and keep interest in men's tennis in Great Britain alive.

Murray-mania reached fever pitch on 20 June when Roger Federer hit the first ball to start Wimbledon. Even music magazines ran articles on Murray, poring over the choice of music he played on his iPod as he walked onto court. It was revealed that the Black Eyed Peas, The Proclaimers and Eminem were his three favourite artists, and there was much debate on how music could inspire sportsmen and women to success. 'The mood I'm in determines what I will listen to on court,' said Murray. 'If I have been waiting around for a while, maybe because of rain delays, and need to get pumped up straight away, I will listen to something like The Proclaimers or the Black Eyed Peas. If I am in a rush going on court and being hurried for whatever reason, I'll listen to stuff which helps chill me out. I listened to the Black Eyed Peas song "Let's Get It Started" when I played at the Stella Artois, and I also like "Lose Yourself" by Eminem. Both of these songs really get me up for a match.'

His game against Bastl was scheduled for the first Tuesday of the tournament, and by his own admission, not playing on the first Monday was a good break, allowing him more time to soak up the atmosphere and prepare for the occasion. As he trained at Aorangi Park, the practice court complex at Wimbledon, he got a feeling of the huge interest in him from the British crowd. 'Not having to play on the first Monday is a stroke of luck,' he said. 'That extra day off will give my ankle an extra 24 hours to heal, and I will have more time to prepare on grass as I want to be at my very best.

'My preparations were disrupted when I had to miss the Nottingham tournament because of injury. Many people forget that my three matches at the Stella Artois tournament were the only competitive ones I have ever played on grass. It would have been useful to get a few more under my belt at Nottingham, but it was not to be.'

Some of the most respected figures in the British game were quick to try and take the pressure off him going into the Bastl match, not wanting him to be affected by the growing expectation levels. David Felgate warned: 'Just keep it in perspective. Andrew Murray is a great talent, but let the kid get out there and just enjoy his moment. He is playing at Wimbledon, and I am hoping there are many great things to come for him.'

Before the tournament had started, Murray had agreed to do an exclusive column for *The Herald* newspaper. He was helped by the journalistic expertise of his mother Judy, who was that paper's tennis correspondent for more than ten years before she turned her attention to working with her son. In one article in *The Herald*, Murray revealed how excited he was about playing in the main draw at Wimbledon and talked in depth about his frustration over the injury which kept him out of Nottingham:

> Wimbledon starts today, and I can't wait to get on court to play. It's been a frustrating time for me since I had to pull out of my match against the world No. 20 Thomas Johansson at the Stella Artois Championships with an ankle injury when I was only two points away from victory. Since then I have had to undergo a comprehensive programme of rehabilitation work on my twisted ankle to ensure I'm fit and ready for my first-round match against George Bastl.

Bastl will be a very difficult opponent and is ranked 141 in the world compared to my position of 317. He is an experienced player who beat Pete Sampras at Wimbledon three years ago, and his confidence will be high after making it to the main Wimbledon draw this year through the qualifying tournament. I'm confident my ankle will hold up during the game, but I think I will wear strapping and an ankle protector as a precaution.

With Greg Rusedski and Tim Henman being the wrong side of 30, the British public are looking for a new tennis star, and the fact that I beat Santiago Ventura, Taylor Dent and nearly got the better of Johansson in the Stella Artois means many feel I could follow in their footsteps.

Having that pressure on my shoulders going into Wimbledon doesn't really bother me. When I set foot on court for the first time, I won't be nervous at all. Playing big matches in showpiece tournaments is what you aspire to as a tennis player.

I must admit though the media interest has been incredible and more than I expected, but I like to think I've taken it in my stride.

Murray had so many requests for interviews he had to turn most of them down, especially those early in the morning as he wasn't the best at getting up. 'Most of the requests for interviews going into Wimbledon I have had to turn down,' said the young Scot. 'For example, GMTV asked me to come into their studios at 6.30 a.m. on the Friday morning before Wimbledon started. Anybody who knows me realises I'm not at my best in the mornings. I sent my mum in my place for that one.'

Things were relaxed in the Murray camp the night before the Bastl game, mainly because he was happy in the flat he had rented with his mum. 'We leased a basement flat near the All England Club and have been staying there for three weeks prior to Wimbledon. We moved in before the Stella Artois Championships started and will be there until my involvement at Wimbledon ends.

'Many players will stay in hotels during the grass-court season, which I don't like to do as you don't have the freedom to come and go and eat and sleep when you like. I can fall asleep anytime, anywhere, and to be able to crash in my own bed whenever I feel like is good for me. I have my own room in the flat, but as my mum will tell you, I'm not the tidiest teenager in the world, and within a few minutes, I can make it look like a bomb site.'

According to Judy, his room did look like a typical teenager's, and there were three full boxes of tennis gear supplied by the Fred Perry company, one of his major sponsors, in the hall of the flat. The company supplied all his outfits, which, in the past, had been mainly maroon and navy blue. As you can only wear white at Wimbledon, they had sent Murray boxes of new gear to get him through the fortnight. He also had a big supply of Head rackets, so the flat was starting to look like an untidy sports shop.

The flat in Southfields was also in a good area socially as his brother Jamie, David Brewer, Josh Goodall and other friends stayed nearby. They could all go out for a meal together or the others could visit Murray at the flat. There was also another blessing in disguise. Although he had a new mobile phone, there were still lots of calls from well-wishers, and before such a big match, he wanted peace and quiet. He got that in the flat as he couldn't get any mobile-phone reception. Another bonus was the fact that there was a Starbucks round the corner. He may have had to watch what he ate, but he couldn't resist their chocolate and cream Frappuccino, which is like a big milk shake with cream on top.

The evening before his match against Bastl, Murray ate steak and pasta with tomato sauce. He then studied some videos of his opponent in action. This was not unusual, because as a junior he had known all there was to know about the other players on the tour. Afterwards, he retired to his room to watch *Celebrity Love Island*, *Big Brother* and a DVD of Ricky Hatton, one of his favourite boxers, before falling asleep.

People kept telling him that he should be nervous going into the match, but he didn't feel it, and although he was on edge when he woke up, that was more because of excitement than anything else. Even though the match against Bastl was the biggest day of his tennis life, he didn't exactly jump out of the bed at the crack of dawn in anticipation. Judy had to wake him up at 8.45 a.m., and it wasn't until he had had a shower and listened to some music that he felt ready for the day. He put the sound up full on the music channel on the television, to the extent that Judy had to come in and turn it down when he was out of the room. Needless to say, he turned it back up when she went back to the kitchen. It was a typical scenario any parent of a teenager could relate to, not just the mother of a tennis player.

For breakfast he had two bagels and some banana, strawberry and melon, plus two hydration drinks, before he dispatched his mum to the coffee shop for his favourite chocolate Frappuccino. Before he left, he packed some snacks, just in case he was in a long match and needed energy. He took bananas, mini-Jaffa Cakes and some sour sweets, which he loved. Judy then drove him down to the courts, and after seeing his physio, he hit a few balls with Mark Petchey.

When all this was going on, BBC television ran a pre-recorded feature on Murray. Interviewer Gary Richardson, clearly thinking that the player would take over as the British No. 1, asked Murray whether 'Henman Hill' should be renamed 'Mount Murray'. In response, the young Scot said, 'I am comfortable with the label of the man people think can take over from Tim. In fact, it gives me confidence to think that people have faith in me to be as good as him. As for what to call the hill outside Court No. 1, I'm not really bothered, especially as I haven't even played at Wimbledon yet.'

Such was the interest in his game that he had to take the underground tunnel that goes from Aorangi Park to the locker-room to avoid the crowds waiting outside after his practice session. Once there, he again listened to the Black Eyed Peas song 'Let's Get It Started', which always helped to inspire him. He was told later that a radio station had been running a competition to guess what music he would listen to when he came on court. After he fell and twisted his ankle at Queen's Club, people had suggested 'I Can't Stand Up For Falling Down' by Elvis Costello and 'I Fought the Lawn and the Lawn Won', an amusing take on The Clash song.

Before the tournament, he had made no secret that grass was not his favourite surface. Despite that, playing in the main draw at Wimbledon had always been one of his dreams, and with the match against Bastl fast approaching, his dream was about to become a reality.

The first time he had gone to Wimbledon was when he was ten years old. He had travelled down to the tournament in a minibus along with a dozen pals from Dunblane. He had loved the atmosphere at the All England Club and later revealed that he remembered running after the players for autographs.

No doubt, he would have been pinching himself to think that all over Britain kids were running home to watch him on television, much in the same way as he had done all those years ago when Andre Agassi, one of Murray's heroes, was playing. It must have been a strange feeling for him but one which he would be very proud of.

Murray wasn't the type to get ahead of himself but couldn't have helped but realise that if he beat Bastl, it was likely he would face Radek Stepanek, the No. 14 seed from the Czech Republic, in the second round. The fact that the match was likely to be on Centre Court or Court No. 1 would have been an even more exciting prospect.

Although he may not have been getting too carried away, some of the punters who liked a flutter certainly were. The odds of Murray winning the tournament before the match against Bastl were 250–1, but a string of wagers made in bookmakers in the Stirling and Dunblane area prompted at least one firm to consider reducing his odds. Robin Hutchison of Ladbrokes said, 'Andrew has shown that he can hold his own among the big boys and has been heavily backed in Scotland. Given the odds, we would only need to see people putting a few quid on him to leave us crying into our barley water if he did the unthinkable.

'In all honesty, Andrew has an awful lot to do and that's why he's been placed at 250–1. There are doubts about his fitness at the moment, and it is only his first Wimbledon after all. Tennis fans in Scotland are backing their boy, and we'll face an anxious wait.'

As the hours passed and his time on court approached, Murray would have gone through in his head what he would have to do to beat Bastl. The Swiss player had failed to build on his famous win over Sampras in 2002 and had made six unsuccessful attempts to qualify for grand-slam tournaments since then, before making it into the 2005 Wimbledon competition. Despite his dismal showing in major tournaments, he had been performing consistently on the Challenger Tour and was ranked 146 in the world, 166 places above Murray. 'I realise he will be a difficult opponent,' said Murray. 'He is a decent grass-court player. He does not have a big serve, so he won't blow me away, but I will have to be at my best to beat him. I have heard people say I should beat him, but they forget he has been on tour for 12 years and has had the experience of playing at Wimbledon before, while I am the second-worst player in the tournament based on world rankings.'

Bastl, who also went through his paces at Aorangi Park beforehand, went into the match full of confidence. However, the Swiss national, who was born in Chicago, had made it through the qualifying tournament with a little bit of luck. He had beaten Jean-Christophe Faurel 7–5, 6–7, 6–4 in the first round of qualifying and Marcus Sarstrand 6–0, 6–3 in the second. In the final round, Bastl had faced the experienced American Justin Gimelstob, but he had retired hurt after just one game.

Murray, who was 12 years younger than his opponent and lacked the experience of the older man, was the underdog, but there was only one winner in the match. The young Scot captivated the crowd with a magnificent display of tennis, and he ran out an easy 6–4, 6–2, 6–2 winner.

Although he had been concentrating on the match as he walked out on court, he remembered seeing the Saltire flying alongside the Union flag and appreciated the spectators cheering all his shots. Indeed, they were so much on his side that he felt they were maybe a bit unfair to Bastl, cheering when he made a mistake and staying quiet when he hit a winner. However, he realised that they had been fantastic in their support for him.

Not surprisingly, the win set off some incredible publicity, and Murray-mania at Wimbledon had well and truly arrived. Murray said, 'It was a great feeling to win my first-ever senior match, but I don't want people to get carried away. After the way I was mobbed as I came off court, that may be easier said than done.'

He wasn't kidding. When he had hit the winning shot to take the match, the crowd had risen as one to greet their new hero, and there had been dozens of youngsters waiting at the side of Court 2 at the end of the match asking for his autograph. There were also lots of young ladies screaming marriage proposals at him and asking the young Scot to look their way so they could take his picture.

Before Wimbledon started, Murray had always said that he wanted, as far as possible, to sign every autograph, believing that it was an important gesture. He used to wait to get players' autographs himself as a boy and knew what it felt like to be disappointed when they walked past without signing. He did not want to be that sort of player, and after his match against Bastl, he signed so many that Venus Williams, who was next on court against Eva Birnerova of the Czech Republic, was kept waiting for a short while as a result. When he realised he was holding things up, he left court immediately but kept signing as he went.

It took him a good ten minutes to get through the crowds waiting to congratulate him outside Court 2 after his win. It would have been even longer but a team of security men came to his aid. Later, he explained in his column in *The Herald* why he spent so long signing autographs:

> I go out of my way to sign autograph books of every youngster who asks, and the reason for that dates back to when I first came to Wimbledon with some pals from Dunblane Sports Club. I hung around for ages trying to get the autograph of my hero, Andre Agassi, but I never got near him. I was upset because I really wanted his signature. I know how disappointed I was, and I didn't want youngsters to feel the way I did back then. I can empathise with all of them as I was just like them once, and that is why I tried to sign every autograph after my game against Bastl.

It was a relief for him to get back to the locker-room after his match and have a chance to relax. He plunged straight into an ice bath to help his body recover from the game, then stretched for 20 minutes before being briefed on Radek Stepanek, his next opponent, who had beaten Robby Ginepri in the first round 6–7(5), 6–3, 6–4, 6–2. Murray realised that, once again, he would be the underdog. He was now officially the lowest-ranked player left in the tournament, and Stepanek, who had been on the ATP tour for four years, had much more grass-court experience.

'Let's face it, the hype surrounding me has been over the top, because I haven't really done anything,' Murray said in an interview with *The Herald*. 'I won the US juniors and a couple of matches at Queen's, and now I've won a match at Wimbledon. It's just four or five games and everybody's making it out as if I've pretty much won Wimbledon. Keeping all the expectation surrounding me under control is easier said than done.

'People have told me that Stepanek has a reputation for gamesmanship. I won't let him wind me up, and maybe if he does act up, it will make me play better. With the British crowd on my side, he might even get a bit nervous. That's in the future, though, and the last 24 hours at Wimbledon have given me so many great memories.'

Certainly, the win over Bastl was an incredible moment for Murray and capped a great day's tennis at the All England Club. On the same day that Murray was waltzing to victory, Tim Henman mounted one of the greatest escapes of his Wimbledon career, then took time to pay tribute to the way the teenager, destined to replace him as British No. 1, had played. The Englishman clawed his way back from two sets down to beat Jarkko Nieminen 3–6, 6–7(5), 6–4, 7–5, 6–2 in his 50th match at the All England Club. Beforehand, he had watched part of Murray's match on television. 'Andy has a big future, and the more British players we can get at this level the better,' said Henman. 'I thought Andy would win, but he pretty much took George Bastl apart. He's 18 and didn't have any lapses in concentration, and that's impressive. His head is screwed on, and he's the one British player who is going out there and performing at the moment.' He also went on to predict that the young Scot would beat Stepanek.

The day after Murray's victory over Bastl, the press and media went into overdrive. Gary Richardson, the BBC presenter who was to become a frequent house guest of Murray's during his time at Wimbledon, turned up at the young player's flat in the morning and interviewed him as he read the headlines about himself in the newspapers. Sitting there in his Barcelona football top, he looked like a typical teenager: his hair all over the place and the papers strewn all over the floor.

As the BBC film crew panned round Murray's flat, Mark Petchey could be seen flicking through the papers in the background. He didn't say anything on that occasion but more than made up for it later in the day. Petchey is one of the most articulate men in tennis, as demonstrated by the fact that he is employed by Sky Sports as a tennis commentator. However, when he spoke to journalists by the practice courts at Aorangi Park, he unintentionally placed more pressure on Murray, saying that his new charge had the potential to become a bigger sporting superstar than Wayne Rooney. Although Murray was playing down his chances of beating Stepanek, it was clear that Petchey thought Murray had a great future in the game, regardless of how well he did against the man from the Czech Republic. 'Andy has the "X factor",' Petchey said. 'He can be as good as Wayne Rooney. England may never win the World Cup, but Andy may win Wimbledon. He may be a bigger star than Rooney. If he wins here or at one of the other three grand slams, then why can't he be bigger? Andy seems to deal with everything in a pretty special way, just like Rooney. He is so strong and has so much inner belief, and, obviously, he will improve, because he is only 18.'

Petchey put Murray through his paces on the practice courts for an hour that Wednesday afternoon and said afterwards that the ankle problem which had troubled his player going into the tournament had completely cleared up. Later in the day, Murray played doubles with Englishman David Sherwood, but the British pair lost to Martin Damm of the Czech Republic and Mariano Hood of Argentina in straight sets, 6–1, 6–4, 6–4. However, Petchey pointed out that the doubles contest had been a worthwhile exercise as every match on grass was a bonus for Murray. Petchey also said that the 18-year-old Scot had more potential than Tim Henman had shown at the same age and Wimbledon 2005 was just the start of what promised to be a glittering tennis career. 'Tim was nowhere near where Andy is at the age of 18,' said Petchey. 'Nobody said Tim was destined to win a grand slam. He was not talked about in the same way people talk about Andy.

'Everybody wants the new Tim Henman to be here tomorrow. Maybe Andy will get there quicker than we think but a couple of years seems reasonable. He is not as ready physically as other players around his age, such as Rafael Nadal or Richard Gasquet, but he just needs a bit of time.'

Petchey said Murray's self-confidence and strong character had allowed him not to be overawed by all the attention which surrounded him at Wimbledon. 'Being on a show court at Wimbledon against Stepanek will not faze him. In Andy's own mind, he was destined to play on big occasions and challenge for the big prizes,' said Petchey. 'That is because he was a great junior, winning the Orange Bowl in America and then the US Open junior championship. His pedigree as a junior is so high, he looks at the top players and thinks, "Why am I not playing where they are?"'

Rafael Nadal, the French Open champion at that time, also felt that Murray could make it to the top. 'He is playing good just now, and although he needs to improve and some things he can do better, I believe he can make it into the top ten,' said Nadal, who lost in the second round at Wimbledon. 'I have known Andy for four years from when we played in junior competitions, and he can do very well in the game.'

Murray allowed himself a grin when it was mentioned to him that Petchey thought he could be a bigger star than Rooney. 'I don't know about being as big as him, but I must keep doing what I'm doing on the court and playing well,' said the Scot. 'Some guys want to be famous, but I don't like it so much. I just like playing tennis.

'I'm under no illusions that it will be difficult to beat Stepanek as he is in the top 15 in the world and reached the semi-finals at Queen's Club. I really don't think I have much chance of winning. I have to play one of my best matches and hope he doesn't play as well as he can as my tennis is not as good as his. I need him to play badly, and if the crowd gets behind me, then I might have a decent chance.'

On the Wednesday evening, Murray returned to his flat and had a glimpse at Stepanek's playing record, which illustrated why the man from the Czech Republic was such a formidable opponent. Stepanek had taken the world No. 2 Andy Roddick to three sets in the semi-finals of the 2005 Stella Artois Championships, before losing 6–3, 2–6, 6–2. On the way to the last four, he had beaten Greg Rusedski and the up-and-coming French player Richard Gasquet. Another notable Stepanek scalp had been Mario Ancic, whom he had beaten in the first round of the Rome Open in May 2005. He had also run other top players close in matches since the turn of the year. It had taken Rafael Nadal three sets to beat him in the quarter-final of the Rome Open, while he had taken Sébastien Grosjean to five sets in the French Open, before losing 6–1, 4–6, 3–6, 6–3, 6–4. Stepanek had played well on all surfaces in 2005, reaching the final of an indoor tournament on carpet in Milan in February of that year, which he lost to Robin Soderling in three sets, 6–3, 6–7(2), 7–6(5). He had also been a semi-finalist at a hardcourt tournament in Sydney in January 2005, which he lost to Ivo Minar of the Czech Republic in straight sets, 6–1, 6–2. His record in grand-slam matches was also consistent, and he had reached the third round six times in twelve majors.

Czech journalists said that they had not been in contact with Stepanek and had no idea where he would be preparing for his game against Murray. He had been, at times, accused of gamesmanship but Mark Petchey believed that was because he never had a set game pattern, and it was difficult to work out a strategy against him, which caused his opponents to become frustrated. 'We have heard about the way he goes about things on court, but he is a good player who plays within the rules,' said Petchey. 'I will watch a tape of him and discuss his style of play with Andy. Andy has seen a lot of him so he knows what to expect.

'He cannot let himself get irritated as I realise Stepanek does things which can take your focus away from hitting tennis balls. He is a great competitor, and I have nothing against him personally. He has made the most of his talent, and I have great respect for how he plays the game. He plays with lots of slice, can change the pace of a game quickly and is a difficult player to play against. Andy realises he has a tough game on his hands.'

Despite his good record, Stepanek apparently aggravated many of his fellow professionals on court. When he played Andy Roddick at Queen's Club in 2005, the American had pointed out that Stepanek was taking a long time between his first and second serves. Even Tim Henman, who usually keeps his counsel about other players, had said in the past that he was 'cynical' about some of the Czech player's antics. Many players believed that Stepanek intentionally used stalling tactics to break up his opponent's momentum, something Murray realised he had to guard against. He was also hoping that Stepanek, a mercurial player at best, would be affected by the partisan crowd, which would be strongly in favour of the Scot.

Stepanek admitted to not knowing much about Murray going into the match. 'I saw him play in Queen's Club, and he did play a couple of good matches,' he said. 'It's my job to keep winning, and I just concentrate on myself, regardless of who is on the other side of the net.'

Although he may have laughed about it afterwards, Murray's moment of glory was almost scuppered by a chicken curry. He had the meal the evening before the match against Stepanek at a friend's house. He had then gone to bed at a reasonable hour but woke up at 4 a.m. feeling dreadful as a result of his carry-out meal. He was hot and sticky and couldn't get back to sleep. Talk about bad timing. This was the night before the biggest game of his life, and here he was tossing and turning in bed. He was so concerned that he got Judy to call his physio, who came around to check on him. Murray downed a couple of painkillers at around 8.40 a.m., and it was recommended that he regulate his temperature. He was told to take a hot bath at precisely 37 degrees, and when he got out, he was to walk about with ice cubes in a towel wrapped around his neck to cool him down.

As this was a problem they had not envisaged, Judy had to go to a pharmacy to buy a thermometer so she could check the water temperature to ensure it was at precisely 37 degrees. Murray, who was left alone while his mum went to the chemist, then fell asleep. He slept until noon, giving him some much needed rest. When he got up, he took the recommended bath, before sticking the towel with ice cubes round his neck and walking around the flat.

The sleep and the bath made a big difference, and at around 1 p.m., he started to feel as good as ever. He had some pasta and a couple of hydration drinks plus a couple of nectarines. He was ready for action.

The match against Stepanek was his first on a show court at Wimbledon and that had its advantages. It meant he could practise on one of the outside courts rather than wait his turn at Aorangi Park, which was usually very busy. It was a great feeling for Murray to be practising on Court 10 with Petchey, and they had a good hit in peace, although he didn't mind signing autographs when he came off.

After his warm-up, Murray went straight to the dressing-room to wait for his game to be called onto Court 1. While there, he watched some of Tim Henman's second-round match, and he was sorry that the man he looked up to and who had given him some great advice was beaten by Dmitry Tursunov of Russia, 3–6, 6–2, 3–6, 6–3, 8–6.

Once again, Murray walked out on court listening to the same Black Eyes Peas track, which was becoming his lucky song. It was only later that Murray heard that Tracy Austin had claimed on BBC Radio that he had kept Stepanek waiting at the net before the match started. If it had happened, it had not been deliberate. He had been focused on his match, listening to his iPod, and hadn't been conscious of what was going on around him.

At stages during the game against Stepanek, he felt a bit weak but that didn't show in the first set, which he won 6–4 amid a huge tide of emotion from the British crowd. Once he won the second, by the same 6–4 score line, he got a bit more energy, perhaps because of the confidence his lead had given him. Feeling ill on court isn't pleasant, especially when you have television cameras trained on your every move, and there were times during the match that Murray wasn't at his best, partly because of the after-effects of the dodgy chicken curry he had had the night before and partly because of slight dehydration.

He played a reasonable game, but Stepanek made more mistakes than Murray and that was the difference. The 6–4, 6–4, 6–4 victory was a great performance, and at the end of the match, the Court No. 1 crowd went wild.

The man from the Czech Republic had got on his opponent's nerves a bit, but the Scot had managed to keep his anger in check. 'People had warned me about his gamesmanship, and they were spot on,' Murray said later. 'He kept staring in my face when I missed the ball, then he started going up to the net and touching it when he hit a drop-shot to try to put me off. When I got a net cord at 5–4, I did it back to him. I think his antics made him look a bit stupid, and we didn't say much to each other at the end.'

It was another great win for Murray, and his family and close friends, including Laura Middleton, a respected Scottish tennis coach, celebrated in style. Judy and Laura had a few celebratory glasses of Pimm's in the bar, and a journalist in the post-match press conference described Andy's mum as 'cool'.

Reaction from the London-based media was huge. Ivan Speck of the *Daily Mail* described Murray's performance as 'simply breathtaking'. What he wrote summed up Murray's style of play perfectly:

> If tennis was as ridiculously easy as Andy Murray made it look against Radek Stepanek, why aren't we all bestriding Wimbledon with our genius? Keep the ball within the lines and hit it to where your opponent isn't. The art of perfect tennis, according to Andy.
>
> Set of tools required – skill, racket-head control, hand-eye coordination and utter belief in your ability to execute the strategy. Murray has the lot. Yet, perhaps it is the commodity which does not inhabit his mind which is the secret of his staggering success.
>
> Negative thoughts, the kind which accumulate with defeats and fester inside the brain only to resurface in critical moments on court, are mercifully absent in the 18 year old. Let's hope they remain alien to him.

The way Murray floated around Court 1 against Stepanek showed his real quality. And Boris Becker, the former Wimbledon champion, was also quick to praise the young Scot's performance. In a television interview, Becker said, 'He looks as if he has begun to own Court 1 already. Andy played against Radek Stepanek like it was a junior Wimbledon match against a player from Ecuador, instead of the No. 14 seed. That's his secret.

'He's so cool and relaxed inside, so poised, that nothing seems to faze or affect him. It was his first time on Court 1, and by the third, set he was controlling the place and the atmosphere.

'He was getting tired in the third set and shook his arms around, as if to say "Let's get this party started again". His mental approach

Murray, aged 13, and his Great Britain teammates at the ITF's 14-and-under Team Championships in Prostejov, Czech Republic, August 2000. Left to right: Andy Murray, Jamie Murray, Tom Rushby and team captain Laurence Kelly.

(© Stephen Wake.)

A 15-year-old Murray in full flow during the Scottish Junior Championships in Edinburgh, where he and Andrew Kennaugh won the doubles title.

(© Rob Eyton-Jones.)

Andy and his fellow British players take time out during the US Open junior competition, September 2004. Left to right: Jamie Murray, Andy Murray, Miles Kasiri, Jamie Baker (bottom left) and Tom Rushby. (© Roger Parker/Fotosports International.)

Murray mid-match at Junior Wimbledon 2004, where he made the third round. A year later, he would reach the third round of the men's competition. (© Susan Mullane/Camerawork USA.)

Joy and relief for Murray as he beats Sergiy Stakhovsky 6-4, 6-2 to win the US Open junior title in September 2004, crowning a glittering junior career. (© Susan Mullane/ Camerawork USA.)

Murray speaks to journalists at Edinburgh airport on his return to Scotland after winning the US Open junior title, September 2004.
(© Alan Peebles/Scope Features.)

'That was rubbish, wasn't it, Mum?' A dejected Murray trudges off court after losing to Marin Cilic in the semi-finals of the French Open juniors, June 2005.
(© Susan Mullane/Camerawork USA.)

Murray with Leon Smith, who coached him for six years and remains one of his closest friends. (Courtesy of Leon Smith.)

Wimbledon discovers a charismatic new hero to cheer as Murraymania sweeps the All England Club in June 2005.
(© Ken Passley/Fred Perry.)

Murray casts a happy glance up to the players' box after beating Radek Stepanek to make the third round.
(© Fred Mullane/Camerawork USA.)

Judy Murray watches from the players' box on Centre Court as her son loses in five sets to David Nalbandian at Wimbledon, June 2005.
(© Roger Parker/Fotosports International.)

Murray tries to compose himself with the help of official Mike Morrissey during a 'vomit delay' in his five-set win over Andre Pavel at the 2005 US Open.
(© Roger Parker/Fotosports International.)

The Murray brothers join forces for Scotland as they take on an English team of Greg Rusedski and David Sherwood in the Aberdeen Cup exhibition event.
(© Rob Eyton-Jones.)

Murray feels the heat of the Australian summer in January 2006. His first trip Down Under proved to be a trying time for the teenager.
(© Roger Parker/Fotosports International.)

Tim Henman smiles despite being given the runaround by Murray during a practice session at the Australian Open, January 2006.
(© Roger Parker/Fotosports International.)

Murray celebrates his first ATP Tour win after beating Lleyton Hewitt in the San José final. (© Mark Lyons/ Fotosports International.)

Murray enjoys a lighter moment during his post-match press conference in Memphis after losing in the quarter-finals to Robin Soderling, February 2006. (© Fred Mullane/Camerawork USA.)

Mark Petchey, Murray's former coach, in pensive mood while watching his charge in action in Memphis, two months before their split. (© Fred Mullane/Camerawork USA.)

Murray at the ATP/WTA Tour awards gala in Miami, March 2006. He narrowly missed out to his friend Gael Monfils in the Newcomer of the Year category. (© Fred Mullane/Camerawork USA.)

Murray reminds Rangers what they missed out on by showing off his soccer skills during a rain delay in Indian Wells, March 2006. (© Roger Parker/Fotosports International.)

is the reason why he's still in the tournament. Now he should do exactly what he's been doing all week long. He should eat the same food, drink the same water, whatever – stick to his routine!'

On the middle Saturday of Wimbledon, and with Henman and Rusedski out of the tournament, the spotlight was on Murray as the only Brit left. To add to the hype, he was due to play former Wimbledon finalist David Nalbandian in the third round on the hallowed Centre Court.

Nalbandian had a good Wimbledon pedigree. He had burst into the public's attention when he made the Wimbledon final in 2002, although he had lost to Lleyton Hewitt. Making the Wimbledon final had made him a national hero back in his homeland of Argentina as he had been the first man from his country to make the final of the greatest tennis tournament in the world, and in his home city of Cordoba, he had both a bus stop and a hot-dog stand named after him! On his way to the third round of Wimbledon 2005, Nalbandian had beaten Raemon Sluiter of the Netherlands in straight sets, 6–2, 6–2, 7–5, then Karol Kucera of Slovakia 6–2, 6–4, 6–3 to set up the meeting with Murray.

'I can't wait to play him,' said Murray. 'Everybody says there could be up to 8 million people watching my match live on television, but that won't bother me a bit. It's just me and him on court as far as I'm concerned. As you would guess, I never expected to make the third round at Wimbledon, let alone play on Centre Court, but here I am.'

Before the match, Murray received texts from Tim Henman and Greg Rusedski wishing him luck. He also got a good-luck message from Alex Arthur, one of Murray's favourite boxers, and since then, the pair have gone on to become close friends.

Judy's phone was red-hot as well. About 30 texts arrived within minutes of her son hitting the winning shot against Radek Stepanek, and they didn't stop arriving until he set foot on court against Nalbandian. Family and friends back in Scotland had called to say they had been watching him in action on television and that everyone north of the border was rooting for him. Emilio Sánchez, who had helped Murray's game so much when he was in Spain, had also been saying nice things, which the young player appreciated.

Playing on Centre Court so early in his career was an exciting prospect and came with other perks, which included being allowed to use the top locker-room, an honour usually reserved for the top-seeded players. Murray felt a little embarrassed by being able to use it, but he was realistic enough to know that just because he had beaten Stepanek did not mean he was automatically a top-class player: 'I don't feel I have earned the right to be in the top dressing-room, and it has not sunk in being around the top guys. My feelings on that issue haven't changed since I beat Stepanek. It still doesn't feel right being around the best players in the world, as they are all top 50 or so, and I'm not even in the top 200. I want to be in their dressing-room by merit on a regular basis.

'For instance, not many players in the top dressing-room think they are going to get beat, but I do. I'm not a negative person, but I still think Nalbandian should beat me. OK, I know I said that before the game against George Bastl in the first round, and also before Stepanek, but I'm not joking when I say people still shouldn't expect too much.

'Bastl and Stepanek were more than two hundred places above me in the rankings when I played them, while Nalbandian was a Wimbledon finalist only three years ago. He is also much more consistent than Stepanek, and, because of that, he should be looked upon as the firm favourite.

'I know his game very well. I had six months out of tennis last year with a knee injury, and I saw him on television many times. He is a solid player, particularly from the baseline, and is a tough opponent.'

That was all true, but Murray had the fact that he had reacted positively to the big-match atmosphere in his favour, and playing on a show court would help rather than hinder him. Not surprisingly, he also kept away from chicken curry, the dish that had made him feel unwell before the Stepanek encounter, this time round, and he felt in great fettle going into the match.

Murray practised at four o'clock the day before the game with Mark Petchey at Aorangi Park and felt good during his workout. He wore a Barcelona top with the name of Ronaldinho, his favourite football player, on the back. Nalbandian, who was on a nearby court, looked across to watch his young opponent. The Argentinian was probably trying to work out what Murray looked like in the flesh, because he had told the press he knew nothing about him.

Murray was the first British player since Greg Rusedski in 1995 to outlast Tim Henman at Wimbledon, demonstrating how consistent Henman had been at the tournament compared with other home-grown players. It was just before the match with Nalbandian, when that statistic was mentioned to him, that Murray made it clear he felt Henman had been given an unjustifiably bad press. 'I don't feel people have any right to criticise Tim, as he has played well at Wimbledon, and I was very sorry to see him go out in the second round,' he said. 'He has regularly made the quarter-finals and semi-finals here, and his record is incredible and very consistent. To get into four semis and four quarter-finals at the All England Club is something he doesn't get enough credit for.

'I think I can handle the pressure pretty well, but it's nothing compared to what Tim has had to endure, and he has done so well despite that. I would accept Tim's record at Wimbledon, as long as I won either the French, Australian or US Open, but you can't take anything away from what he has achieved here and the way he has handled himself.

'He has been unlucky, because he had Pete Sampras to contend with when he started his career, then Lleyton Hewitt came along and now Roger Federer. He was never the favourite for Wimbledon because of the quality of the other players, yet he still always played well.'

In the excitement over Murray's performance in the main Wimbledon draw, everybody had forgotten the fact that he was eligible for the junior tournament: 'It will be a great moment for me playing Nalbandian, but what people have forgotten is that, if I get beat, I am still young enough to enter the junior tournament at Wimbledon. But to be honest, I'm not sure I will enter it now. I find it tough to get in the right frame of mind for junior tournaments at the best of times. Imagine what it would be like for me playing in junior Wimbledon after all that has happened to me in the main tournament. It might be worth me taking next week off, provided, of course, Nalbandian beats me, so I can prepare for the two Challenger tournaments I play after Wimbledon. However, the decision about whether I play in the juniors is for another day. My main concern is my match against Nalbandian on Centre Court.'

The *Daily Record*, Scotland's biggest-selling daily newspaper, spoke to Andy's dad Willie before the Nalbandian match and ran a picture story about the young star on their front page. Willie told the paper, 'I'm so proud of him, Dunblane is proud of him and I hope the country is proud of him.'

Holding up a poster of his son, which the *Daily Record* had printed in the paper, Willie said, 'I watched at home as Andy won on Thursday against Stepanek, but I need to be there in person to support him on Saturday.'

Speaking after a round of golf at Dunblane New Golf Club, he told the *Record*, 'I had more than a few drinks to celebrate that win, and I hope I'll be doing the same after his game on Centre Court.'

Rumour had it that the *Sun* newspaper tried to sign up Murray but found he was 'patched up', having already reached the maximum number of sponsors any player can display on their clothing. Wimbledon banned excessive advertising, so, instead, they had to settle for getting his coach Mark Petchey to wear a baseball cap with the name of the paper written on it as he sat in the box when Murray took on Nalbandian on Saturday, 25 June.

It turned out to be a match full of drama and one which the crowd at Centre Court and the millions watching on television would always remember. For two thrilling sets, Murray looked on course for an upset. In the end, the Argentinian, seeded eighteenth, won a dramatic five-set battle 6–7(4), 1–6, 6–0, 6–4, 6–1, but it was a contest from which Murray learned a lot. Only his fitness let him down, which wasn't surprising considering he had never played a top-level five-set match before. His spirit was strong, but his body ultimately proved unwilling. At the end of his five-set marathon and three hours and eleven minutes of drama, the young player slumped exhausted into his seat on Centre Court. During the match, which was undoubtedly a defining moment in Murray's career, he showed he had the shots, big serves and mental toughness to succeed. What he did not possess, just seven short matches into his senior career, was the stamina to go along with it.

The final set was one way traffic, only occasionally diverted by Murray's dogged determination to drag his ailing body around court until his last drop of energy was exhausted. An ATP trainer was required to help rejuvenate Murray's tired body during an injury break between the fourth and fifth sets. As he lay prostrate on the grass receiving attention, he looked a tired young player.

What went on before his legs gave in had been nothing short of spectacular. Murray had been beating Nalbandian at his own game, trading ground strokes and mixing in slices and changes of speed to confuse his more experienced rival. It was a game of magnificent returns, the pair sharing two breaks of serve apiece in the first seven games. And when it came to the first-set tie-break, it was the reigning US Open junior champion who held his nerve.

Murray rattled through the second set with the loss of just one game, but it was just after that that his lack of conditioning began to tell. He had never played for so long in such an important match, and his energy simply disappeared. Nalbandian took the third set to love, Murray seemingly choosing to let the set go and conserve what little energy he had left.

The fourth set showed that he had made the correct decision, and the crowd roared their approval as he competed toe to toe with the Argentinian. It was incredible to watch Murray, who had looked down and out after the third set, battle back so brilliantly. 'Come on' he repeatedly screamed as he broke Nalbandian's serve early on to take a 2–1 lead. He then held his own serve in a game which seemed to show a shift of momentum back in his favour. However, Nalbandian is a cool character and, despite being under the cosh, remained calm.

Meanwhile, all around Centre Court, the usually sedate crowd was going crazy, carried along on the wave of emotion generated by the young Scot. Some covered their faces in their Scottish flags, and Sir Sean Connery, sitting in the Royal Box, was punching the air when his fellow countryman hit a winning shot.

As the fourth set progressed, Murray had a great chance to win the match. Three break points came and went on the Argentine's serve in the ninth game of the set, points that would have given Murray the chance to serve for the match. Instead, Nalbandian used all his experience to dig deep and take the set 6–4. The trainer was called to help Murray before the final set, but the damage was done, and Nalbandian moved in for the kill, easily winning the deciding set 6–1.

Despite the defeat, Murray received encouraging words afterwards from players he respected, including Jimmy Connors, Boris Becker, John McEnroe and Martina Navratilova. Mentally, if not physically, he handled the match against Nalbandian very well.

Along with Sir Sean Connery, there had been some other big

names shouting encouragement from the Royal Box. Former Olympic stars such as Sir Steve Redgrave, Jayne Torvill, Audley Harrison and James Cracknell had all cheered him on, and Murray acknowledged their support: 'It was really humbling that people of such stature watched me play. I hear Sir Sean was really getting into the match and on his feet a few times when I won crucial points, which was great. Imagine having 007 on your side!

'I also had my family and friends who travelled down from Scotland on the day to support me, and the crowd in Centre Court gave me a great ovation. I was disappointed I couldn't win it for them.'

Later, Murray said that there were two reasons why his body had let him down. One was the fact that he had never played a five-set match before and doing so was a step into the unknown. The other was that it was just growing pains, as his body took time to adjust to a growth spurt, that had caused him problems. In saying that, he didn't lose sight of the fact he had been up against Nalbandian, a top player, or that he had outplayed and outran him for the first two sets, albeit at a physical cost.

After the game, he was knackered – pure and simple. When he tried to stand up for a shower, he was unable to. His legs buckled, and he was forced to sit down. He remained seated for a full 15 minutes, waiting for his legs to start working again. After that, he did his round of media interviews and went back to a barbecue at the house near Wimbledon that was rented by his management company, Octagon. He then returned to his rented flat with Judy, because his time at Wimbledon wasn't over just yet. He may have been out of the singles, but he was still going to play in the mixed doubles with Shahar Peer, a promising young player from Israel.

As he sat in the flat on the eve of his mixed-doubles match, he stayed up late watching boxing DVDs and reflecting on how his life had been turned upside down by his play during the summer of

2005. 'Maybe my life deserves to be turned upside down a bit,' he said. 'I did very well this week, and it's not every 18 year old playing in their first grand slam who manages to get to the third round and then takes an ex-finalist of the tournament to five sets. I think my life will change a lot, but maybe I deserve that for my efforts.

'As a tennis player, you must have belief in yourself, and, to be honest, I've always had that. I heard someone suggest I looked like the type of player who felt he was destined to play on Centre Court and challenge for titles, and that's the way I feel.

'The way I played at Wimbledon, beating George Bastl, who had beaten Pete Sampras in the past, then getting the better of Radek Stepanek and then taking Nalbandian to five sets, suggests to me I could progress in the game quicker than I expected. In saying that, I have to take things one step at a time and not get too carried away just yet.'

His prize money for the singles tournament was £25,510, more money than he had ever won before. Inevitably, people asked him what he was going to do with the money and any other sponsorship cash which might come his way. 'I don't drive, so I won't be buying a car,' said Murray. 'In fact, I don't need anything really as I have everything I want just now. I had been thinking of putting a deposit down on a flat in Barcelona, where I went to the tennis academy, but still have to make up my mind on that one. I might do that as I could rent it out when I wasn't there. I must admit, I'm not ready to live on my own just yet. I'm much too messy, as my mum will tell you.

'Looking to the bigger picture, I hope my exploits have inspired youngsters all over Britain to play tennis. I love tennis, and one of the reasons I play the game is to try to encourage more people to play. Hopefully, the way I am on court helps people enjoy tennis a bit more, and they might not just think it's a pretty dull sport. When you have people screaming at the top of their voice and throwing their rackets around a little bit, they might get into it.'

The good news for Murray was that his performance at Wimbledon moved him into the top 220 in the rankings, a position high enough to earn him a place in the qualifying competition for the US Open in August 2005. However, before he could ponder his future in more detail, he had to focus his mind on his mixed-doubles match against the pairing of Lucas Arnold, from Argentina, and Emmanuelle Gagliardi, from Switzerland, which was to be played on Monday, 27 June. Played on an outside court, it was standing room only for the first-round game, which had taken on new meaning following Murray's run at Wimbledon. Stewards had to clear fans from the steps overlooking the court as everybody crammed in for a good vantage point.

Neither Murray or Peer had ever previously played any mixed-doubles matches. Peer had seen him in Davis Cup action against her country and sent him an email asking if he wanted to team up. Their inexperience showed, and they were beaten 6–3, 6–4. Despite this, both players enjoyed the experience.

As he walked off the court in defeat, the crowd mobbed him, asking for his autograph. Murray obliged them before struggling to make his way back to the locker-room. At least 100 people stood on the steps near Court 3 simply to get a glimpse of him and girls flocked to him and took pictures on their mobile phones to send to their friends.

Afterwards, Murray described his performance as 'rubbish', which was not far from the truth but understandable after his heroics in the singles. 'I didn't know what to do as I hadn't played mixed doubles before and was a bit scared about hitting Shahar,' he said. 'It was a shame I played so badly. I was rubbish, although I played a bit better in the second set.

'I was amazed all the people turned up to watch. There were so many standing outside waiting, I couldn't move at all. Because there were other matches going on, I thought they might be interested in someone else. I wasn't expecting so many people. When I got off court, I couldn't move.'

When he was asked about all the female attention, he said, 'That's the best thing about this. It's great.'

He was asked to give an interview with the international press after his mixed-doubles match. Wimbledon officials said that they thought it was the first time in living memory that an unseeded player, who had just lost a first-round mixed-doubles match, had been asked to give such a conference.

Murray made it clear that his success so far would not make him rich overnight, despite reports in the press that he stood to make £1 million in the coming year through sponsorship deals because of his play at Wimbledon. 'Financially, this week won't make a huge difference as I signed my contracts at the start of the year, and you can't change your contracts after six months,' Murray said. 'They're all quite long. Financially, I can't really do anything else, because I have both of my patch sponsorships in place [Robinsons and Royal Bank of Scotland], my clothes [Fred Perry] and my rackets [Head].'

After Murray ended his interest in Wimbledon, Frank Dick, the Scottish fitness coach who had worked with Boris Becker when the German was at his peak, expressed an interest in working with the young player on his long-term physical training strategy. Murray had only a vague recollection of who Dick was, but once he was told about the trainer's pedigree, he admitted that he was delighted that a man with such a good track record had been in touch. Becker was one of the greatest players of his generation and to have one of his backroom team interested in working with Murray was another boost and an indication of the young Scot's growing standing in the game.

The physical development of his game was vital, and he took advice from Tim Henman, who told him that he had started working with a physical trainer four or five years too late. It was a piece of information that stuck in Murray's mind.

Ilie Nastase also offered advice during a BBC television interview. The Romanian, who won the US Open in 1972 and the French Open in 1973, made it clear that Murray had to get his conditioning right before he could consider calling himself a top player. He said Murray's game was good and his head was right, but there was a question mark over his fitness. He added that of all the facets needed to be a great tennis player, the physical side of the game was the easiest thing to improve.

He wasn't telling Murray anything he didn't know, and the young player felt all the talk about his lack of fitness had been blown out of proportion. 'I am satisfied I'm doing everything right just now, but, obviously, it's hard to keep to a physical-training programme when you are on the road and not playing in the main ATP events week after week. It's OK when I play at places like Wimbledon, where they have the best facilities. However, I've spent my time at junior level or on the lower-level tours, where training facilities are hard to find, and when you do find them, they aren't that great.

'If I am in Barcelona, at the tennis academy, I have a set routine. I will play three hours on clay in the morning and then stretch a while before going for lunch. I'll maybe have a little sleep after lunch then perhaps play for another 90 minutes in the afternoon or go to the gym.

'I feel my stamina is pretty good, but I'm always trying to improve that as well. I go road running, take time on the treadmill or do a skipping session when I can. My Wimbledon experience simply highlighted the parts of my body I need to strengthen. For instance, I need to be stronger in the legs and in my buttock muscles. That is because when I have to get low to the ball, it puts that part of the body under more pressure. At the higher competitive levels, these muscles are made to work even harder. I have not done much weight training as I am still growing, but I do a lot of press-ups, sit-ups and squat thrusts.'

The other area Murray needed to work on was his upper-body strength. You could see in the tough matches, such as the one against David Nalbandian on Centre Court, that he was inconsistent on serve. Part of the reason for this was his lack of strength. He needed to push into his serves more to give himself extra power. His best serve during Wimbledon was 132 mph. To get it up around the 140-mph mark, he would require stronger arms and shoulders, but this would put great stress on his muscles. Andy Roddick, who is one of the biggest servers in the game, puts a massive bag of ice on his shoulder after he has been playing or even practising. It was something Murray would have to work on in the future.

After eight days which had changed his life for ever, Andy Murray packed his bags and left Wimbledon. Before he said goodbye, there were still a couple of things left to do that would give him a thrill. First up, he had to visit the Wimbledon Museum so that he could give them his outfit from his third-round match against David Nalbandian to be put on show. The racket used by his childhood hero Andre Agassi when he won Wimbledon in 1992 and the outfit worn by Boris Becker when he lifted the trophy for the first time in 1985 were already in the museum. Murray admitted that it was amazing to think that his gear was to be displayed alongside items belonging to the greats of the game.

After that, he practised for 90 minutes, did some work for The Royal Bank of Scotland and then got a call from the BBC to do an interview with Sue Barker. He would have loved to have said that it was because they really wanted to talk to him, but he wasn't daft and realised that they probably just needed somebody to fill in time because it was raining. Whatever the reason, he really enjoyed it, and the pair had an interesting chat.

Murray wasn't nervous about speaking to Sue but was on

tenterhooks before the next interview he had planned. Being based in Barcelona, he was always trying to improve his Spanish. When a Spanish television station asked him to talk to them about his performance at Wimbledon, he wanted to give it a bash. He had to talk slowly but did OK, and they understood what he was trying to say.

The next morning, he flew to the USA with Mark Petchey to play a grass-court tournament in Newport, Rhode Island, but before he left London, he reflected on the interest the public were now showing in him. 'Before the tournament started, I could walk around Wimbledon no problems at all,' he said. 'After I won a couple of games here, things changed. Now, I can't walk down the street without people asking me for my autograph.

'One thing which has been fun is the fact that some girls have been shouting out they want to go out with me. I was told there was lots of that going on during my mixed-doubles match. All I can say is, that's OK by me!'

Before leaving, Petchey was asked what he thought of the young man he was about to coach and travel round the world with and whether he thought he had caused problems by comparing Murray to Wayne Rooney. 'We live in a society where you are going to get asked questions like that, and you cannot dodge them,' said Petchey. 'I qualified my comment, but journalists are going to grab the headlines. It is part and parcel of what Andy has decided to take on in life. Expectations are always going to be high on him, whether you mention Rooney or Muhammad Ali in the same sentence. The kid is going to have to live with expectations from now on in.

'I was hugely impressed with how he handled himself but not surprised. He is such a student of tennis. As I have got to know him over the last couple of weeks, I've also learned that he is a student of other sports like boxing, which he loves. He studies boxing and the tactics involved. That is how his mind works. He doesn't get thrown off his stride, because he stays with his tactics, and that is why he is so solid in the big moments. I am looking forward to working with him.'

When Roger Federer beat Andy Roddick in the Wimbledon final, Murray was already in the States. He left the All England Club with a wealth of experience under his belt and the knowledge that he needed to improve his fitness. Next up was another rarefied tennis venue. Newport, Rhode Island, was an idyllic setting for his next tournament and the perfect place to pick up where he left off in SW19.

10

COAST TO COAST

SOME PEOPLE MIGHT BE UNDER THE IMPRESSION THAT ONE GRASS COURT LOOKS much like another, but only people who had never stood on Centre Court at Wimbledon and listened to 13,812 people in full voice – certainly not anyone lucky enough to have played there. The grass laid down at the Hall of Fame Championships at Newport, Rhode Island, is the same length and colour as the stuff he played on over 3,500 miles away in London, SW19. For Andy Murray, though, it might as well have been growing in another universe.

His third-round, five-set defeat to David Nalbandian was still the talk of Wimbledon when Murray and Mark Petchey boarded a plane to the USA to try to keep hold of the extraordinary wave of momentum that the British grass-court season had provided. Murray's first task was to try to forget the sights and sounds of Centre Court and steel himself for weeks on end of hard graft in successive tournaments in North America. Newport, one of two ATP Tour events which had offered him wildcards in the wake of his eye-catching success at home (the other was the clay-court event in Gstaad), seemed to be the perfect place to start.

Newport's candy-striped awnings and twee New England signage is a gentle (and genteel) sort of a grindstone to get back to, but anything would have been a comedown after the thrills of Wimbledon. For one thing, he was a relative unknown outside the UK and hadn't yet won a match on the ATP Tour when he wasn't on home soil.

Murray wasn't daunted, but there were plenty of people who were worried for him back in the UK. On the final weekend of Wimbledon, almost every Sunday newspaper carried a preview of Murray's trip to Newport, and it seemed that everyone with any connection to British tennis (most of whom Murray had never met) was being asked their opinion of the 18 year old. For all those who were singing his praises, there were plenty who were either critical of his perceived lack of fitness or scornful of the optimism about him, predicting that he would be simply another flash in the Wimbledon pan.

A piece in the *Independent on Sunday* was typical and featured interviews with David Lloyd, Roger Taylor and Tony Pickard, three former British Davis Cup captains, all of whom voiced doubts about Murray's fitness, his emotional on-court demeanour and whether he was capable of building on his success at Wimbledon. 'Pickard is convinced that, after what he calls "the glamour trip to Newport", the urgent need is for Murray to get back to his own level,' wrote the *Independent on Sunday*'s Ronald Atkin, before quoting Pickard as saying, 'He is off now to play some Challengers in the US, and if he can win a couple, that would set the fire. It would mean he has taken away an awful lot from Wimbledon. But he has never won a match at Challenger level yet, and that worries the hell out of me. It is a very important month coming up for him.'

Pickard's grasp of statistics might have been a little tenuous (Murray had already won several matches at Challenger level by that stage of his career), but he was right about the last bit, even if his pessimism proved to be misplaced. Perhaps he was haunted by the ghosts of British players past: the endless names who would perform above themselves in the spotlight of Wimbledon, inspired by being on prime-time television and playing in front of a home crowd, but revert to mediocrity once the Wimbledon fortnight was over. Anyone with a passing interest in the gloomy fortunes of British tennis could reel them off: Chris Bailey, who came close to beating former world No. 2 Goran Ivanisevic in the first round in 1993 yet never got his ranking above 126; Miles Maclagan, who once pushed Boris Becker to five sets at the same stage; Barry Cowan, who had Pete Sampras on the ropes in round one in 2002; and the list goes on.

Yet there is an important reason why Murray didn't join that roster: he had won two rounds before losing a close match against Nalbandian, which gave him a huge leg-up in the rankings and therefore something more concrete to build on, rather than just 15 minutes of fame. He proved that he had more in common with Tim Henman, who, as a 21 year old ranked No. 62 in the world, found himself in a fifth set against the then reigning French Open champion Yevgeny Kafelnikov in the first round of Wimbledon in 1996 and did the very un-British thing of actually winning the match.

'I think it was early on in the fifth, we were at the change of ends, and I was probably down a break, and I suddenly thought to myself, "Oh, God, I've got to win this," because there have been quite a few British players in the past that have been remembered for great losses at Wimbledon,' Henman later revealed. 'And I just thought, "I just don't want to be associated with that," because I also knew that I was much better than them.'

The week after Henman made his breakthrough at Wimbledon – he went on to reach the quarter-finals after beating Kafelnikov – he played in a Europe/Africa Zone Group II (the equivalent of the third division) Davis Cup tie in Accra, Ghana, helping Great Britain to a 5–0 win with only his teammates cheering for him. After standing on Centre Court with all those people shouting for you, the following weeks will always be an anticlimax, but what marks the good players out from the mediocre ones is how they cope with what happens next. Like Henman, Murray would cope just fine.

Not that the Scot was exactly anonymous in Newport, given that some of the British press corps had followed him to the aptly named New England. There were seven journalists in all, though only one of them, Alix Ramsay, was a regular tennis writer, the rest having been hastily sent by their editors to cover the biggest story in British sport that month. Greg Rusedski, who had won the event twice before in front of a nearly empty press box, walked into the interview room in Newport, took one look at the assembled hacks and grinned, knowing full well who they were there to see.

Murray, who began the week ranked 213, played his opening match against the world No. 126 Gregory Carraz in front of, according to one estimate, about 250 people. It didn't seem to matter: he beat the 29-year-old Frenchman 6–4, 7–5, though he pointed out afterwards that it hadn't been nearly as easy as it looked.

'My coach [Mark Petchey] was there, and he's the most important person for me,' said Murray. 'He got me gee'd up. It was quite difficult to play because it was windy, and I had balls bouncing over my racket. But it's not difficult to get fired up for ATP tournaments – I mean, this is just my fourth one. I was happy when I won, but it was difficult to get into any rhythm, so I just had to concentrate on holding serve. I did that pretty well.'

After getting used to the perfectly manicured lawns of Wimbledon, Murray was more troubled by the bad bounces on Newport's rather scruffier grass courts than he was by Carraz, though he was keen to point out afterwards that beating higher-ranked players shouldn't yet be viewed as routine for a player of his inexperience. 'I know a lot of people were expecting me to win, but it's not as easy as that,' he said. 'The guy's a very good player. For me to win against him is one of the biggest victories of my life.'

Rusedski won his opening match, too, which meant a potential all-British quarter-final to look forward to, though Murray would have to find his way past another French opponent first, the mercurial but talented Anthony Dupuis, then ranked 111.

When rain fell and delayed the start of the match for an hour, it hardly helped Murray's cause, as it made the court damp and ensured that the ball would stay far lower than he finds comfortable. From the off, he was having to pick the ball up off his shoelaces rather than make time for his shots, a state of affairs which, together with the bad bounces, left him frustrated with the court and the effect it was having on his tennis.

It's worth noting that it was only his eighth senior match on grass, a surface which it takes many players years to learn to play on. As he had explained during the French Open a few months earlier, the perception that British players are all grass-court experts by virtue of nationality alone is largely a myth these days. 'I don't think it's an advantage being British and playing on grass. The only thing that helps is that you have the crowd there [at Queen's and Wimbledon],' he explained. 'If you look at the tournaments, basically, people from other countries come over to play Queen's and Nottingham and Wimbledon. The Brits maybe play one challenger before on grass on top of that. It's not like they have so much more practice or they practise on it a lot, because there's only four weeks of tournaments.'

Murray lost 6–4, 6–1 to Dupuis, playing poorly and leaving no one watching in any doubt as to his mood. He then vented his irritation at the state of the court to the attendant press pack, saying things which, in retrospect, it might have been more politic to have said off the record, given that the very tournament he was criticising had given him a wildcard. 'They didn't put any cover on [the court] when it started raining,' Murray said. 'They used blowers, but the court was still damp. The ball bounced so low. I can't play when it's like that. Here the ball bounced high . . . skidded through, was dying. That's the worst tennis court I've played on in my life, by far.'

Rusedski, like almost every other high-profile player on the tour, has made similar mistakes in the past in publicly letting off steam after a defeat, and he was quick to point out that the young Scot was, at that stage, still getting used to being under the scrutiny of the press pack. It was for this reason that he should be allowed the odd injudicious comment or two. 'I've done that. I think everyone has done that,' Rusedski said. 'It's just youth, and it's also a desire. He expects to do well; he expects to win. That's a good thing. He'll grow up from that, and he'll learn to handle those situations. It shows that he has the passion, and he wants to win.

'He doesn't go out there scared. He goes out there to win every time and believes that he can beat whoever he's playing. That's what makes the difference between someone who does OK and someone who does well out here, and that's what sets him apart from the younger British players that we have. Don't be too hard on him. He's had a great start. He's had a good Wimbledon, a good Queen's and he's won a match here, outside of Wimbledon. That shows that he can get away from all the hype and all the support and still play well, so that's a positive.'

Rusedski, incidentally, went on to win the title in Newport for a third time, the only man in history ever to do so. Only Alix Ramsay stayed to watch him do it. When she'd finished interviewing him, Rusedski's mother quietly came up beside her and said, 'Thank you for staying.'

That week, Murray also gave an interview to *The Times* in which he attempted to get those writing, talking and reading about him to maintain some sense of perspective about what he had achieved thus far. 'I hate losing for a start,' he said. 'I don't think I've played any tournament hoping to come second best. What I want to do is really try to win every match. I actually believe I can go right to the top. I feel really motivated to go on and do it. Things have got a little over the top recently, because I still don't think I've really done anything yet. OK, I won the junior US Open, which was good, and I had quite a good Wimbledon. I've won four or five matches so far, but some people have acted as if I pretty much won Wimbledon. Obviously, my results so far have been quite good and some people are calling me the new British hope. That bit doesn't bother me. I just need to try to keep doing it on the court.'

The next place to do that was Aptos, a palm-tree-lined outcrop of Santa Cruz, in northern California, which meant a six-hour flight across the US, a step back down to Challenger level and a switch to the more familiar surface of hardcourts.

The event, held at the Seaside Sports Club for the last 19 years, is the longest-running Challenger tournament in the United States and has a total prize-money pool of $75,000 to be shared between a draw of 32 players, which is not small by Challenger standards but which seems modest when you consider that Murray's efforts at Queen's and Wimbledon had just earned him $64,255.

The Challenger Tour is not a place for flash hotels and limousines either – just like the rest of the players, Murray and Petchey lodged in a family home for the week, sharing a room. That is not to say Murray felt playing a Challenger was beneath him – quite the opposite, in fact. He was well aware that his ranking was still too low to have secured him a place in the main draw without a wildcard.

Murray went about his task in Aptos with professional zeal, happy to be back on his favourite surface and, perhaps, a little relieved at having shed the travelling British press pack, albeit temporarily. He ripped through his first-round match against Frederic Niemeyer of Canada 6–2, 6–4, then played Marc Kimmich, a lucky loser from the qualifying rounds, after the young Australian helpfully knocked out the second seed, experienced American Justin Gimelstob. Another straight sets win put Murray into the quarters, where he was to take on Israeli Harel Levy, who had been ranked as high as No. 30 in the world.

However, Murray had hit his stride, and he made light work of Levy, notching up a 6–4, 6–0 win, thus limiting his time in the hot Californian summer sun. Saturday saw him look equally commanding against Bobby Reynolds, who was ranked 94 places above him at 111 in the standings. Reynolds fell 6–4, 6–3, and Murray had played his way to an all-unseeded final against little-known American Rajeev Ram, who had also required a wildcard because his ranking (291) was too low to get him into the draw on merit.

Murray absorbed the pressure of being favourite like an old pro, though Ram pushed him hard in the first set. The underdog had two game points at 4–5, only to see Murray rip two returns past him and take the set with a screaming backhand winner down the line. The second set was more straightforward, and Murray wrapped up the victory 6–4, 6–3 to secure the biggest title of his career thus far. Having never previously got past the quarter-finals of a Challenger-level event, he had won his first Challenger title without dropping a set, earning himself 60 ATP ranking points – enough to push him to well inside the world's top 200 for the first time.

'Andy has been playing very well and has been on a bit of a run this summer,' Ram said afterwards. 'I want to congratulate him. He is tough to beat when he is returning and making passing shots so well.'

'I had to work hard to make the right shot. Rajeev was getting to passing shots that nobody else has been getting to. It seemed like he would just stick out his racket, and the ball would come back,' said Murray, who might also have given Petchey a bit of good-natured ribbing. His then coach had played Aptos three times (in 1990, 1991 and 1992) and managed to win only one match!

With his ranking now up to 164 and his confidence bolstered by the career breakthrough he had enjoyed in Aptos, Murray headed back across the US to the mid-western city of Indianapolis, where he had been granted a wildcard into the ATP Tour-level event held there. He and Petchey flew overnight after he won the title, arriving in Indianapolis on the Monday morning. It had been a sleepless night, and Murray conked out for 13 hours. It was a badly needed mega-nap, perhaps, but one which he later admitted upset his sleeping pattern for the following few days.

As well as having to negotiate the jetlag that comes with transcontinental flights across the US, Murray was also having to cope with swapping between different levels of tournaments. Like a boxer constantly having to step up and down between weight classes, each week required an adjustment for Murray, both in the level of opponents and in his expectations and those of the public back home, which wasn't always educated in the different levels of tournaments he was playing.

To put the difference between the Aptos Challenger and Indianapolis ATP Tour event in context, the total prize-money purse at the ATP Tour tournament was $575,000, more than seven and a half times what was on offer in California, and both the quality of the entrants and the ranking points on offer reflected that disparity.

At that stage of Murray's career, winning a round at an ATP Tour event was still a significant achievement, but he managed that in his first match in Indianapolis with a 6–4, 6–2 win over unseeded American Jesse Witten, a late replacement for injured Brazilian Flavio Saretta, who would probably have provided far tougher resistance. The second round saw him take on another American, this time the 16th seed, Mardy Fish. On a stiflingly hot day at the Indianapolis Tennis Center, Murray struggled to contain Fish, whose mammoth serve is probably his most testing weapon. The Scot did well to level the match at a set apiece and was even up a break in the third set, so although he walked off the court having lost 6–4, 4–6, 6–4, he had little reason to be upset.

Indeed, he seemed to be thoroughly enjoying his American sojourn, especially the brief tastes he was getting of the relative high life of the ATP Tour. He was particularly impressed with Indianapolis, which is renowned for treating its players well. 'Over here, it's better,' he said, having indulged his love of go-karting in between matches. 'It's absolutely unbelievable. You stay at great hotels; you get to play in front of big crowds. There is internet in the players' lounge – everything.'

But it was back to the relatively spartan conditions of the Challengers next for Murray and yet another plane journey, this time north to Canada. The first was a Challenger in Granby, which is about 45 minutes' drive south-east of Montreal, right in the heart of French-speaking Quebec, and is famous for its marshlands and not a lot else. It would hardly be on the itinerary of most travelling 18 year olds, but Murray was all business as he battled through to the quarter-finals before Gregory Carraz, whom he'd beaten in the first round in Newport, gained revenge on him.

From Granby, he and Petchey headed back west to another Challenger, this time in Vancouver, which had a prize-money purse of $100,000 – the most any Challenger can offer – and a strong field because of that. By now, Murray was starting to feel tired from the combined effects of travel, playing and possibly some of the residual emotion of all that he experienced at Wimbledon. He came through his first match OK, against Marc Kimmich (one of his victims in Aptos), but had to battle through his next one, against American Cecil Mamiit, before winning 6–7(4), 6–3, 6–4 to make it through to his third consecutive Challenger quarter-final to play Paul Baccanello, another Australian. Murray played well in the first set, winning it for the loss of just two games, but let things slip to allow Baccanello to take the match to a deciding set and then ended up losing it in a frustrating tie-breaker. It was time for a day off.

The next destination on Murray and Petchey's whistle-stop tour of North America was Binghamton, in upstate New York. The tournament, a $50,000 Challenger, has played host to the likes of Lleyton Hewitt, Paradorn Srichaphan, Max Mirnyi and, in its inaugural year in 1994, a 19-year-old Tim Henman. Played in a recreation park in the middle of the small provincial city, the Binghamton Challenger was to provide Murray, who was now ranked 145 and therefore seeded second, with an eventful and ultimately successful week.

Murray had taken a couple of days off to rest after arriving from Vancouver. Suitably recharged, Murray shrugged off hot, sultry conditions to rip through his first match against Harel Levy, whom he'd beaten in Aptos, winning 6–3, 6–1. 'It's hot here – a lot hotter than Vancouver,' Murray observed afterwards. 'I quite like the courts. They are pretty quick, but the ball comes up quite high, and I can attack in a lot of the points.'

He took those good vibes into his second-round match, but it was to provide a sharp contrast to the rout of Levy. His war of attrition with Harsh Mankad, the world No. 256 from India, was a gritty, tense battle which very nearly put Murray out of the tournament and forced him to save a match point in the second set tie-breaker. After an exchange of breaks midway through the first set, Murray, who grew increasingly frustrated with his own standard of play, then put in a poor service game at 5–5 to effectively give the Indian the lead. Petchey gave credit to Mankad for denying Murray any time to find the rhythm he was lacking: 'I thought Harsh did well to keep Andy rushed.'

Much the same thing happened in the second set, but this time, thankfully, Mankad's nerve failed him when he went to serve the match out, and he instead handed Murray a break with two galling errors. The Indian player then led 5–1 in the tie-breaker before Murray, faced with defeat, found the inspiration that had been lacking earlier and fired off five straight winners. He also saved a match point at 7–6 with a rasping backhand. A big first serve and a return winner gave him the set and broke Mankad's spirit. From then on, it was a gallop downhill towards a 5–7, 7–6, 6–0 victory after two hours and twenty minutes.

'I was surprised I could turn that around,' Murray admitted afterwards. 'I didn't play that great today. I think the key was that when I had to, I played pretty well. But on the smaller points, I got myself in bad positions and was a bit lazy and tired.'

Encounters like that are won by experience and match hardness, something which can only be acquired by undertaking the kind of relentless run of tournaments which Murray and Petchey were on. As well as tightening up his competitiveness and amassing ranking points, the succession of matches was also a way of improving Murray's fitness, the cause of such fevered debate during the grass-court season. His new-found conditioning was to be severely tested when rain fell heavily at Binghamton, washing out most of Friday and forcing Murray to play two matches on Saturday, something he had never previously done at any level.

In stifling temperatures, Murray had first to play world No. 196 Alex Bogomolov Jr., whom he beat 6–4, 6–4, then Brian Baker, another American, in the semi-finals with a little over two hours off in between. Murray beat Baker, ranked 221, even more comfortably (6–2, 6–3) to put himself in his second Challenger final inside of a month.

'I played two matches in one day in 35 degree heat and 90 per cent humidity, and during the first match, Bogomolov was sitting down between points in the first set because it was that hot,' Murray later recalled, 'and he's a pretty fit guy himself.'

Despite his gruelling Saturday, his body and mind seemed more than alert to the challenge offered by 22-year-old Colombian qualifier Alejandro Falla, ranked 233 in the world. Murray won the match 7–6, 6–3 to give himself another replica trophy to put in his already overflowing suitcase.

'Alejandro has gone through qualifying, so he's played a lot of matches, and he started out very well. I managed to hold serve pretty well today, and I played a pretty solid match,' Murray said afterwards. 'I've won against some good players – I've beaten seven or eight guys inside the top two hundred. I think I'm ready. Maybe physically I'm not in as good shape as a lot of the guys inside the top 100, but I think my tennis is there. This isn't the same as winning on the ATP tour, but winning these tournaments gives you a lot of confidence, because there are still a lot of good players here.'

Murray had proved that he could beat those 'good players' with no rampantly patriotic British crowd, no TV cameras and no movie stars in the players' box cheering him on. After the event was over, the tournament website received the following, rather touching email from a gentleman in Dunblane who had taken a special interest in its enthusiastic and comprehensive coverage:

> A note to thank you for keeping us, here in Scotland, up to date with Andy's progress at Binghamton. Due to all his tennis activities, we rarely see him nowadays, so the up-to-date pictures were indeed a bonus. I hope his tournament success at Binghamton is another big step in his quest for a top 100 ranking. Thank you again for your excellent coverage.
> Sincerely,
> Roy Erskine (Andy's proud grandfather).

Having proved himself at Challenger level for the second time in a month, it was time for Murray to step up to the big league again at his first Masters Series event in Cincinnati. Masters Series events are

187

the nine most prestigious tournaments on the ATP Tour outside the four grand slams and are worth more in ranking points and prize money than ordinary ATP Tour tournaments. To receive a wildcard into a Masters Series draw is a huge bonus for a player ranked 153 in the world, especially since no one ranked outside the mid-60s usually gets in without one.

The wildcards Murray received in the US were one tangible upside of the media coverage and attention he got over the summer, since it persuaded tournaments that he was a draw-card for garnering international coverage for their event. In the long term, it was to mean a period of adjustment while he got used to being covered week in, week out by the written press, TV and radio, but as he was on the way up, the slavish attention of the much-maligned British media came in very handy.

The Cincinnati Masters is not held in Cincinnati at all but in the unprepossessing town of Mason, Ohio, a huddle of strip malls, hotels and fast food outlets which exists solely to service the nearby Kings Island theme park. Kings Island is such a feature of the place, including the tennis tournament, that its most terrifying ride, the Drop Zone, which simulates an elevator plummeting towards the earth, towers over the tennis centre and can be seen from the centre court, the only other landmark on the otherwise flat mid-western horizon.

Despite its rather peculiar location – or perhaps because of it – the tournament thrives, drawing in punters from all over the region to watch a world-class field in a large and imposing venue. Past champions include Pete Sampras, Stefan Edberg and Patrick Rafter, and the sports fans of Mason, Ohio, have had their share of decent tennis down the years, while the players adore the access they have to the nearby golf course and therefore tend to return year after year.

The nature of Masters Series events is that only the very best players and a small selection of wildcard entrants are eligible to play, which invariably means that the old cliché about their being no easy draws really does apply. To make the jump from a Challenger event to a Masters Series tournament, as Murray did, is a sizeable leap in class. As fate would have it, he drew a familiar foe in the first round in the shape of Taylor Dent, the American serve-and-volley specialist whom he had beaten in such style at Queen's. Dent, who is half Australian, is a cheerful, affable fellow, but after being humiliated at Queen's, he would have been unimpressed to see Murray's name beside his on the draw sheet. Murray played every bit as well against him as he had done in London – if not better, since Dent put up a good deal more resistance than he had done previously – and won the match 7–6, 7–6.

Afterwards Murray said, 'I'd already beaten him once this year, so I knew that going in I was going to have a chance. I would just have to put a high percentage of first serves in, which I didn't do so well in the first set but did much better in the second. Also, I knew I was going to have to return well, and that's one of my strengths. I think, in the key moments, I returned very well. I like playing against serve–volleyers, because returning is one of the best things that I do on the court. So, playing against him, it kind of suits me a bit more than him playing against me. So, yeah, it was probably one of the better guys I could have played in the tournament.'

Murray's nonchalance afterwards, and the fact that he had already defeated Dent that summer, disguised just how significant a win it was. When you are the world No. 132, winning matches at a Masters Series event is not to be taken for granted, and neither is rolling over a good player who is ranked No. 23 in the world on his home turf in straight sets.

There was a small and rather comical reminder of just how new it all still was for Murray at the end of the first set against Dent when he needed the toilet, and instead of being taken back to the locker-room by a linesman in the usual fashion, he followed the official to a public restroom instead. Fortunately, there wasn't a queue. 'The guy who was taking me there told me to go in that one, so I just went,' he explained afterwards, not quite understanding why the journalist posing the question thought it was noteworthy enough to ask about. 'It was fine. There was no one there.'

If Dent was a significant obstacle to overcome, there was an even bigger one to get past in the second round in the huge, muscular shape of Marat Safin, the 2000 US Open winner and then reigning Australian Open champion. The giant Russian, who had beaten Roger Federer in the semi-finals to claim the title in Melbourne, is widely regarded as one of the most talented players of the modern era, even if his explosive temper and succession of injuries means that he will probably never be the most consistent. He was to be the first grand-slam champion that Murray had ever played.

'It's been pretty big for me. I won two tournaments – two Challengers – and I'd never been past the quarter-finals of a Challenger before I came here,' said Murray, reflecting on what had been a tumultuous few weeks. 'It's given me a lot of confidence. This is the third ATP tournament that I've played since I've been here. To be around these guys – and obviously tomorrow I get to play against one of the best players in the world – is a great experience for me.

'I see myself losing pretty comfortably against Safin. But I'm just going to go out there and try and play a pretty solid match, not make too many mistakes, and hope that he has an off day so I can cause him a few problems. But it's going to be very difficult. He's one of the best players in the world. I've got a lot of respect for him. He's one of my favourite players as well.'

Murray did lose, 6–4, 1–6, 6–1, but it wasn't exactly comfortable for either of them. Safin was wild and wonderful in equal measure but looked in deep trouble when Murray levelled the match after whipping through the second set. For Murray, the pain he felt in his shoulder throughout the match was a worry, especially with the US Open qualifying competition just a few days away.

'I hurt it in the third game of the match hitting a serve,' he said, 'and after that it was one of the reasons why I didn't serve so well. Every time I hit the ball, I got a bit of pain just at the front of my shoulder. It's not too bad, but it was a little bit annoying. I don't think it will be too bad. I've never had a problem with my shoulder before, and, obviously, I could still continue the match. I was still serving hardish, but it was just a little bit sore. The physio doesn't think it's too bad, and I should be OK to play the quallies next week.'

Like the rest of his American summer, the time spent on court against Safin was an education for Murray, both in the way the Russian hit the ball and also in the circumstances of finding himself involved in such a huge match a long way from home. 'Playing on the centre court here against Safin compared to playing in a Futures tournament, where there's three or four players watching, against someone who's ranked 500 is just completely different. I felt a little bit nervous today before I went on, because I have never played against anyone as good as him. Obviously, he's quite intimidating. He hits the ball pretty hard, and he's won a grand slam this year. So, you don't know how you're going to play or how you're going to deal with everything because you've never played against someone as good as him. But I think I did OK.

'It was quite difficult playing against someone like him, because he puts a lot of pressure on your second serve, and he's got such big ground strokes – it's quite intimidating. I mean, he's absolutely massive. He's obviously a great player. It's difficult to settle down early on. You have so much respect for his shots that you can sometimes go for too much. His backhand is his best shot, so you try to stay away from it too much and play to his forehand, but that's a great shot as well. Obviously, he's got a better game than me – he's a better player – so it's difficult to keep up with him for three sets.

'I'd still say the gap is pretty big between the guys outside of [the top] 150 to the guys inside. Then, obviously, the guys in the top 20 are all great players. I think between 20 and 100 there's not that big a difference, but the guys inside the top 20 are very consistent – they don't give away cheap points. To get into the top 20 you have to win a lot of matches, so it's always going to be difficult to beat them.'

The fact that it was getting less difficult had much to do with the hard graft he'd put in since Wimbledon: the twenty-two matches in seven different countries played in seven weeks. It was this experience which meant that he entered his next grand-slam tournament, the US Open, a fitter, stronger, more experienced player than when he left SW19.

11

A QUALIFIED SUCCESS: US OPEN 2005

BEFORE THE 2005 US OPEN, THE USTA SPENT A LARGE CHUNK OF ITS PROFITS painting all 28 of the courts at Flushing Meadows a fetching blue with a green trim. Little did they realise that before the tournament was out an 18-year-old Scotsman would come along and decorate one of the show courts in his own distinctly memorable way. The images of Murray throwing up on the Grandstand court during his first-round match against Andrei Pavel ended up sprayed across the back pages of most national newspapers and almost all of the Scottish ones, a peculiar testament to what was another important breakthrough for the young player.

He arrived in New York in less than optimistic mood, having spent the previous eight weeks travelling and playing the longest stretch of tournaments he had ever had to contend with. He was also quietly seething that negotiations behind the scenes between Wimbledon and the USTA had not resulted in him getting a wildcard, something which, as the reigning junior champion, he might have felt entitled to. After weeks of travelling and playing and with an injured shoulder to worry about, having to play three matches in qualifying was the last thing Murray needed. With a flock of US tennis players to nurture, the USTA is not prone to helping those without an American passport, though, and so he was reliant on the All England Club agreeing to a deal which the USTA had brokered. Under the American proposal, Murray would have received a wildcard in exchange for an American getting a free pass into Wimbledon 2006.

Such deals are commonplace between the grand slams, especially since part of their remit is to help up-and-coming players from their own country. Roland Garros and the Australian Open have a similar arrangement, and Wimbledon previously had a deal with the Australian Open as well, under which Britain's Elena Baltacha once got a wildcard for the event in Melbourne. As much as those precedents were persuasive, the All England Club was unwilling to give up a wildcard slot to an American which might otherwise go to a British player.

'It was very disappointing that the USTA wanted to give me a wildcard and Wimbledon didn't want to trade,' Murray told a small group of British journalists. 'I felt that I had done enough that Wimbledon might step up for me. I could understand if the USTA wanted to give all their wildcards to American players but they offered a trade. It's disappointing when the tournament [Wimbledon] doesn't want to help you.'

Mark Petchey, who had been with Murray for every step of his North American odyssey over the summer, was equally unimpressed but philosophical. 'I personally don't think Andy needed the experience of trying to qualify here after everything else he's done over the summer,' he said. 'Physically and mentally it's been a really demanding few weeks, not just because of the matches he's played, but we've also been criss-crossing America between matches. He could have done with a few days off instead, but we just have to get on with it, don't we?'

Petchey is a keen student of the ranking system and knew that Murray also had little to gain in winning three qualifying matches, since the allocation of ranking points for qualifying rounds at the grand slams is relatively meagre. Only by qualifying and then winning matches in the main draw could Murray improve his ranking, which stood at 122 that week.

'I think he is getting tired, and he could probably have done with a week off, but it wasn't to be,' Judy told *The Herald*. 'I hope he hasn't overdone it, but if he doesn't perform well next week, it's not the end of the world. It's still been an amazing summer, and he's learned so much. The wildcards he got have been a big bonus, but qualifying will be another good experience, because it will do him a whole pile of good to find out what it's like to battle his way through to the main draw.'

The only non-American to get a wildcard was an Aussie, 1997 finalist Mark Philippoussis, who'd won a total of eight matches in his last eight tournaments and ended up losing in straight sets to Karol Kucera in the first round.

As Judy predicted, battling was certainly going to be the order of the day. As the last days of August heralded the start of the three rounds of qualifying – which meant three best-of-three set matches in four days – Murray's shoulder was still giving him problems, particularly when he reached back to hit his serve. A scan on the injury, which he had sustained when losing to Marat Safin a week earlier in Cincinnati, revealed no permanent damage, and medical advice suggested that no further harm could be sustained by playing through the pain.

'The physio says I'll be fine, but we'll just have to wait and see,' Murray told reporters whom he ran into in one of the many grey-painted corridors that snake through the bowels of Arthur Ashe Stadium. 'I've had a few days off, and I only practised properly for the first time on Monday and have been taking it easy on my serve. My shoulder hurts a bit when I serve or when I put my hand behind my back, but I think it will be OK.'

Qualifying was due to start on Wednesday, 23 August, but Murray was given the first day off by the schedulers. At first glance, it seemed helpful to have a day to rest up in the salubrious surroundings of the Omni Hotel in Midtown Manhattan where he was staying, but it meant potentially playing three matches in three days, which was going to test his reserves of energy and his pain threshold to the maximum.

Things could have been an awful lot worse, though. The night before he was due to play 20-year-old Israeli Dudi Sela, Murray got into one of New York's trademark yellow cabs outside the hotel where his physio Jean-Pierre Bruyere was staying. Murray had been having treatment on the shoulder and was on his way back to the Omni when the cabbie decided, as only a New York taxi driver can, to jump a red light. However, he wasn't quite quick enough and was forced to slam on his brakes, causing Murray to go flying into the plastic partition which separates the driver and passenger. Thankfully, Murray got out of the cab with nothing more than a bruise on his head and a mild dose of whiplash, and although he was worried about how his body would feel the next day, he woke up on the morning of his match feeling fine.

He was scheduled to appear last on Court Seven that day, which necessitated hours of waiting around and created the possibility that the conditions would be cool and damp as the humidity, which characterises New York in August, faded. Such conditions, as anyone with a bad back, a bum knee or, for that matter, an injured shoulder, will tell you, can stiffen the joints and exacerbate existing problems.

Qualifying week at a grand slam can seem strangely quiet, with most preparations already in place (save for the odd sound of sawing or hammering as final touches are added) but crowds are nowhere near the levels seen once the tournament gets properly under way. The No. 7 subway train is not yet full as it ferries sports fans and commuters to and fro on the 45-minute journey from Midtown Manhattan to Willets Point, the stop shared by Flushing Meadows and Shea Stadium, home of the New York Mets. Instead, it's as though the tournament has made a false start, with the action and attention centred on random outside courts, while the Arthur Ashe Stadium and the other show courts remain eerily empty.

In spite of the hurdles which seemed to have been placed in his way, Murray beat Dudi Sela 6–4, 6–4 under the lights, much to the delight of the small but noisy crowd which sat courtside to cheer him on, most of which was made up of fellow British competitors in qualifying (including Arvind Parmar, Jonathan Marray, David Sherwood and Jane O'Donaghue), Murray's Davis Cup captain Jeremy Bates and, of course, the ever-vocal Judy. Sela, too, had his fair share of support, largely drawn from New York's thriving Jewish community. Sela had been two years ahead of Murray in the juniors, but he appeared a good deal less experienced. He was slow to adapt to the conditions, and Murray went a break up. Although Sela broke back immediately, three beautifully crafted lobs secured another break of serve for Murray at 4–4, and he served out the first set. Another early break of serve in the second set put the match well out of Sela's reach. Meanwhile, in the huge empty press room (few journalists come to cover the qualifying rounds), a small group of British hacks typed feverishly, trying to get the result into the last, post-midnight, editions of the UK papers.

The shoulder held up, just about, but the discomfort Murray was obviously feeling was apparent to anyone who watched his second match the following evening on Court 11 against 23-year-old Paolo Lorenzi of Italy. A cheerful journeyman who fills his off-court time by training to be a doctor of sports medicine, Lorenzi's studies would have undoubtedly taught him to interpret an opponent wincing and taking power off his serves as a sign of shoulder trouble, but Murray played well enough to keep the Italian at bay.

As if the shoulder wasn't irritating him enough, there were a slew of line calls which had him howling out his frustration. Qualifying is the unglamorous end of a grand slam, a place where it isn't just the players who tend to be the lesser lights of their profession. Line judges are often what might politely be called the 'B team', and their job is made no easier when matches are played under floodlights and their eyes have not had time to adjust to the conditions. For all that, though, some of the calls were almost farcically bad.

Murray grumped and winced and did his best to avoid Lorenzi's flashy forehand, while the Italian – who, in fairness, received just as many terrible calls as Murray did – didn't help his cause by serving so badly that one of his second serves landed in the park next door. It was not a match for the scrapbook, but another grafted win in straight sets was exactly what was required.

By the time his third and final match arrived on the Friday, Murray was the last Briton in the qualifying rounds. Yet again, he was scheduled late in the evening, but the fact that he was playing a semi-famous name – at least to British tennis fans – in Giovanni Lapentti and on Court 4 helped draw a crowd and added a sense of occasion. Lapentti, whose brother Nicolas made the top ten in 1998, is famous for breaking the hearts of British tennis fans when, at the age of 17, he came from two sets down to beat Arvind Parmar in the final rubber of Great Britain's Davis Cup promotion/relegation tie on Wimbledon's Court No. 1 in July 2000. Lapentti's win consigned Great Britain to Europe/Africa Zone Group I and elevated Ecuador to the Davis Cup World Group. Though Tim Henman and Greg Rusedski returned the favour by beating the Lapentti brothers in their home town of Guayaquil the following year, Giovanni's place in British tennis history was assured.

Court 4 always attracts a large crowd because its stand overlooks the practice courts and it is situated opposite the administrative offices and players' entrance to the Arthur Ashe Stadium, making it a tempting place for staff, players and media to watch a match.

They had to be quick to find their seats for the first set: it took just 17 minutes as Murray punished Lapentti's shortcomings. Murray, unsurprisingly given the run he'd been on, looked match sharp and ruthless, but Lapentti could scarcely get a ball in court. He won just eight points in the first set to remind everyone why he had failed to build on his famous British upset. Five years on, he was twenty-two yet still only ranked 138 in the world.

He did a little better in the second set, which was neck and neck until the tie-breaker when Murray, anxious not to be pushed to a third set, stepped up a gear to become the first British man in 35 years to qualify for a grand slam tournament and the second youngest British man to do so in the open era. Not for the first time, Murray's achievements had the ITF communications team, as keen as ever to assist the frantic British journalists on deadline for last edition, sifting through the record books to find the last British man to qualify for a grand slam. For the anoraks, it was Stephen Warboys, who qualified for Wimbledon in 1970.

Despite making the main draw, there was no whooping in celebration for Murray, just a handshake for Lapentti and the umpire and a weary trudge through the small crowd back to the locker-room with the BBC's tennis correspondent Jonathan Overend trailing in his wake in the hope of getting Murray's thoughts on what he had just done. Murray hardly had the strength to pull himself together for an interview, only managing the meek but eloquent quote, 'I'm still fighting after playing eight weeks in a row.' He would speak to the media at length once he'd had a decent night's sleep and time to reflect on his efforts.

'In my first match, a lot of people came to watch. I don't know exactly how many, but there were a lot of people, and there were a lot of Israelis supporting Sela,' he explained to the eight or so travelling tennis writers who had joined him in a comfortable corner of his hotel lobby to hear his thoughts. 'It was probably the second round that was the toughest to get up for, because the guy I was playing wasn't that good. I felt a little bit tired when I woke up in the morning, [but] I managed to get through that, and yesterday, obviously, the stadium was packed. The guy I was playing is a good player. He's won a lot of matches this year, and it wasn't really that tough to get up for it. This is my favourite grand slam. I'm pretty happy about playing it as an 18 year old. It's a pretty good achievement. Since I came here the first time as a junior, I always wanted to come here and play in the seniors. I just didn't think it was going to happen so quickly.'

By then, the news had come through that he was playing Andrei Pavel in the first round. The Romanian, then ranked No. 39 in the world, was a likeable veteran of the tour. Aged 31 and with two children (the elder of whom is six, closer to Murray's age than Pavel is), he represented the other side of the generation gap.

'I do feel like I earned my place in the main draw rather than just getting it for free,' said Murray. 'I've got a pretty decent draw. Pavel is a very good player. He's not having his best year, but he's pretty solid. I'm really looking forward to playing. I've got a pretty good record playing on these courts. I'm hoping I'll be back in good condition for Tuesday. Hopefully, my shoulder will get much better. I know it's going to be pretty tough. It's going to be hot, and playing a five-set match against a guy with as much experience as Pavel is going to be pretty difficult. I feel pretty good now. I was in a bit of pain last night, but I had a good night's sleep, and I know I've got at least three days off. It's good to know I've got a chance to rest.'

By the time Murray got on court in the late afternoon of Tuesday, 30 August, he was already the last British man standing for the second grand slam in succession. Just as he had done at Wimbledon, he outlasted both Tim Henman and Greg Rusedski. Henman had been first to go, beaten by his consistently bad back and Fernando Verdasco, who punished the Brit's restricted movement to win 6–4, 6–2, 6–2. 'Every time you engage a muscle, which is basically on every shot, you feel like someone is prodding you with a knife,' said Henman, his uncharacteristically dramatic description speaking volumes about both his pain and his frustration. Rusedski followed him out of the tournament within a couple hours, losing 7–5, 7–6, 6–3 to the in-form American James Blake, who had come fresh from winning his first (and home) title in Connecticut. Both Henman and Rusedski, as had become customary, had the good grace to set aside their own disappointment and wish their young compatriot well before he headed out to play his match.

On the day of the first-round match, Murray took to the Grandstand court, one of the most unusual venues at any of the grand slams. It is flanked on one side by the adjacent Louis Armstrong Stadium and on the other by low stands which create a noisy, intimate atmosphere. Its lack of corporate or allocated seats lends it a freewheeling, slightly disorganised air, but the front row is only a few feet away from the players, so it has the capacity to create the most compelling of atmospheres when the match warrants it. Those who sat in the wooden bleachers at the Grandstand court that day were to witness one of the stadium's more memorable contests.

The match began mid-afternoon, but the pair would stay on court long enough for night to fall, and although the weather started off being muggy and cloudy, it later changed to cooler and windier conditions (it was hurricane season on the Eastern Seaboard, after all).

Murray looked sprightly compared to his weary, irritable demeanour during qualifying, and he started with brisk efficiency, winning the first set 6–3 after a crucial break in the eighth game with the aid of a neat stop volley on set point. He was playing with an audacity and authority that had Pavel, the old campaigner, sighing wearily as he returned to his chair at the end of the set. The Romanian, though, didn't seem inclined to be railroaded by a player more than 12 years his junior and broke in the first game of the second set to give the contest legs.

Murray went a break up early in the third but, to his evident fury (his racket was bounced off the court more than once), Pavel broke back and then went to 5–3 as the younger player's serve went AWOL. At that point, with an inexperienced opponent looking as though he might have fatally lost his composure, the Romanian must have thought that he'd done enough to see the young interloper off.

'I had so many chances on his serve, even in the second set, and I didn't take them. I had a lot of 30-all points,' Murray said afterwards.

However, far from being bowed, Murray seemed to find an extra burst of energy at the beginning of the fourth set, which was a remarkable feat given the miles in his legs from the preceding weeks of tennis. The fist-pumping, ferocious player that the smattering of British fans courtside would have remembered from Wimbledon a few weeks earlier, was soon drawing Pavel into his web then punishing him with pouncing winners. Anyone taking a passing glance would not have been able to tell that it was Murray rather than Pavel, a veteran of nine US Opens, who was the debutant.

The young Scot won the fourth set in a blur, but the drama was yet to fully unfold. Pessimists who had watched his fitness and lack of experience fail him against Nalbandian were bracing themselves for a let-down in the fifth, forgetting perhaps, that while his exertions since then had tired him, they had also made him far fitter and much more match tough. He may have been going into only the second fifth set of his career, but he was better equipped to cope than the detractors assumed.

He went a break up to lead 2–1 and sat down for the change of ends with the satisfaction of a man in command of a fifth set, an unfamiliar feeling for the teenager. As he stood up to walk back to his side of the court, he took a swig of the electrolyte drink which Petchey had prepared for him, only to suddenly and violently vomit all over the court. Pavel, whose chair was nearest, moved to get his racket bag out of the way with such haste that he threatened to break the land speed record, the linespeople suddenly looked queasy, and there was an audible gasp and some very British cries of 'Eurrrghhh'. The photographers, lined up on one side, had the perfect shot, and their motor shutters whirred away, taking what was one of the more memorable shots of the tournament. *The Herald* covered their inside back page with a side-on action shot of him throwing up, which must have made delightful breakfast-time reading for the people of Scotland. As the late-night sports editor on duty there put it at the time, 'We've got a great shot of the sick.'

Murray was as surprised as anyone, looking at the bottle quizzically, then waiting, embarrassedly, while the ball kids attempted to clear the mess up. In all, the delay was about 15 minutes long, sufficient to give Murray a certain amount of infamy and a unique place in US Open folklore.

Vomiting on court has a certain cachet at the US Open ever since Pete Sampras repeatedly threw up while playing Alex Corretja in the 1996 quarter-finals and went on to win the title. The US Open website's Erin Gell summed up the amused and bemused reaction to the incident around Flushing Meadows in the opening line of her match report: 'With the overcast skies, a rain delay seemed entirely possible. But a vomit delay?'

'I took a glucoside sodium drink, which is supposed to stop you from cramping. I was a little bit tired at the start of the set, and I started to drink it. Always when I take it, I start to feel a little bit sick. And there I took too much. I felt like I was going to burp and then threw up,' he explained, with a smile. 'I didn't feel sick. I felt fine. I was just walking and . . . It's that drink. I'd been drinking a different one, which is just supposed to keep you hydrated, then this one is supposed to stop you from cramping. It's got sodium and salt and everything in it. I just felt like I was going to burp, and then everything came up.

'It was pretty funny. I was just a little bit annoyed at the time because I was getting a bit of momentum. Then, obviously, I had to stop for 15 minutes. It's the worst thing [that can happen] when you're starting to get tired, because your body goes down and then you can cramp. But I'm sure I'll find it funny tomorrow.'

The delay nearly proved costly. Pavel had looked as though he'd been tiring at the start of the fifth set but returned to the cleaned-up court rejuvenated. By contrast, it took Murray a couple of games to get the momentum back.

'Yeah, it definitely helped him more than it did me,' said Murray. 'I had a lot of momentum. I had just broken him, so I was pretty disappointed when I threw up. That's why I was angry when I was on the court. That stuff always makes me feel like that. Then, obviously, to take a break of like 15, 20 minutes when you're a break up in the fifth set is the last thing you want.'

Pavel won the next two games to go 3–2 ahead before Murray held, vitally, to level the score at 3–3 and ensure the change in momentum was only temporary. At deuce in the next game, the match took another dramatic twist that sent the crowd, which was already enthralled, into overdrive. Murray hoisted up a lob which landed in the far corner, on the opposite side of the court to umpire Tony Nimmons's chair. The linesman called it out, Nimmons overruled and Pavel exploded in outrage, remonstrating with Nimmons at length. According to their guidelines, umpires are taught only to overrule a 'clear mistake', which usually means a ball which lands near them or is so far in or out that anyone could call it. Having made what was a marginal decision at best, Nimmons felt the wrath of Pavel, while the crowd – being as unreasonable and fickle as only an emotionally

charged mass of people enthralled in a five-set tennis match can be –
seemed unable to decide who was in the right and therefore ended up
booing everybody. Murray won the next point to seal the break, at
which point Pavel exploded again, ranting at Nimmons throughout
the change of ends and earning himself a point penalty in the
process.

Murray, still relatively new to the heat of five-set battles, watched
on, unsure of how to react. 'It was a bit strange, because, obviously, he
got the point penalty. I was thinking whether or not I should say to the
umpire, "Leave it. Give him the point back," but it's pretty difficult
when you're 4–3 in the fifth set. You start to think a lot of things: "If I
go on to lose this match after giving the point to him, I'm going to feel
pretty bad." I think he had a pretty good go at the umpire, so I don't
know if he deserved it or not. I didn't hear exactly what he said, but
he was having a go for the whole of the change of ends.'

Pavel was still rankled, even an hour later: 'The match had started
to be interesting again, put it this way. Then there was that call from
the umpire, which I saw as out, and I got really frustrated, because,
you know, it is a far corner, and the ball was really slow. I mean, it
was very difficult to overrule that ball at that time of the match. I got
a little bit upset. He was just pissing me off because he came with
that overrule. For him to overrule that, especially at that time . . . that
was pretty bad.'

Pavel was still furious, and there was more booing, jeering and
general muttering when Murray went to serve at 4–3 and promptly
double faulted. It was a nervous mistake which was, somewhat
unsportingly, cheered by some in the stands. At 30–30, the game and
the match appeared delicately poised, but Murray hit a thunderous
forehand winner to go ahead 40–30. He then hit a lob – ironically, the
very shot which had caused the furore in the first place – to take a
5–3 lead.

When Pavel held comfortably in the next game, it was the mark of a wily old competitor wishing to put the pressure on his younger, less experienced opponent to serve out what was then one of the biggest wins of his career. Needless to say, the tenth game of that fifth set was fraught with tension, short on first serves and a test of Murray's resolve. When Pavel mustered up a break point, an already tortuous match seemed to be taking another twist, but the Romanian misfired horribly, and although he saved one match point with one of the best backhands of the match, Murray was not to be denied. When Pavel's last backhand clunked into the net, Murray could finally relax. After three hours and eighteen minutes on court, he had earned a 6–3, 3–6, 3–6, 6–1, 6–4 victory and his first-ever five-set win.

As he ran to the net to shake hands, he put his finger to his lips in a gesture of defiance, shushing those critics who had rounded on him after his cramping problems in the match against David Nalbandian at Wimbledon. The likes of Alan Jones (Elena Baltacha's coach) and Tony Pickard (a former coach of Greg Rusedski and Stefan Edberg) were by no means the only ones who had passed comment on Murray's fitness during the grass-court season, but their remarks had stung more than some others.

'I did OK for someone who can't play past three sets,' said Murray, having barely sat down for his post-match press conference. 'For me, after what everybody said about me at Wimbledon after I lost against Nalbandian – "He's not fit enough. He doesn't work hard enough" – to win a five-set match from two-sets-to-one down is just slightly different than winning any other matches. I feel like I proved a lot of people wrong. That's why I quite enjoyed it. You learn from experience. I knew that I was in good shape. I worked really hard on the practice court. This is my tenth week in a row. I just won a five-set match. It's just pretty disappointing when you play your first match over five sets and everybody is so negative about it. And I think today I kind of showed that I'm not in such bad shape.'

When asked if he was surprised that an 18 year old played so well against him, Pavel had some gracious words about his conqueror after the match, but he also provided a welcome dose of perspective about Murray's progress. 'Are you surprised that Nadal is No. 2 in the world right now?' asked Pavel, rhetorically. 'It's a young generation. There are a few guys that are playing very good. You should compare him with Nadal, I guess. I don't know. He played a good match today. I couldn't get rhythm with his game. He plays really smart. He played these really slow balls that I didn't like. I hope he's going to do well. Next time we'll see. Maybe next time I will play different. This is my first time I played him. It's always, you know, difficult playing a young kid that is just coming out and is playing good, because you know all the pressure is on your shoulders. He has nothing to lose. He fought, and winning a five-setter match is good for his age. I think he is a great player.'

Henman has often remarked that playing in the US comes as a relief after the tension and heavy emotional toll of Wimbledon, and while the US Open crowd was at its most boisterous during his match against Pavel, Murray found it far easier to cope with than the British crowd at SW19. 'It's obviously great having so many people supporting you, but it does put a lot of pressure on you,' said Murray. 'I feel pretty good here. I like the courts. Obviously, there are not so many people here. It's a little bit strange. I almost felt like I had to get so fired up at Wimbledon. And then, here, it's a little bit different, because the crowd really, really does help you a lot. They just make so much noise, and it's much easier to play when it's like that, when they're not all for you, because you don't feel like you have to please them or you have to win – they're just enjoying the match. I think it's much easier playing here than it is back in Wimbledon.'

The schedulers afforded Murray a much-needed day off on the Wednesday, giving him a vital 24 hours to rest his still painful shoulder and allow his body to recuperate before his second-round match against Arnaud Clement. It also gave him the chance to get reacquainted with John McEnroe, who was taking an increasingly keen interest in his career. 'He said a couple things to me,' Murray revealed the following day. 'You can ask him – it's probably better. But he's a lot of help. It's great to have somebody like him supporting you, someone like him who wants to work with you and wants to help any time he can.'

Clement had, like Murray, come through qualifying to garner a big win in the first round. The diminutive, quick-footed Frenchman had beaten former French Open champion Juan Carlos Ferrero, who had made the US Open final in 2003. Clement, who'd shown his gumption by saving two match points in his second-round qualifying match against Danai Udomchoke, told French journalists that he was looking forward to facing Murray: 'I've seen him play on grass, and he's good even though he's young. He has a lot of good qualities, so I guess it's going to be a tough match.'

The 27 year old had been out of form during most of 2005, but he was runner-up to Andre Agassi in the 2001 Australian Open final and had got as high as No. 10 in the world rankings. One of the fastest men on the tour, he was also renowned as a baseline sprinter who delighted in moving his opponents around. Murray might not have been playing against Ferrero, but Clement was more than capable of providing another gruelling physical and mental test for the young British hope, who went into the encounter knowing a win was probably enough to take him inside the top 100 for the first time.

'I played well the whole summer, and I think I've improved on what I was doing badly at Wimbledon, so I'm really happy with the way things are going,' said Murray as he looked ahead to his contest with the Frenchman. 'I've got one more match to win here to be in the top 100, so I'm really looking forward to playing. Clement's pretty small, so he's going to be very consistent. He's very quick on the courts and intelligent, so I'm going to have to play a pretty clever match: not go for winners too early and just wait for the right opportunity to go for my shots. It'll be a pretty fun match, because both of us like to use the angles and change the pace.'

Within minutes of play getting under way in the now familiar surroundings of the Grandstand court, Clement was doing just that, peppering his thoughtful, determined defence with occasional flashes of brilliance. His patience seemed to have no end, and while Murray's game is built around a similar mix of pragmatic resistance and killer finishing, he frequently blinked first in the longer rallies early on, making the final error when impatience got the better of him.

Clement broke for a 3–1 lead in the first set, and he wrapped it up courtesy of another break of serve at 2–5 after only 33 minutes. The second set was almost impossibly close, with Murray saving a hatful of break points before Clement got the advantage he had been pushing for at 3–4, Murray having double faulted on another break point. He was gifted a chance to claw his way back into the match, however, when Clement blew the next game, dropping his serve to love and finding himself back on serve instead of sitting pretty with a two-set lead.

It seemed to bring Murray into the match, and he held serve twice, the second time to love, to force the tie-breaker, which he was marginal favourite to win given the turn in fortune the match seemed to have taken. The tie-breaker went with serve until 3–2 when Clement slammed back one of Murray's serves for a clean winner to get a mini-break. It was a lead which was consolidated when Murray missed a forehand on the next point. If, as is often said, tie-breakers are a tennis equivalent of a penalty shoot-out, then Murray was, ironically enough, suddenly cast in the role of England. Little wonder he howled out his frustration.

As Kate Kirwan wrote in *The Herald*:

A less stubborn competitor than Murray might have folded in the third set, content that the match had slipped beyond his grasp. Instead, he began to play better, living with Clement in the longer rallies, serving more consistently and attacking with verve and panache at the net. He broke to go 4–2 up to push the match into a fourth set, and a by now packed and noisily animated Grandstand court was willing him to push Clement further still.

He came close to doing that at 5–4 in the fourth set when he held three set points on his opponent's serve. A flashing forehand from Clement hugged the line on the first and left Murray flailing at thin air, a hefty first serve saved the second, and a forehand from Murray landed millimetres long on the third. It was a tiny mistake which characterised the narrow margins separating the world's best players from victory and defeat.

With both players now performing at something near their peak, the match tingled with tension, but as the fourth set tie-breaker approached, it was Murray who still had the appetite to go on the attack. An audacious lob in the second point landed in the corner to give him a mini-break then his serve and some wayward hitting from Clement did the rest.

By this time, the crowd were rowdily cheering Murray on, desperate for a dramatic comeback story. As well as the tennis fans so tightly crammed into the Grandstand court, which the stewards had long since closed off to any more spectators, the players' box was also full. Richard Gasquet, who is on chatting terms with Murray and Clement, his fellow Frenchman, was one of those who came to watch with his coach.

And so Murray found himself, for the second time in three days, in a fifth set. Having won his first five setter only forty-eight hours previously, he seemed to be about to tick off another achievement by coming from two sets down for the first time. To put it in context, this is something that Tim Henman has done only four times in a thirteen-year career and didn't manage for the first time until he was twenty-five years old, the second time being a further four years later.

However, serving at 15–0 in the second game of the decider, and after three hours and forty-two minutes on court, Murray felt the unwelcome return of an all-too-familiar feeling as cramp gripped his right leg. Unable to play on without treatment, he summoned trainer Per Bastholt to the court, but sustained massage on both thighs only eased the immediate discomfort. As Murray knew from the bitter experience of having had the same thing happen to him against Thomas Johansson at Queen's, the cramp was merely a symptom of fatigue in his legs and the legacy not just of the near-four hours he had just spent on court but also the three hours and eighteen minutes against Pavel.

He could put up little more than token resistance after that, and the disappointment and frustration was written on his face as he limped through the next five games, unable to move effectively from side to side or bend his legs to put the requisite power on his serve. As he explained afterwards, 'I didn't actually get any more cramp after I got treatment, but I couldn't move. Mentally, I lost it after I got broken. I just got really, really tired. It completely drained me of everything.'

His 6–2, 7–6, 2–6, 6–7, 6–0 defeat after four hours and two minutes was a depressing and annoying way for his summer in the US to end, especially since it raised the old issues about his fitness just when he seemed to have laid them to rest by beating Pavel. 'I didn't start off well, and then from second set to fourth set, I thought I played pretty well,' Murray said. 'I fought hard. It's not easy coming back from two-sets-to-love down when you're playing someone who's playing as well as he is. In the fifth set, when I got broken, I ran out of gas. I got a bit tired after that. I think coming back from two-sets-to-love down is mentally pretty difficult. And because I played so many tournaments, I found it difficult after I got broken, because I've been working really hard the last nine, ten weeks. It's more mental than anything. It's quite difficult after ten weeks to play two five-set matches in a row. Like, mentally, to go through everything in the Pavel match, then to go two-sets-to-love down not playing so well, then to come back, then to start the set badly is pretty difficult. Physically, it's really, really tough.

'I didn't really enjoy the start – the first set. I was playing badly. He's quite frustrating to play against, because he doesn't make many mistakes. He doesn't hit the ball very hard, but he plays pretty close to the lines, and you end up going for shots that you shouldn't. But from the second to the fourth set, I enjoyed it a lot. It was a good match. I think the crowd enjoyed it as well.'

Inevitably, comparisons would be drawn with the Nalbandian match, Murray's body having seemingly let him down when he appeared to be in a winning position again, but the circumstances were quite different this time around. Murray had played twenty-seven matches since the beginning of Wimbledon, competing week in, week out for nine weeks (eleven if you include Wimbledon), often in stifling humidity and at a level of tournament which he wasn't used to. He was also playing his tenth set and his seventh hour of tennis in three days when the cramp struck. Such details mattered little to the columnists back in the UK, who rushed to their laptops to pour scorn on the fitness of an 18 year old still learning his trade.

'I'm not as disappointed as I was after the Nalbandian match, because I proved to myself in the first match that I was fine to go five sets,' countered Murray. 'I think it's kind of normal after ten weeks, after playing a five-set match, then to play another tough one, to get a little bit tired.'

Murray had been scheduled to play an ATP Tournament in

Istanbul the following week, but, wisely, he had opted instead to take a few days' rest in New York before flying home to get ready to play in the Davis Cup against Roger Federer with Greg Rusedski, Alan Mackin and David Sherwood in Geneva.

It had been a long and exhausting July and August, full of new and not always pleasant experiences, a period which had culminated in yet another eventful trip to Flushing Meadows. His long, hot summer was over, but he could look back with satisfaction and look forward with justified optimism.

'It's a pretty good effort, expecting a wildcard, then getting told a few days before the qualifying starts that . . . Wimbledon didn't want to do a trade. Mentally, that was pretty tough as well. I think I did well coming through and then winning my first five-set match,' said Murray. 'I didn't play that badly against Clement, apart from the first set. He's playing very well. I don't think I did a bad job today, and I'm pretty happy with what I've achieved here.

'I'm happy with what I've done since before Queen's. I'd never won an ATP match until then. I was about 357 in the world. After this week, hopefully, I'll be around 110, getting close to the top 100, which is what I wanted to do at the start of the year. I've learnt a lot about myself the last three months: about my tennis and what I need to work on. I learned I could cope with playing with guys that are in the top 100 in the world, and I'm good enough to get there. It's never that easy. I always believed I could do it, but it gives you an extra bit of confidence when you win matches in grand slams and ATP Tour tournaments, and you beat some guys that are in the top 50. But now I just want to get into the top 100, and I'll be happy.'

12

ANDY'S SWISS ROLE FOR BRITAIN

MURRAY HAD BEEN LOOKING FORWARD TO THE DAVIS CUP WORLD GROUP QUALIFYING match between Great Britain and Switzerland ever since the draw had been made in May 2005. Representing his country was a big enough kick, and having the chance to face world No. 1 Roger Federer for the first time made the tie an even more exciting prospect. The possibility of facing Federer was the kind of challenge Murray relished with a passion, and he would have been unfazed at the prospect of facing the greatest player in the world.

When the draw was made, Jeremy Bates said he was pretty satisfied: 'There were some very tricky teams that we could have drawn, and Switzerland away is definitely preferable to some of the options we could have had. You know you are going to have to play exceptionally well to progress. We would have loved to be at home, but it could have been Spain, Chile, the US or Sweden away.

'Having said that, the Swiss are a formidable team with or without Roger Federer playing. It will be tough, but I believe it is a tie we can win. Whoever we were matched up with didn't matter too much. It is just good to be in the World Group play-off stage again, playing against great tennis nations. That is undoubtedly where Great Britain wants to be.'

Bates prepared his team well and took them to Thonon-les-Bains, on the shores of Lake Geneva for a training camp. Situated in the north of Haute-Savoie, in the lower Chablais region, it was the perfect place to prepare for the match ahead.

There was a great atmosphere in the British camp, and between practice sessions, Murray took a few British pounds off the other players on the golf course. His teammates joked that he was a bit of a bandit, playing off a handicap of 17, and made it clear that if Tim Henman, who played off four, had not retired from Davis Cup tennis, the young Scot wouldn't have won as much money as he did.

It was on the shores of Lake Geneva that Murray first talked in detail about how he felt his lack of fitness at Queen's Club and Wimbledon had been overplayed in the media. He also said it had never been the career-threatening problem that it had been portrayed as. 'Let me get this whole thing into perspective. I work hard and just had a few problems in a couple of five-set matches, because I was not used to them,' he said. 'I just cramped in the games I struggled in, and that is in the past. Going into the Davis Cup match against Switzerland, I feel absolutely fine.'

Jeremy Bates dropped heavy hints on the Monday before the tie took place that Murray would go head to head with Federer on the first day of the Davis Cup match. Although the draw wasn't going to be made until the Thursday, Bates made it clear that Andy was more than capable of holding his own against the world No. 1. 'Andy is chomping at the bit to play Federer,' said Bates as he arrived in Geneva from the team's training camp. 'He can't wait to get out there.'

Murray always believed he could compete with the best and had shown his potential at Queen's Club, Wimbledon, the US Open and in a series of Challenger tournaments in the USA, but had yet to face an opponent approaching the class of Federer, let alone the great man himself. While Murray had played well at the aforementioned grand slams, Federer had won both at a canter. His victory at Flushing Meadows had even prompted Andre Agassi to hail his conqueror as the greatest player he had ever faced. The Scot was unperturbed, however, by the thought of facing the man from Switzerland on his home soil.

Although this was a British Davis Cup team, it was one with its biggest ever representation of Scots. Wimbledon officials laughed when it was suggested to them at one time that Scotland could make up a full Davis Cup team and the tie could one day be held north of the border. However, looking at the side which arrived in Geneva showed that that idea was becoming closer to reality. Alan Mackin, who was born in Paisley in Scotland, was recalled after a two-and-a-half-year absence. His one previous Davis Cup appearance came in the visit to Australia in February 2003 when he lost in straight sets to Mark Philippoussis, who later that year reached the Wimbledon final. His singles ranking had improved dramatically in the run-up to the Davis Cup match against Switzerland. He started 2004 as the world 589 but had made his way to within the top 300. And to add to the Scottish contingent, the first reserve in Bates's team was Jamie Baker from Glasgow.

With Tim Henman retired from Davis Cup tennis, the side was led by Greg Rusedski, while Yorkshireman David Sherwood completed the squad. Morale going into the match against Switzerland, despite the difficulty of the tie, was high. Jeremy Bates had been British captain for eighteen months and boasted two wins to one defeat since taking over from Roger Taylor. Bates's team beat Luxembourg in his first match in charge back in April 2004 before the disappointment of

217

losing to Austria in a play-off for World Group membership five months later. Bates, a former British number one and six times National Champion who twice reached the last 16 of Wimbledon, enjoyed his finest moment as Davis Cup captain when he guided the side to victory in Israel on 4–6 March 2005.

Bates believed the Scots in the squad would cope with the pressure of the Davis Cup and come through with flying colours. He also revealed he would have no problems playing Murray every day if necessary. 'The whole tie this time around, with the team I have got, has given me more options than I have ever had,' he said. 'Tactically, it'll be a tough decision which way round to play the matches, but I have no hesitation in playing both Greg and Andy three days in a row if need be. It's just a question of working out the best way forward.'

Bates said he hadn't made up his mind about the doubles partnership and admitted he wasn't sure whether to play Rusedski with either Murray or Sherwood or ignore Rusedski and choose Murray and Sherwood: 'Things to consider are points like should Andy play day two and day three, and not have him play day one? Would he be better in the doubles if he had played on the first day? Should I play him on all three days, which wouldn't be a problem? The permutations are endless, and, as of yet, I have not made up my mind.'

Bates admitted the 'Federer factor' would be huge given his total dominance at the US Open and his standing in his native country. 'Federer is rightly one of the biggest sportsmen in Switzerland, and his win at the US Open will heighten the home interest in the tie,' said Bates. 'It's fantastic to be playing against him in his own country, but we are under no illusions how difficult a match we are facing.'

The Swiss side, led by Federer, also included Stanislas Wawrinka, George Bastl, Michael Lammer and doubles specialist Yves Allegro. A look at their track record showed that they were a strong team and had good experience, but Bates believed his side could give them a run for their money. He also made it clear that Murray and Mackin were comfortable on indoor clay courts and believed they would give a good account of themselves whoever they faced. 'Murray is very comfortable on the surface and has spent a lot of time on clay as has Alan, who has based his whole game around the surface,' said Bates. 'With a player like Federer, whether it is his favourite surface or not doesn't matter as he's so versatile he can adapt.'

Although Murray had captured the headlines, Bates said that Mackin was playing well and looking forward to the match. 'I've spent a lot of time with Alan and his dad this year,' said Bates. 'He's doing his own thing, which we embrace 100 per cent, and he's been picked on merit.

'He has stepped up to playing bigger tournaments with good results, and he wants it really badly. He's always put the work in. There has never been any question over his attitude or commitment. He's the most professional guy you can imagine.'

The draw for the tie was made on the Thursday in a hall a short walk away from the Geneva Palexpo complex, where the match was taking place. Both teams attended and rather self-consciously walked to the front of the hall after being introduced individually to the assembled media.

Jeremy Bates struck the first psychological blow with his bold decision to pitch Alan Mackin, ranked No. 262 in the world, into the opening day's singles against Federer, rather than rely on the experience of Greg Rusedski. Some felt it was a shrewd move with Murray taking on the under-pressure Swiss second-ranked player Stanislas Wawrinka. It was a calculated risk as Great Britain had to win at least three of the rubbers to overcome their opponents. His decision piled the pressure on Murray, who it was assumed would beat Wawrinka.

Interestingly, whether through far-sightedness or coincidence, Murray had predicted such a match-up against Wawrinka during his post-match press conference after beating Andrei Pavel in the first round at the US Open, a few weeks before the Davis Cup tie. 'Maybe I won't play against Federer on the first day,' Murray had said. 'We've got to try and bully their worst player, who is obviously Wawrinka. He's still top 60 and a very good player, but Greg beat him a few weeks before the US Open. Possibly me and Greg will play doubles on the second day. I'm just trying to think of the best way of winning against Switzerland.'

His comments suggested that before they even arrived at their training camp or took up residence in Switzerland the British team had a rough idea of what was going to happen in Geneva. Bates believed that keeping Rusedski fresh to play doubles with Murray could give Britain the upper hand and would prove to be a master stroke. His further plan was to put Rusedski in for Mackin in Sunday's final reverse singles which would put the British number one up against Wawrinka.

'I'm really comfortable loading all the pressure on Wawrinka, and I hope he does not get a good night's sleep before facing Andy,' said the British captain, who had adamantly refused to give any clues to his team selection before the lunchtime draw for the first tie between the two nations in twenty years. 'I believe the way we have set up our team will help our chances. It transfers all the onus onto Wawrinka.

'We have spent the last eight or nine days preparing for the tie, and it's obviously a very tough and difficult match as we are playing against somebody like Federer. To look at the tie realistically, we are looking at winning the doubles and two singles matches against their No. 2 player. Of course, we will fight for everything we can get against Roger as well.'

Certainly Bates's tactics seemed to have the desired effect in terms of confusing the Swiss team. On hearing the British line-up, Wawrinka immediately turned and looked at Federer with an expression that suggested he was thinking, 'Who is Mackin?' The two Swiss players then embarked on a long conversation that did not go unnoticed by the British captain: 'They were not expecting what has happened, so from that point of view, playing with the team this way around puts a lot of pressure on Wawrinka to perform, especially as he is playing Andy.'

Wawrinka's world ranking had slipped to No. 60 the week of the tie, but that still put him 50 places above Murray, who had yet to experience singles play in the Davis Cup. Wawrinka, a former French Open junior champion, sounded confident and insisted he was not disturbed in any way by Bates's decision to pitch him in against Murray.

Federer admitted he was taken by surprise by the move and conceded he knew next to nothing about Mackin. Rather than rest on the afternoon before the tie, he spent it working on his laptop computer, looking up the competitive record of the 25-year-old Scot.

'I have got nothing to lose,' insisted Mackin. 'Clearly, it's a big match, and Roger has been beaten less than a handful of times this year, so I just intend to go out to enjoy the match and see what happens when I'm out there. It's a wonderful opportunity for me and one I wasn't really expecting, but I cannot really think about it too much. I was at home watching television when Federer won both his Wimbledon and US titles.'

Despite the female president of the Swiss Tennis Federation introducing Bates's line-up as the team from England, there was the novel situation of having two Scots filling the first-day singles roles. 'We are playing for Britain, which I don't mind, but I don't want anybody to think we are representing England,' said Murray. 'I think playing Wawrinka is going to be a tough match, because he is in the world's top 60, reached the final of an ATP tournament in Gstaad a few months ago when he lost to Gaston Gaudio and made the third round of the US Open, beating Mariano Puerta on the way, so he is obviously playing very well, but if I play one of my best matches, I think I can win.'

The schedule of play for Friday, 23 September, was Federer v. Mackin, followed by Wawrinka v. Murray. On the Saturday, Federer and Allegro would play Rusedski and Murray in the doubles.

The fact that Mackin and Murray were selected to represent Great Britain on the first day of the tie brought great interest back in their home country. Most of the intrigue surrounded Mackin's match with Federer as the Scottish public were fascinated by the fact that a man from Paisley ranked 262 in the world and relatively unknown in his own country was playing the world No. 1 in a top tennis match. The Swiss player had lost just three times in 2005, and Mackin's career earnings of £70,565 at that point were eclipsed by the 2005 Wimbledon and US Open champion's £10.7 million.

Mackin and Murray both made it clear they were delighted to be Scots representing Great Britain and proud that they had been selected for the first day's play. Mackin said, 'Both Andy and I feel strongly about being Scottish, but this is about being part of the British Davis Cup team, and we will give it our best shot.'

The make-up of the Scottish-dominated team raised a smile from Federer when he was asked about it. 'This is a Scottish team and a British team,' said Federer. 'I have never been to, and I do not know much about, Scotland. All I know is that it is very green, has great scenery and my football team, Basel, played a Champions League qualifier match over there and lost to Celtic.'

Federer admitted he knew little about his Scottish opponent and had expected Jeremy Bates to nominate Murray to play him. 'I was taken a bit by surprise by their team selection,' said Federer. 'I thought I would be facing Murray first and am a bit surprised, but very pleased, I am not facing him.

'Murray is still young and that is his great strength. He will be improving day by day, week by week, month by month. He gains more experience every time he steps on court. Expectations are high, but he needs some more time.

'I will be hot favourite against Mackin. I remember him a bit from the juniors, but that was a long time ago, and the danger I have with Mackin is that I do not know how he plays his game now.'

Mackin believed he could at least give the world No.1 a decent game. 'I have nothing to lose as everybody knows how good a player Roger is, and he has only been beaten three times this year,' he said. 'It is a wonderful opportunity for me. Hopefully, I can go out there and play well.

'I have played big Davis Cup matches before and felt I did OK, although I lost to Mark Philippoussis in three sets when we played Australia in 2003. I have been improving steadily, and this is a big challenge.'

Jeremy Bates admitted that he did not expect Mackin to beat Federer but felt he would give him a good match: 'Everybody knows how good a player Roger is, and, to be honest, whoever comes up against him is in a no-win situation. I have spoken to Alan, and he will have to play with aggression to match him. We need to have Alan in a great state of mind, pumped up and ready to give it a go. As for Andy, we believe he can do well against Wawrinka, and we want to put pressure on Andy's opponent.'

Murray was quietly confident and had no regrets about not playing Federer, which would have given him the chance to compare his game to the best in the world. 'It doesn't bother me as I realise I have a difficult opponent to overcome in Wawrinka,' he said.

The British camp was full of optimism on the Friday morning, but once play started, things went badly wrong. Mackin never came close to beating Federer, and at one point, there was every possibility he would be whitewashed 6–0, 6–0, 6–0. Thankfully, he took two games in the final set before losing 6–0, 6–0, 6–2. Mackin was simply outclassed by the majestic play from the man from Switzerland.

The Swiss maestro is usually the most diplomatic of players, but in interviews conducted with the Swiss press after the match, he was critical of the level of Mackin's performance: 'I was shocked as he is a professional. I did not think I would get away that easily. It was my easiest match since I played an inter-club fixture over five years ago.

'I had never won a match 6–0, 6–0, 6–0, and I used that as a motivation to keep me going and to keep my focus against him. I knew I was a big favourite, but it wasn't easy going into the match, because I couldn't remember the last time I played someone ranked so low. It would have been a disaster for me if I had lost, so there was a lot on the line, but now I'm just happy to have lots of energy left for the rest of the tie.'

Federer's comments wounded Mackin, who sought to put a brave face on the heavy defeat which was inflicted in just 75 minutes: 'Not many players get the chance to come up against the world No. 1 in the Davis Cup singles. He hits the ball at an incredible speed and finds great angles. After experiencing that, I should learn from it and maybe things will be a bit easier when I face my next opponent on the Challenger Tour.

'At the time, I was concentrating hard, and it is only now that the game is over that I can look back and say I enjoyed it. I had a couple of game points which I did not capitalise on, but the match went very fast, and some of the shots Roger played, particularly when I had him on the run, were just too good. He could up his game when needed.'

The spotlight then fell on Murray and his match against Wawrinka. The pressure was really on the young Scotsman as Bates had put his faith in him and changed the team around to accommodate him.

Bates had suggested that Wawrinka might crumble under the pressure of playing Murray in front of his home crowd. Instead, Wawrinka found inspiration from the circumstances – and possibly by being underestimated by the British team – and emerged victorious in two hours seventeen minutes. As ever, Murray put in a spirited performance but was always up against it after starting slowly. He lost the first set 6–3, and he took the second to a tie-break, which he lost 7–5 after having led 3–0 with two mini-break points. In the final set, Murray was a break up and had his chances, but Wawrinka put down some powerful serves and some delightful cross-court shots to close out the match 6–3, 7–6(5), 6–4.

'I know many people thought I would win, but Wawrinka doesn't get into the top 60 in the world without being a good player,' said Murray. 'I thought I played OK against him, although I didn't serve or return as well as I would have liked.

'It wasn't the best of starts, and I didn't do too well as he went 5–1 up in the first set, but after that, I played a bit better and did well for a while. I know people were looking to me to win, but the only pressure I felt was the pressure I put on myself.'

Wawrinka was diplomatic in victory and tipped Murray to go much higher up the world rankings. 'I slept well before the game, and although I got a bit nervous when I stepped out on court, I kept it together well,' said the Swiss player. 'For me, it was my greatest win, but it wasn't easy.'

The Murray defeat was a body blow to the British side, who had hoped to beat Switzerland to make it into the elite Davis Cup World Group but saw their chances of achieving their goal fading fast. They were now required to win the three remaining rubbers, starting with Murray and Rusedski against Federer and Allegro in the doubles on the Saturday. Should they manage that, Britain would still go into Sunday's final round of singles 2–1 down, and Murray would have to achieve the near-impossible task of beating Federer to give Rusedski the opportunity to clinch victory against Wawrinka in the final tie.

Jeremy Bates said, 'It's disappointing to be 2–0 down after the first day. I think the last match between Andy and Wawrinka was obviously very tight, but Wawrinka managed to play fantastically well on the big points. As I said on the Thursday before the game, it was always our plan to win the doubles and win the matches against

Wawrinka, but it is unbelievably difficult to do that when he is playing that well.'

After going 2–0 down on the opening day, there was criticism of Jeremy Bates's decision to rest Rusedski and play Mackin against Federer as it had put pressure on Murray to beat Wawrinka. With hindsight, Bates may have wished he had forced Wawrinka to face Rusedski and had either rested Murray or offered him the chance to face Federer in singles.

The debate was fuelled further by Switzerland's Davis Cup coach Ivo Werner. 'After the draw, I thought it was even better for us, because I knew that if Stanislas had to play Rusedski, he would have found it tough,' he said. 'Stanislas needs a rhythm and Andy gave him that, whereas Greg would have not have given him that – he would have mixed it up.'

However, many people thought that the British captain should not be criticised for having been bold enough to try to find a solution to the problem of beating a team that contained Federer. An indication of his importance came during the Saturday's doubles match when, once again, he was the star man for Switzerland, overshadowing Yves Allegro, while Murray was the more consistent of the British pairing. The young Scot returned serve with aggression and verve and volleyed well, and while Rusedski's serve was a more potent weapon than his teammate's, Murray was by far the better British player for much of the match.

Murray's only moment of culpability came at 5–6 in the first set, when a poor service game allowed the Swiss team to break his serve. The British pair hit back to claim the second set 6–2 and should have won the third after fighting their way into a tie-breaker with the help of a moment of on-court anger from Rusedski. At 4–2 down, he lost his temper when he thought an Allegro serve should have been called a let and then celebrated a winning point by pointing at the Swiss pair and shouting provocatively. The 6,500 people in the hall put down the noisy plastic sticks which had been issued to them all, and which they had been irritatingly banging all through the match, and began booing instead. 'Both Andy and I play off emotion, and sometimes we show what we feel on court,' said Rusedski when talking about the incident later. Federer, perhaps a little rattled by Rusedski's antics, dropped his serve at 5–3 up, but he later made the Britons pay in the tie-breaker. He combined neatly with Allegro to take three points on the Brits' serves and wrestled the momentum irrevocably in Switzerland's favour, allowing them to win the third-set tie-break with the loss of just one point.

The fourth set was one-way traffic, and the Swiss team won 7–5, 2–6, 7–6, 6–2 with lots of room to spare. The victory gave Switzerland a 3–0 lead, ensuring that Britain would play their Davis Cup tennis in the second division of the competition in 2006.

Playing in the Davis Cup was part of the learning process for Murray, and that weekend, while disappointing, formed another vital part of his development. He clearly had great respect for Rusedski, and although it had taken them a set and a half to gel as a doubles team in what was their first competitive match together, their on-court rapport at least gave Jeremy Bates options for the future.

Morale was low in the British camp on the Saturday evening after the tie was lost, but they still had to go through the formalities of the final day's play. On the Sunday, Murray was rested, but Britain hoped to restore some pride in the final two meaningless matches. However, David Sherwood was beaten in straight sets by George Bastl, 6–3, 6–0, in just 52 minutes, while Alan Mackin lost to Stanislas Wawrinka 7–5, 7–6(5) to round off a humiliating 5–0 team defeat.

Murray had mixed opinions about being rested on the final day of the Davis Cup tie. He would dearly have loved for the tie to still be alive, which would have given him the chance to play Federer. On the other hand, he was due to travel to Bangkok later that same day to take part in the Thailand Open, where he was scheduled to face George Bastl, the man he had beaten at Wimbledon, and not playing meant he had an extra day's rest before his long flight.

Murray was in a relaxed mood before leaving Switzerland as he reflected on topics ranging from whether the next Davis Cup tie should be played in Scotland to whether he would win a £400 bet with his teammates that he could break into the top 100 by the end of 2005. Regarding the venue for the next tie, he said, 'It doesn't make a difference to me as I am playing for Great Britain, and it does not matter where it will be played. Playing in Scotland would not give me an extra edge, but, obviously, it would be great.'

An LTA spokesman said that no venue had been decided for the next Davis Cup tie at that stage and that a decision would be made after they found out who their opponents were and if they were due to play at home or away.

Murray also revealed that his biggest regret of the weekend was the fact he didn't get the chance to play Federer in what would have been a fascinating match-up. Federer also spoke of his regret at having not faced the up-and-coming star of British tennis. 'It was a pity we didn't play each other,' said Federer. 'Watching him in his two games, he behaved really well, and we will have some battles in the future.

'He looked very relaxed, and his attitude and technique was sometimes good, sometimes not so good. Although there are areas he can improve upon, he has real potential. He had a good return and volleyed very well. He surprised me at times.'

For two weeks, Bates had looked at Murray closely and had no regrets about making him the most important player in the team for the match against Switzerland ahead of Rusedski and made it clear he might do so again. 'Andy is playing at a different level, and his quality of play is well above his ranking of 110,' said Bates. 'Everybody thinks he should go on a smooth curve upwards, but when you are coming through, there are always stages of huge improvement, then you take stock, then improve some more. He is now getting to the stage of being on a fast, straight line going forward.

'You see a lot of talented 18 year olds, but it is in the mind that Andy has the advantage. He has a strong mind and is very mature. It is not easy to walk out on Centre Court at Wimbledon or play in the Davis Cup, but nothing seems to faze him. I remember when I first went on Centre Court for mixed doubles, I found it very daunting. You either have to love it from the word go or learn to love it, and he has loved it from the word go.'

Bates said that he hoped having Murray in the fold would inspire other young British players to become even better and encourage kids to take up the game. 'Andy can inspire other players coming through the ranks as he is about their age,' he said. 'I hope he does have an influence. He certainly gets on with all the young players, and they are great together. They have a laugh and listen to the worst music you can imagine.

'From a Davis Cup point of view, if we had Andy alongside Greg Rusedski and Tim Henman playing three or four years ago, we would have been playing and winning rounds in the World Group.'

The future did look bright for the British Davis Cup squad thanks to the emergence of Murray. The result against Switzerland was a bad one for team morale but a learning experience for everybody involved, and Murray certainly came out of the tournament a better player. However, even he could not have predicted what lay ahead when he flew out of Geneva on his way to Bangkok for the Thailand Open.

13

BREAKTHROUGH IN BANGKOK

WHEN ROGER FEDERER WAS ASKED, DURING SWITZERLAND'S DAVIS CUP TIE in October 2005, to talk about Andy Murray he made a prediction: 'I think we'll have many battles in the future.' Federer is a wise and thoughtful fellow, but even he cannot have believed that his words would prove so prescient, so soon.

As he boarded a plane in London bound for Bangkok that Sunday night, still weary from a gruelling and ultimately disappointing Davis Cup weekend, Murray must have wondered where he was going to get the energy from to get through his first match, let alone the week. He had been given a wildcard into the Thailand Open and was about to play only his eighth ATP Tour event. His first priority was to pick up enough ranking points to break into the top 100, gain a little experience and make the 12 or so hours spent in economy class getting there worthwhile.

The prospect of coming home a week later ranked nearly forty places better off, having beaten a string of higher-ranked players and having giving Roger Federer a run for his money in the final, was more than he could have dreamed of as he dozed through the flight to Thailand. Dreams, though, have a habit of coming true when you are as talented and determined as Murray.

He landed in Bangkok on Monday morning, local time, and, like most of those in the draw who had been on Davis Cup duty over the weekend, had the luxury of a day to sleep off the combined effects of the weekend's exertions and jetlag before playing his first match on Tuesday at the appropriately named IMPACT Arena. Incidentally, the 12,000-seater concert and sports hall, which is about 30 minutes' drive outside the city, boasts an address as memorable as its name: 99 Popular Road.

By a somewhat bizarre coincidence, Murray's first round match was against another Swiss player – as if he hadn't had enough of them over the weekend. This time it was George Bastl, then ranked 124 to Murray's 109, who had been in the Swiss Davis Cup team but was only involved when he beat David Sherwood in the meaningless final rubber. Bastl had been a familiar face when they were reacquainted in Geneva, having been Murray's first-round victim at Wimbledon just over three months earlier. On a reasonably quick indoor court, Murray walked into the match as favourite to repeat that win and gain a measure of revenge on his nation's behalf for its Davis Cup drubbing.

The 6–2, 6–4 victory over Bastl was routine enough, a performance of admirable efficiency under the circumstances. 'It was pretty tough as I only arrived on Monday and didn't have much time to get used to the courts and the change of surface, but I played pretty well,' Murray said afterwards. 'George had the same trip as me from Geneva, so it was the same for both of us. I played very solid. I don't think he made many mistakes, but I returned really, really well.

I think I got at least two points in every one of his service games. He may not have played his best match, but I played really, really well.'

Victory over Bastl allowed Murray to bank a few more ranking points and move a step closer to his goal of the top 100, which would be in his grasp if he won his next match against Sweden's Robin Soderling, seeded fourth for the tournament.

Soderling is three years older than Murray and, like him, had been an outstanding junior (he won the Orange Bowl title in 2001) before making steady progress in the pros. An adept baseliner with a liking for indoor tennis (he had gone unbeaten on indoor carpet the previous season), Soderling was a sizeable obstacle in the way of the ranking goal which Murray had set himself at the start of the year.

When a cocky 17 year old ranked 411 in the world announces at the start of a season that he believes he can get inside the top 100 by the end of the year, the world tends to be divided between those who admire his confidence and those who think he is getting a little ahead of himself. Murray made it clear that he didn't mind what people thought – this was a definite intention rather than a fanciful ambition. 'I knew the top 100 was a pretty realistic goal,' he said later. 'I'd played pretty well at the end of the previous year, and I knew I was going to get my chances around Wimbledon time.'

Ask most young and upcoming tennis players what their goal is and breaking into the top 100 will usually be one of the first things they mention. It is a target to aim at and something to motivate them during hours on the practice court and at scruffy little tournaments in places they would rather not be. If there is a universal marker for 'making it' as a tennis player, getting your ranking into double figures is probably it. It is a sign to peers, sponsors and the public that you are the genuine article. Tim Henman took until he was 21 to do it and Greg Rusedski was 19, but both recall it as a significant moment in their careers. As well as an accepted benchmark of success, being ranked higher than 100 also has practical implications:

it can be the difference between playing week in, week out on the Challenger circuit or the ATP Tour, where the players, prize money and ranking points are better and where the rate of achievement tends to escalate. It can have a financial impact, too, as many endorsement deals have built-in bonuses for reaching certain milestones – breaking into the top 100 being one.

Perhaps because of what was at stake, the match against Soderling proved to be a struggle from start to finish. Murray exchanged breaks with the obdurate Swede in the first set before squeaking out a tie-breaker to give himself breathing space. His head was pounding, so much so that he called for the trainer before the second set got under way in the hope of finding relief.

'I wasn't feeling that great towards the end of the first set,' he explained afterwards. 'I took a timeout and got some medication from the doctor. I had a really sore head. I don't know why.' Any psychologist worth his or her salt would probably have hazarded a guess – the proximity of a longed-for goal can have a strange effect on the mind and body.

Whether it was the headache pills or the knowledge that he was a set to the good, Murray felt well enough to go through it all again in the second set, trading breaks once more before turning up the gas in the tie-breaker. 'I thought I played a pretty clever match,' he said later. 'I used my slice pretty well, and I didn't give him so much pace, which I think he likes. I returned well in the first set and when I had to in the second. I thought I could have served better and maybe attacked a little bit more, but it was a pretty big match for me, and I'm just happy to come through.'

For 'pretty big' read 'absolutely huge', though his knack for understatement extended to the text message he sent his mum, who was back in Dunblane following the scores on the internet. 'I did it, Mum' was all it said.

He was a little more forthcoming in his press conference

afterwards, reminding those who had doubted his word on the subject that he hadn't just delivered on his promise to get to the top 100 by the end of the year, he had done it with two months in hand: 'I said at the start of the year, "That's my goal." After the first couple of months, a lot of people told me I should have kept quiet, but I'm pretty happy with myself now. Getting to the top 100 at 18 is a pretty big deal.'

Murray's elevation up the rankings – he was the youngest British man to break into the top 100 since 1974 – did not go unnoticed back home, and Davis Cup captain Jeremy Bates was one of many to join in the chorus of praise. 'It's a big boost to everyone but most of all for Andy himself. It has happened phenomenally quickly, considering where Andy was at the start of the year, but it's no great surprise,' said Bates. 'The signs were always there that Andy would become a top-class player. It is terrific to see another British player in the top 100. It's a fantastic effort by Andy, and not only has he shown the class to be able to do it but the ability to stay there as well. He is not going to rest now – he has tremendous drive and fortitude, and he will keep going for it.'

Having achieved his major aim for the year and felt the accompanying sense of relief, Murray was then free to tackle his first quarter-final on the ATP Tour, in which he would play third seed Robby Ginepri, a handsome American best known for being the ex-boyfriend of British actress Minnie Driver. Ginepri's relationship with Driver and a lot of female attention threatened to be the only notable items on his CV until he reached the semi-finals of the US Open in September 2005 and proved that he was more than just a pretty face.

Despite Ginepri's pedigree, Murray walked on court with a spring his step. A little over three months earlier, while playing in Cincinnati, he had revealed his sense of unease in the locker-rooms of the ATP Tour, saying that he felt as though he didn't yet deserve to be there amongst the likes of Soderling, Ginepri, et al. 'It doesn't feel right. When I walked into the locker-room the first time I got here, it just didn't quite feel right. I'm still not in the top 100,' Murray had admitted. 'I think it takes a while to get the respect. Until you start beating some of the best players, you don't get the respect of the top guys.' Now he could hold his head up high – he felt like he deserved to be there.

That's not to say it was an easy win over Ginepri – far from it. Despite breaking in the opening game of the match, Murray lost the first set after 27 minutes and had to battle throughout the second set. Then, with the set tied at 4–4, he fired himself up (thanks, in part, to arguing vociferously against a line call in the previous game) and somehow managed to get the break which was to turn the match on its head. He served his way to a deciding set in the next game.

The third set was just as edgy, at least until Murray, who'd served under relentless pressure throughout, mustered another important surge of adrenalin, this time accompanied by two forceful slams of his racket on the squeaky hardcourt beneath his feet. It did the trick, giving him the break and a 4–2 lead, and three games later, it was the American who was blaming his tools, cracking his racket down in frustration as he again lost his serve and with it the match.

'Winning against two top 50 players in a row is a pretty big deal for me, and to get to my first semi-final is also great,' Murray said afterwards. 'I said after my last match that I would have to serve better than I did on Thursday if I wanted to win, and I think I served very well. I attacked when I had to and after the first set, played pretty much perfectly.'

To give Murray's first ATP Tour semi-final an extra frisson of excitement, as if it needed it, his opponent was not just a national hero in Thailand but one of the more talented and charismatic players on the ATP Tour, Paradorn Srichaphan. Anyone who thinks British tennis players have pressure on them should have a chat to Srichaphan, who bears not just the hopes of his country but of the entire Asian region – about 4 billion people. When Srichaphan reached the fourth round of Wimbledon in 2003, the streets of Bangkok were reportedly empty at the time of his matches, as Thais everywhere crowded around television sets. Srichaphan, who is nicknamed simply 'Ball' in his home country, is credited with having started a tennis boom in Thailand which saw racket sales leap by 40 per cent between 2003 and 2004. Like Boris Becker in Germany in the 1980s and '90s or Stefan Edberg in Sweden, Srichaphan is not so much a tennis player as an icon. Little wonder he is officially recognised as a cultural ambassador for his country.

Scotland's own icon in the making couldn't have been more excited about playing Srichaphan in his home town and in front of 12,000 adoring Thai fans. It was also the biggest match of the teenager's career to that point – one in which the prize was a final against Federer, an idol to anyone who has ever played tennis.

Srichaphan has been ranked as high as No. 9 in the world and plays with a verve and flair that is hard to resist when the inspiration strikes him. With a noisy, worshipping home-town crowd all around him, he could hardly be anything less than inspired. For this reason, Murray's first task was to contain Srichaphan long enough to quieten the baying fans a little. Things didn't go to plan immediately, and Srichaphan's flashy shot making earned him an immediate break of serve. Murray broke back straight away, which at least quelled the crowd a little.

Murray was barely clinging on through the first set, whereas Srichaphan's belting serve allowed him to hold with ease. The young Scot looked weary and leaden-footed and repeatedly found himself at deuce or worse when it was his turn to serve. The pressure told in the tie-breaker when Murray saw two incendiary returns fly past him and then double faulted to go 1–5 down. Four points and a smashed racket later, he was a set down and wondering why all of his hard work had come to nothing.

Players with less of the terrier within might have allowed their head and spirits to drop. Instead, Murray dug in, scraping through most of the time and showing occasional flashes of brilliance at moments of danger. At a set, 3–4 and 0–30 down, he seemed to be losing the fight, but four points on the bounce and a healthy streak of obstinacy kept him in the match. He got to 30–30 in the next game, and although he didn't break serve, it was the closest he had got to doing so for about an hour. It must have allowed him to hope, even if the pain he suddenly felt in his right hand during the game was a worry.

He held on his own serve to take the set to 6–5 and called for the trainer, who examined the hand but found no serious damage – something which was borne out by the way Murray ripped the through the next game as though he had simply been toying with the Thai thus far. His sudden change of gear clearly rattled Srichaphan, who plonked an easy volley into the net to surrender the second set and take the match into a decider.

Srichaphan is a big, athletic jack-in-the-box of a man, so it was hard to imagine that he would be about to lose a war of attrition to a willowy adolescent who had repeatedly been accused of being unfit. Yet somewhere around the middle of the third set, the Thai's stamina began to wane, and despite treatment for cramp at 3–2, his movement became increasingly laboured. His naturally exuberant game can look very flat very quickly when he loses momentum, and Murray's patient, well-thought-out court craft eventually wore his opponent down, both physically and mentally. By the end, Srichaphan's lucky red shirt – the colour is regarded as a portent of good fortune in Thailand – was dark with sweat.

'Obviously, the crowd wanted him to win,' said Murray afterwards. 'I just had to block it out, but I really enjoyed it in the end. The support all week has been very good, and even against Paradorn, they were really appreciating my good play as well as his.

'I didn't start off so well – I was serving rather badly and gave him some chances in the first set and a half – but I changed the way I was playing, and I think that threw him off. Towards the end of the second set, I started to hit my ground strokes a bit better, and it paid off in the third. I felt good physically. Paradorn was doing a lot of running in the second and third sets, and I could see he was getting a little tired.'

Murray broke to go 4–2 up, and buoyed by the knowledge that he was minutes away from his first ATP Tour final and the longed-for match against Federer, he didn't lose another game, sealing the 6–7, 7–5, 6–2 victory with an emphatic winner.

At that moment, thousands of miles away, the Murrays' neighbours in Dunblane must have wondered what on earth was going on next door. 'I nearly fell off the sofa at home when he made it through to the final against Federer,' Judy later revealed. 'I was dancing around the living-room in my dressing gown and slipper socks.'

Federer had beaten Jarkko Nieminen 6–3, 6–4 earlier in the day, so Murray had walked on court knowing that a meeting with the world No. 1 would be his prize for beating Srichaphan. It was hard to tell which he was more excited about – making his first ATP Tour final or the prospect of a meeting with the Swiss maestro.

'To play against the best in the world, and possibly the best ever, at only 18 is a dream come true,' Murray said, with a touch of uncharacteristic gushiness. 'I just have to concentrate on making a good start, getting a few games under my belt and taking it from there.'

With his tongue firmly in his cheek, Mark Petchey said, 'Andy hasn't lost a pro-final yet, so something's got to give tomorrow. Roger, if he plays his game, is virtually impossible to beat, but Andy will go out there with a game plan. Whether it'll work, I don't know.'

It was always going to be unlikely that it would work well enough to stop the streak Federer was on: he had won his last 23 finals, going back to July 2003, and had won 31 matches in a row, which was one of the longest winning runs in the open era. He had already won ten titles (including Wimbledon and the US Open) during the season and lost only three times, to Marat Safin, Richard Gasquet and Rafael Nadal. To say the odds were stacked against Murray was like saying that Federer was quite handy with a racket.

It was a moment to celebrate for Murray regardless of the fact that he was going into the final with his name already traced onto the runner-up's trophy. Not only had he made an ATP final, but he managed it far sooner than even the most optimistic of his supporters could have predicted. To put the rate of Murray's progress into context, Tim Henman played thirty-four ATP Tour events before he reached his first final, whereas Murray was playing his eighth. From starting the year ranked 411 and the tournament ranked 109, he was guaranteed to end it at or around the 70 mark, the biggest jump of any player on the ATP Tour that season.

'Before Queen's or Wimbledon, if somebody had said I was going to be in the top eighty in the world in three months, I would have said I'd got no chance,' said Murray. 'But I got a lot of self-belief after I won against some really good players at Queen's and Wimbledon. Then I went over to the States and played some smaller tournaments and had a lot of confidence, and I won a couple of them. So it's been a pretty good three months for me. I wasn't expecting it, but I always believed I could get to the top. It's a pretty big deal, and I'm happy with what I've done.'

Federer and Murray walked on court together, as is the custom, but during the first set, the old cliché about man against boy certainly applied. It was hardly surprising that Murray took longer to settle than the 24-year-old Federer, who was playing his 41st final at ATP Tour level. The Swiss player ran up a 3–0 lead courtesy of some indifferent serving from the teenager, who appeared a little overwhelmed by the circumstances and by the reputation of the man in the white headband, prowling menacingly on the other side of the net.

'It's quite intimidating playing a player like Roger, who's one of the greatest ever. You don't get the chance to see players like him much nowadays,' Murray later admitted. 'I was a little bit nervous at the start, but once I got going, I was OK. I was 40–15 on my first service game, but I played a few loose points. That might have settled me down a bit, but once I got my first game, I started playing OK. I maybe could have returned a little bit better in the first set, but it was always going to be tough.'

He had to battle to hold serve at 1–4 down in order to keep the first set score line respectable. Although the breakpoint he mustered as Federer served for the set was quickly snaffled away, it at least suggested that Murray has beginning to feel his way into the match. Federer, with the ruthlessness of a champion, broke in the opening game of the second set to further dampen Murray's confidence, yet it was to take more than that to put the Scotsman away. He broke the Federer serve − not something that many players can claim − to restore parity at 3–3, then traded enough blows with Federer from the baseline to lift the atmosphere in the IMPACT Arena as the crowd realised that Federer, who had humiliated Andy Roddick 6–4, 6–0 in the preceding year's final, was at least going to have to work for his latest trophy.

However, with the set tied at 5–5, the relentless pressure on Murray's serve again told as Federer came at him with the combination of touch and aggression − which must feel a little like being caressed to death − that makes him one of the most accomplished sportsmen of his generation. He snatched his break, then went in for the kill in the next game to earn himself his 77th win of the season, his 11th title of 2005 and the 33rd ATP Tour trophy of his career.

When Federer and Murray had played doubles during the Davis Cup match the previous weekend, Murray had told him, as they shook hands at the net, that it had been an honour to play him. No doubt the Scot felt the same as he went to congratulate Federer before getting his silver runner-up plate. The pair chatted like old friends as they went through the rigmarole of speeches, sponsor's presentations and photographs. Murray's biggest concern at that point was a spot of post-final etiquette and the tough decision whether or not to kiss the local beauty queen who handed him a bouquet. In the end, he blushed a bit, gave her a big grin and a peck on each cheek. Afterwards, he was rather ungallant as he relayed that part of the experience to his mother. 'She wasn't that great up close, Mum,' he said.

'I'm sure she said the same thing about you,' came the retort.

Once the pleasantries were over, Federer sat down for his press conference and promptly admitted that he had been worried by Murray at times, even if he hadn't shown it. 'That was a very tough final today. He was making me work extremely hard in the end. It could have suddenly become a really dangerous match for me,' said the Swiss player. 'I also lost my first final when I made it onto the tour. This time he had to face the number one in the world, but it is great experience for him.'

Reflecting afterwards, Murray said, 'Playing against Federer was the one match when I didn't have a game plan. I had watched him on TV and everyone was saying to me, "He's so good and does everything so well." It was difficult to know what shot to go on, so I just went out and tried to stay with him. Afterwards, I thought that, "Yeah, Federer is an incredible player," but I didn't come off the court thinking, "Gee, he's so much better than me." It's exciting for me that I pushed him close when I still have so much to work on and when I am just starting out on my tennis career.'

The relentless nature of life on the tennis circuit is such that when

Murray had to head for the airport, just as he had done the previous Sunday, he'd barely had enough time to pick up his replica trophy and $45,000 prize-money cheque. He was scheduled to play a Challenger event in Mons, Belgium, the following week, and while he must have been tempted to take a week's rest, he had committed to playing and wanted to honour his promise. Therefore, he had to spend another twelve hours in a plane back to London, followed by three and a half hours on the Eurostar to Belgium. At least he got an upgrade on the plane after staff at the check-in desk recognised him and bumped him up to premium-economy class.

Understandably, his time playing the Elias Trophy in Mons – a rung down in importance, prize money and prestige from Bangkok and held in an unprepossessing sports hall on an industrial estate in a provincial Belgian town – was a somewhat painful experience both literally and figuratively. Every muscle in Murray's body seemed to ache with the exertions of the previous ten days, and he had to squeak through his first two matches with a large dose of determination and confidence and not a lot else. It had been a long and tumultuous season, climaxing in a week in Thailand which had been full of landmarks, new experiences and emotional highs – no wonder he was tired.

He began the tournament ranked seventy-two in the world and seeded seventh, and celebrated with a weary 6–4, 6–4 victory over yet another Swiss player, Ivo Heuberger. The familiar Frenchman Gregory Carraz, whom Murray had played twice earlier in the year, winning one of the matches, followed in the second round. He stuttered a little in the first set against Carraz but eked out a win after playing better in the second. Neither his progress nor his patience were helped by a 49-minute delay while the on-site electricians attempted to fix faulty lights on the indoor arena's roof. With Petchey and Abigail Tordoff from Murray's then management company Octagon watching, along with *Daily Mail* tennis correspondent Ivan Speck and the *Daily Telegraph*'s Mark Hodgkinson (both of whom had been sent at short notice thanks to the latest bout of 'Murraymania' sweeping through the newspaper sports desks), Murray polished Carraz off 7–5, 6–3 to move through to the quarter-finals.

The talented but mercurial Xavier Malisse was next. The former Wimbledon semi-finalist was seeded second at his home tournament and was always going to provide tough resistance to Murray, whose body was beginning to rebel after a gruelling run of matches at ATP Tour level, as well as his two bruising encounters in Belgium. He had been putting up with the various tweaks, aches and pains in the hope of winning another Challenger title and notching up a few more ranking points, but a strain in his left hamstring proved to be an injury too far. After dropping the first set to Malisse 5–7, he made the always difficult decision to retire at 0–1 down in the second set and limped out of the tournament.

It had been another extraordinary few weeks for Murray and some time off – both at home in Scotland (where he hadn't been since the previous December) and at Petchey's house in London – was much needed. He had more events to play, more ranking points to acquire and more milestones to reach before the year's end, but for now, at least, he had earned himself a rest.

It meant he finally had time to digest his week in Bangkok and to plan how to make another of Federer's predictions come true. 'Andy will become a good player,' the Swiss player had said, without hesitation, after the final in Thailand. 'I am sure of that.'

14

HEAD TO HEAD WITH HENMAN

THE MAIN SPORTING OCCASION OF THE YEAR FOR THE PEOPLE OF BASEL IS THE Davidoff Swiss Indoors championships, the third largest indoor tennis tournament in the world. It is an extravagant event staged every October in the St. Jakobshalle arena, just across from the Basel football ground.

The tournament was first played in 1970. It was a low-key affair at the beginning with the first champion being awarded a wristwatch as his prize. From such humble origins, the event grew in stature, and past winners included Björn Borg (1977), John McEnroe (1990), Boris Becker (1992) and Pete Sampras (1996).

The event had always sold out, regardless of who played, but the joy in Basel was unconfined when Federer, one of their own, broke through onto the world tennis stage. Every year, he went out of his way to take part in the tournament, his participation giving the event added kudos. Apart from Federer, the tournament drew the world's best players, but, really, the only person who mattered to the people of Basel was their local hero.

Incredibly, despite his tennis talent and collection of grand-slam titles, Federer had never won the event, although he had two final appearances to his credit, both earlier in his career. In 2000, he lost to Thomas Enqvist in five sets, and the following year, he lost to Tim Henman in the final.

Federer hoped to play in the competition in 2005, arriving on 9 October in his home city to get in some practice and to catch up with his family. However, two days later, a routine training session turned to disaster when he sprained his right ankle. A scan showed that the world No. 1 had damaged ligaments in his foot, and he had to withdraw from his hometown tournament, much to his disappointment, as well as tournaments in Madrid and Paris

His enforced withdrawal did not come quickly enough to allow the organisers in Basel to change their marketing of the event, and they did not have time to remove his photo from the publicity posters. At Basel Airport, Federer's famous face dominated the hoardings, and in every local supermarket and on every tram stop, his picture took pride of place.

The tournament would not be the same without Federer, and the organisers tried their best to think up a way of getting him along. In the end, they decided to present him with an award for his services to tennis, given to him on the final day of the tournament. Such was Federer's commitment, he was delighted to attend but not having him actively take part was a huge blow. Other top players like Rafael Nadal had also pulled out, which left the main draw looking a bit short of real stars.

When the list of seeds was drawn up, it was topped by the Argentinian Guillermo Coria, who was No. 7 in the ATP rankings. Coria's countryman David Nalbandian, ranked No. 10 in the world, was seeded second. The third seed was Juan Carlos Ferrero of Spain, who was ranked No. 19 by the ATP, and Fernando Gonzalez, the Chilean player who was No. 17 in the rankings, was seeded fourth.

They were all accomplished players but not the charismatic superstars the organisers wanted. Losing Federer was a big disappointment, and they desperately needed something else to spark some life into the competition. Their prayers were answered when the first-round draw of the competition was made in Basel town hall on Monday, 24 October.

The organisers knew that Andy Murray was the up-and-coming star of British tennis, and they also knew that he was a box-office draw. They had watched the interest he had generated at Wimbledon and had offered him a wildcard to play in the tournament. It was a decision which paid dividends.

Basel's medium-paced, rubberised court suited Murray's game, and after two weeks off to rest the hamstring he had injured during his last competitive outing at the Mons Challenger, he was sounding typically confident going into the tournament. Having dragged his ranking up from 411 at the end of 2004 to its current high of 71, he was already thinking of his next immediate goal, which was a place in the world's top 50. 'Now I'm playing those bigger tournaments, I think I've got a good chance of making it to the top 50 early next year,' said Murray. 'It's a pretty big jump from where I am, but from now on, I'm hopefully going to be playing ATP tournaments week in and week out, and if you have a couple of good weeks and maybe make a semi-final or even a final, then you can really jump up.'

On the day of the draw, Murray and Guillermo Coria, a man five years his senior and one of his favourite players, were asked to go along to see who they would play. As they sat together, Murray joked that it was a 'certainty' he would get Tim Henman in the first round. However, Coria was first out of the hat and was drawn to face Alberto

Martin of Spain. However, when the pairings for the eighth match were made, the names of Murray and Henman were announced, just as the young Scot had predicted.

Murray had a big smile on his face when he realised he would be facing Britain's best-known player. Henman was seeded sixth in the tournament, and Murray had never played him before in a competitive match, although the pair had practised together at Queen's Club the week before the tournament began and again on the Sunday on Basel's medium-paced indoor courts.

The two players were good friends, and it was always going to be an interesting encounter. Out of the two, it could be argued that the meeting would be more of an ordeal for Murray, considering he had always looked up to Henman. Murray had been Henman's hitting partner for the Davis Cup match against Luxembourg in 2004, and the older man had been impressed by his young teammate's attitude to the game at that time. The pair had formed a closer bond during the 2004 US Open when Murray was on his way to winning the junior title and Henman was en route to the semi-finals.

'Taking on Tim is a match I'm looking forward to,' said Murray. 'I have great respect for him as a man and as a tennis player. He has had a great career, and it will be quite a challenge to play him.'

At various times during his time in the spotlight, Murray had made it clear that he was a long-term fan of Henman's and had often expressed his belief that the Englishman had received a hard time from the British press for not winning Wimbledon. The 18 year old came back to the topic in Basel. 'I don't think Tim gets the credit he deserves,' Murray said after the draw in Basel was made. 'He was consistently in the top 10 in the world and made quarter-finals and semi-finals at Wimbledon. He was a great ambassador for our sport and I could never believe people who called him a failure for he was anything but that.'

Despite the kind words, Murray was excited about having the

chance to take on Henman and made it clear he would be going all out to beat him. Ironically, Murray was set to play Greg Rusedski, who was ahead of both him and Henman in the world rankings, in a Scotland versus England team match in Aberdeen in November, which meant he would play the top two British players within a month of each other. The game between Murray and Henman had much more allure than the match-up against Rusedski as it came in a competitive environment with ATP Tour ranking points as well as pride at stake.

On Tuesday, 25 October, the tournament started in earnest, but the mouth-watering match between Henman and Murray that everybody was waiting for was still 24 hours away. Although BBC television, which had secured the rights to cover the contest, was delighted at the match-up, Mark Petchey wasn't so excited, having hoped for an easier first-round tie. 'The draw is exciting for everybody else,' said Petchey. 'For Andy, it is a bit of a disappointment as there are easier draws than Tim. Playing him is a difficult proposition. I can see why the British public are looking forward to the match, though, coming as it does so late in the season.'

Henman, whose 2005 season had been disrupted by back problems, had a good record in Basel, having won the event twice, and clearly fancied his chances of seeing off the young Scot. However, it was clear that the man who had given so much to British tennis wasn't in the best shape of his life going into the match. His back problem remained and although he came through his practice sessions reasonably well it would be different when the real contest began.

It was shaping up to be a fascinating encounter and although Henman made his name as a serve and volleyer he had other facets to his game which did not get the credit they deserved. He could use slice well, had improved his drop-shots and could win a decent share of points from the back of the court, which was not always the case earlier in his career. However, as he had shown time and time again, at Wimbledon and elsewhere, his concentration could be suspect at times.

To beat Henman, Murray would have to serve consistently, draw on his varied range of ground strokes and keep his mind concentrated on the task in hand. It was unlikely that the teenager would be overawed by the occasion. Indeed, the more passionate the atmosphere, the better Murray was likely to perform.

The evening before the game, Jeremy Bates said that although the match was a big one, it would be dangerous to read too much into the outcome. 'We should not judge Andy and Tim on the basis of this one match,' he said. 'Tim has been on the tour for ten years. When Andy has been on the tour for ten years, that will be the time to make comparisons.'

Bates also said there was no pressure on Murray, despite the fact that he had a lot of expectation on his shoulders following his fantastic summer in 2005: 'It is not a pressure situation for Andy. He has a free shot at the best player that Great Britain has produced in the last 20 years. It's obviously a lot easier when you are the new kid on the block. It is a good situation for Andy, and he will want to do well.'

On the eve of the match, Murray spent his time practising with Petchey at the indoor tennis centre called Paradise, a 20-minute drive from the main venue. The pair of them worked hard, laughing and joking their way through the session. Murray was in a relaxed mood as he went through his paces and had his hair, which he had vowed not to cut until after the 2006 Australian Open, hidden under a Fred Perry cap.

Afterwards, Murray held an impromptu press conference in the hall of the leisure centre as he waited for a car to take him back to his hotel. He claimed he felt no pressure heading into the Henman match despite the fact that everybody knew it would be one of the most high-profile games of his career. Murray said that he believed Henman was the favourite, because of his experience, but was looking forward to taking on the man who had inspired him to play tennis.

'Everybody wants to see us play before Tim retires, and I am not surprised that people are going a bit over the top about the match,' said Murray. 'In another country, like Spain where they have Rafael Nadal, Carlos Moya and lots of other top players, it wouldn't be the same big deal. It's just we don't have that many top players in Britain.

'Playing Tim will be difficult as I have so much respect for him. I have looked up to him for six or seven years, and he inspired me to keep playing tennis. To play him during a tournament is a great opportunity. We know each other's game quite well, so it will be a tough match. He is a world-class player, and if it wasn't for his recent back problems, he would be up there in the top 10. Because we are good friends, it makes the game even more difficult.

'I must try to concentrate and play my own game. Tim has beaten me in practice matches and normally beats me at backgammon, but he is pretty lucky at that. I don't think I have beaten him at anything. In saying that, our tennis matches are normally pretty close. Because this one is in a tournament, there is a bit more pressure on him.'

Henman, meanwhile, talked of the respect he had for his opponent, claiming Murray was 'world class'. Henman said, 'He has risen from more than 400 in the world before Wimbledon up to 70, and he deserves to be called world class. I respect the way Andy plays. Forget the fact we are from the same country. Take the nationality out of the equation and you have a very good player.'

Listening to Henman and Murray talk, you would have thought they had convinced themselves that the upcoming encounter, a head to head the whole of the United Kingdom was looking forward to, was just another match. Henman did a marginally better job of playing down the match between the old and new of British tennis, perhaps because he had more experience of dealing with big matches and the attendant hype which goes with them. 'I have experience of matches between British players from playing against Greg Rusedski, so I am well used to the hype surrounding my match against Andy,' he said. 'My experience in dealing with the media makes me realise what kind of build-up this game is going to get, and I have no problems with that. It is good for the sport that the match is being televised.

'I have tried to tell Andy that both he and I live in a goldfish bowl, and I have told him to try and put outside things aside and concentrate on what is happening on court.

'I know there are 13 years between us in age, but, for me, that doesn't matter. It is the first time I have played Andy competitively, and I know it will be a tough match.'

Wednesday, 26 October 2005, is a date which will live long in the memory of Andy Murray as it was a defining moment in his career. He walked onto the court to the strains of 'I Want It All' by Queen, and the way he saw off Tim Henman in three pulsating sets that afternoon suggested he could have it all in the world of tennis. There was never any doubt beforehand that Murray had the talent, but he showed against Henman that he also had the mental strength to be one of the world's top players.

The on-court announcer introduced the first-round tie as the 'Battle of Britain', but there was little sign of nationalistic fervour as the players walked out on court. One St George's Cross was visible in the crowd, and there were no Scottish Saltires. A few Scottish accents called on Murray to 'do it for Scotland', and he duly obliged by winning 6–2, 5–7, 7–6 in two hours fourteen minutes in what he described as the biggest win of his career. He left with a tear in his eye after the energy-sapping encounter.

During the match, Murray took his supporters, not for the first time, on a roller-coaster ride of emotion. He raced ahead of Henman, winning the first set in just 33 minutes thanks to his consistent serving, punishing ground strokes and overall court artistry. Murray was helped by some dreadful play by the Englishman, who made a terrible start, and it was 18 minutes before he put a score on the board when he held his serve to make it 1–4 to his younger opponent. Some of Murray's passing shots drew gasps from the crowd, while Henman missed simple chances and served erratically. How much the older man was being affected by his back problems was difficult to gauge. He had the problem area taped and seemed to lack mobility at crucial times, though the issues may have been mental rather than physical. He admitted afterwards that despite the difference in experience, it was Murray who had coped better with the situation.

Henman did play better in the second set and was an early break up, but Murray broke back. He then won again on Henman's serve to make it 5–4 and looked as if he would close out the second set. A risky drop-shot at 15–30 was pounced upon by Henman, who won the point and took inspiration from his lucky escape. The Englishman stayed calm and played some of his best tennis in the final two games, breaking Murray again to take the set 7–5.

Henman was in the ascendancy, and the smart money was on him to use his experience to emerge victorious in the deciding third set. However, Murray showed great maturity and shrugged off his second-set disappointment. He plugged away and was always willing to exchange shots from the back of the court. He also cut back on his drop-shots, which had become inconsistent.

Crucially, the teenager kept his nerve when the going got tough in the third set, and when the score reached 6–6 on service, Murray showed composure beyond his years. He broke Henman's serve on the opening point of the tie-break and raced to a 5–1 lead. Henman clawed back a couple of points and at 6–3 down saved a match point, but Murray then closed the match out with a forehand cross-court volley. He had won the tie-break 7–4 and the match in three pulsating sets. He was in tears as he sat down at the end of the contest.

The win was symbolic more than anything else, suggesting that the baton was being passed from Henman, who had reigned supreme in Britain for nearly ten years, to the teenager from Dunblane. Henman and Rusedski may have been ahead of Murray in the world rankings at that time, but the newcomer was closing in on them fast. The victory clearly showed that he had both of the elder statesmen of the British game in his sights. Murray, though, was looking at the bigger picture as his priority was to climb further up the world rankings rather than just being the top player in Britain.

Murray's win created front- and back-page newsaper headlines in the UK and was the top sports story on television and radio. As he entered the interview room after the match, the young player had a big smile on his face. 'This is a pretty special day for me, and I'll remember it for the rest of my life,' he said. 'I have so much respect for Tim, and it's always tough when you feel like that going into a match. He is one of the best players of the past ten years, and to win against him is just amazing.

'I can't really describe how I feel. I tried not to show much emotion during the match out of respect for Tim, but at the end, I couldn't hold it in any more.

'This was the biggest win of my career. If it had not been for Tim and the things he achieved on the tennis court, I might not even be playing the game. He was an inspiration to me when I was growing up, and beating him was a big deal to me.

'I first met Tim when he held a Robinson's tennis clinic when I was about 13. I'm sure he won't remember, but I do. Now I'm playing him and beating him in a tournament. It's amazing.'

Henman looked crestfallen in his news conference but still took time to praise his opponent: 'He has the potential to be a top-20 player, but I won't be if I play like I played against Andy. He has shown he has the mental strength to compete at the top level and is playing well.

'I have no problems about so much being made of our match. Domestic rivalry is good for British tennis, but it is a shame that there are so few of us.'

Neither player, however, would countenance talk that Murray's win signified a changing of the guard in British tennis. Henman said, 'People say that I took the torch, or flag, or baton, or whatever you want to call it, when I beat Jeremy Bates all those years ago when he was the best-known British tennis player. Whatever is supposed to be passed on when a young British player beats an older one, I'm happy for Andy to have it, but such talk doesn't mean very much.'

Back in Scotland, the Murray family and his supporters were celebrating in style. Roy and Shirley Erskine watched the historic encounter with friends at their home in Dunblane and celebrated his triumph with a tipple of whisky. Shirley said, 'It was an exciting match which I found really tense. It was very close. He played the tie-break very well and knuckled down, and we are very proud of him. He has done very well, but we will have to see what happens in the rest of the tournament. We'll have to go through it all again. Roy and I had some friends round, and we're now about to have a wee drink in celebration.'

Greg Rusedski, who had been keeping tabs on the match from St Petersburg in Russia, where he was playing a tournament, was also impressed. Asked what he thought about Murray, he said, 'I think he passed the mental test months before the match with Tim. I think he's just got it. You can just see it with what he's done this past summer, really – and over the last few weeks. Especially going from Davis Cup in Geneva all the way to Bangkok and to get to the finals against Roger Federer.

'He's already proved himself, and I think he's going to be around for a long time so long as he stays healthy. He's still hungry. He's probably going to work hard during the off-season to get stronger. His game suits the way modern tennis is played. I see him having a bright future.'

Next up for Murray was Tomas Berdych of the Czech Republic, who had beaten George Bastl of Switzerland in the first round 5–7, 6–4, 6–2. Berdych had enjoyed a decent season in 2005, and up until the Swiss Indoors, his best results had been on clay in Bastad in Sweden in July when he was beaten in the final by Rafael Nadal, 6–2, 2–6, 4–6.

Observers had grown so used to Murray doing so well that it was easy to forget just how difficult and competitive ATP Tour tournaments are. The draws are stuffed full of players such as Berdych, the world No. 52, who was a talented striker of the ball. Plus there is always the risk that the next match after an emotionally gruelling win will end in anticlimax.

It took Murray about 20 minutes to work out Berdych's game, and once he had learned to stay away from the 20 year old's backhand and began to boss him about from the baseline, the Scot's nerve and game settled. He saved break points at 1–2 in the first set and at 3–3 gained the break which eventually gave him the set 6–4.

He also had chances to break early in the second and was visibly annoyed to have missed them. He then lost a game on his serve. Murray cast frequent frowns and scowls in the direction of Mark Petchey and bounced his racket repeatedly off the court surface. He had lost his rhythm and concentration at that stage, and the second set was more one sided with the Czech player taking it 6–2 in just 36 minutes, and it seemed the momentum was with him.

However, just as he had done against Henman, Murray pulled himself together at the moment of greatest danger and pushed on, breaking Berdych's serve to love, when it was 3–3 in the third set, with the aid of a double fault from his opponent. In the end, he ran out the winner 6–4, 2–6, 6–4.

During the match, Murray had overcome three dodgy line calls and an ungracious opponent who'd complained on several occasions in a way that threatened to break the Scot's momentum. Because of his antics, the Swiss crowd, which usually isn't very demonstrative, threw its support behind Murray. And in spite of Berdych's tactics, the young Scot had kept his nerve to secure another creditable victory.

The win over Berdych was as significant as the Scot's success over Henman and was another great learning experience as he had passed another stern mental test.

It was an indication of Murray's standing in the tournament that his next game against Fernando Gonzalez was given an evening start in order to allow Swiss television and Eurosport to make it their match of the day. Gonzalez was a likeable Chilean and had beaten players of the calibre of Carlos Moya, David Nalbandian, James Blake, Greg Rusedski and Mario Ancic earlier in 2005. He had come to Basel in good form and had beaten Andreas Seppi of Italy, 7–6(3), 6–3, and Michael Berrer of Germany, 6–4, 7–5, to set up the quarter-final meeting with Murray. In the Madrid Masters, the tournament before Basel, he had reached the quarter-finals and was hitting the ball well.

The match promised to be an exciting one, involving two charismatic characters, but it was Gonzalez who went into the match as favourite. The players arrived on court at 8.34 p.m. in front of a capacity crowd. Although Murray was the man of the moment after his wins over Henman and Berdych, the crowd didn't see him at the height of his powers against Gonzalez, although they did see a decent game of tennis. In the end, the sheer power of the Chilean's forehand, his subtle touch and drop-shots, and great use of spin, secured him the match.

The perfect example of Gonzalez's superb forehand came at 3–3 in the first set, just when Murray seemed to be making headway. The young Scot was 30–15 up on his own serve when a forehand screamed past him. After that, he hit two bad shots in a row to lose his service game and allowed Gonzalez the upper hand. It was no surprise that the Chilean player went on to take the first set 6–4.

However, Murray hung in and rallied superbly in the second set. Gonzalez blows hot and cold during matches, and Murray took advantage of his opponent going through a chilly period to take the second 6–3 with a combination of clever cross-court shots and consistent serves. His ability to keep going was graphically illustrated in the third game of that second set when he faced four break points but never wilted and ended up holding his serve.

Murray had complained of feeling stiff and sore after his win over Henman, and it seemed his exertions against Berdych and the constant grind of facing the big-hitting Fernandez was taking its toll. The man from Chile put down some thumping serves and forehands in the third set, and Murray struggled to cope with his sheer power. He hit his thighs with his racket as if willing them into life but still looked increasingly sluggish, especially when Gonzalez broke to take a 2–0 lead. It was an indication of things to come, and Gonzalez built on the momentum he had created to take the deciding set 6–1.

Although well beaten, Murray returned reasonably well, particularly in the second set, despite Gonzalez serving superbly well. For Gonzalez, it was a hard-fought victory and proved the spur he needed to go on and win the tournament. After Murray, he beat Dominik Hrbaty of Slovakia, 6–0, 6–3, before beating Marcos Baghdatis of Cyprus in the final, 6–7(8), 6–3, 7–5, 6–4.

The fact that Murray had managed to take a set from Gonzalez showed how far the young Scot had come in just a few months, especially as the man from Chile had played some great tennis during his winning week in Basel.

Afterwards, Murray said, 'I served OK but felt I made mistakes in the rallies against him. I found it a bit difficult to get into a rhythm. It was a strange sort of game, and I kind of lost the feel for the ball in the third set. His serve was difficult to read, as he was slicing some of them, but I felt I did a good job of working out his ground strokes. I don't feel too bad, as it has been a good week for me, but I was really disappointed how easily I lost the third set. On the positive side, though, I have played nine ATP tournaments and lost just once in two sets against top guys.'

Murray admitted that it was now likely he would return home to Scotland for the first time that year and then go abroad to prepare for 2006 and the Australian Open in January. 'I am in better shape now than when I was at Queen's and Wimbledon in the summer and have learned a lot in a short time,' he said. 'I'm going to speak to my coach, but it's likely that I will take some time off now to get ready for the new season. I'll go home for a while and find somewhere hot before going to Australia in January.

'I'd like to play in Sydney before the Australian Open in Melbourne, but I think it's just the top 60 players who are allowed in for Sydney and I'm around 70 just now, so that might not happen, but, obviously, I will play some tournaments Down Under before the Australian Open starts.'

After the match, Murray sat down with the journalists who had travelled to Basel to watch him in action against Henman to give them his views of 2005. 'A pretty good effort' was his typically understated assessment of his stellar season. He had come a long way since his promising performances at Queen's Club and Wimbledon, but goodness only knows how downbeat he would have been if he hadn't just hauled his ranking up two hundred and eighty-seven places in five months, made a final and a quarter-final in his last two ATP Tour events, and beaten his hero Tim Henman. It was reassuring to see that for all his exhilarating precociousness Murray had yet to show the slightest hint of getting carried away with himself. Both his nature and his upbringing guarded against the purchasing of big houses, Ferraris or any of the other trappings that successful sportsmen his age sometimes indulge in. 'I'm happy with the two wins that I got in Basel, but I'm not too happy with the way that I played. I could have played better, and I have certainly played better over the past few months,' Murray said, summarising his week in Switzerland. 'If you are coming through and winning against guys who are ranked higher than you and are in the top 50 and not playing your best tennis, then from that way of looking at it, I've got to be happy, but I know I can play better, and there is still a lot for me to improve. At least this year I played in nine ATP Tour tournaments, and I've only lost in two sets once. I've got to be pretty happy that I haven't lost badly against any of the top guys.'

For those watching Murray close up since his breakthrough, it had been both thrilling and astonishing to watch his fitness and form blossom after Queen's, when he had accepted the wildcard which had proved to be the start of an extraordinary run. What followed was an explosion in his popularity and a burst to the third round of Wimbledon, two Challenger titles on the American hardcourts, qualification for the US Open, where he won his first five-set match amid criticisms of his fitness, and a first career ATP Tour final against, of all people, Roger Federer. In Basel, he also added a highly emotional and personally significant victory over Henman, a man he named as his 'inspiration', to his list of achievements.

Basel was the last ATP tournament of 2005 for Murray, and he left Switzerland full of confidence, secure in the knowledge that he had managed to beat one of the United Kingdom's top two established players. He would find out in less than a month how he would do against the other. He played Rusedski in two sold-out exhibition matches in Aberdeen over a November weekend. He lost his first match against the left-hander and won his second, although Rusedski was carrying an injury in both. However, because it was not a tour event, little could be read into the results.

At his press conference after his second match against Rusedski in

Aberdeen, Murray claimed that the LTA had hampered his brother Jamie's tennis career for a few years when he was a promising teenager. 'My brother is very talented,' he said. 'He was No. 2 in the world when he was around the age of 13. He then went down to an LTA school in Cambridge, and they ruined him for a few years. It was their fault.' Murray will always stand by the statements he made about Jamie but has made it clear that he was not having a go at the LTA in general, just their operations in Cambridge at that time.

The match against Rusedski, part of a Scotland v. England tennis contest televised by Sky TV, was Murray's final one of 2005 and brought down the curtain on a remarkable year. For a few days after the competition in Aberdeen, he relaxed with his friends in London before flying to South Africa to prepare and acclimatise for the Australian Open. The warm weather in South Africa provided the perfect conditions to help him prepare for the searing heat awaiting him in Melbourne, where the first grand slam of 2006 was due to be held in January.

15

BROTHERS IN ARMS

*For ten months, Mark 'Petch' Petchey was Murray's coach, confidant
and companion, the man who took an 18 year old without an ATP Tour
win to his name and turned him into a champion. Their spectacularly
successful partnership began on 6 June 2005 and ended on 14 April
2006, Good Friday.*

BY JANUARY 2006, MARK PETCHEY HAD JUST SPENT SEVEN MONTHS LIVING CHEEK BY
jowl with his eighteen-year-old charge: sharing a room with him,
sitting next to him on flights, spending Christmas with him, being
repeatedly beaten at PlayStation games by him and even having him
as a part-time lodger at his house in Wimbledon.

'It's been fun for both of us,' said Petchey of the journey they had
taken together to that point. 'We do get along really well, and that's
a large part of the relationship. You have breakfast, you have lunch,

you have dinner together and you're on the road for four weeks, or, as we were in the States over the summer, nine weeks. You'd bloody better get on, otherwise it's going to be a short relationship or a very boring one. We share a sense of humour and that helps, but you can't let all that stuff get in the way when it comes down to the difficult times and when things aren't going so well – you've got to have a solid enough relationship that you can tell each other home truths when things aren't going right. We've had a few of those but, hopefully, not too many.'

Speaking to the *Daily Telegraph* in October, Murray said, 'It's almost like having a big brother with me. We are very competitive, and we do pretty much everything together – pool, darts, backgammon, whatever. Mark has already gone through what I'm going through now, and he understands me as a person. Some people were quite surprised when I decided that I wanted to work with Mark, but they don't realise how good he was. I have a lot of respect for what Mark did in tennis. He is the main reason why I have done so well. Mark gets me to make notes after every match so I can look back on the notes the next time I play the opponent. And Mark has been so helpful with putting game plans together.'

Turn the clock back to June to the first day of the Stella Artois Championships and Petchey's first match in charge of Murray. The new coach sat courtside to watch his young player beat Santiago Ventura and score his first-ever win on the ATP Tour. Afterwards, Petchey stopped outside Court No. 1 to talk to the press, speaking in serious, thoughtful tones about Murray's potential and how well he took to what was a new and daunting situation. As well as looking after Murray over the grass-court season, in what was then to be a temporary arrangement, Petchey was planning to continue in his roles as manager of men's national training for the LTA and pithy television and radio pundit. It wasn't surprising, then, that he talked a good game, though the journalists hanging on his words couldn't help but notice the small, bright-pink rucksack he was clutching while he spoke, unmistakably the property of his daughter, who was pulling impatiently at her father's trouser leg as she waited for him to finish.

It was a telling vignette of the difficult juggling job that Petchey – not to mention his wife Michelle – had to undertake in order to make his coaching relationship with Murray work. When they decided during Wimbledon that their arrangement should be permanent – it was announced on 2 July 2005 – Petchey gave up his job with the LTA and came to an agreement with his other employers, Sky Television, to balance working as a coach and a commentator. Yet the wrench of leaving his wife and young family to travel with an 18 year old was not so easily negotiated away.

'It is a huge commitment,' said Petchey in January 2006. 'I think that's something that can get lost with some people when they look at the lifestyle of someone who travels around the world. It is difficult when you've got a family, and it's not something I jumped into lightly last June. There is still a lot of soul searching, because you don't get those years back with your kids, and Andy knows that. It's always a tear for me, and we'll just have to try and do the best that we can with it, but it's not easy.'

Chris Bailey, Petchey's close friend and colleague, had no doubts as to how strong the bond between Murray and Petchey had become seven months into their coaching relationship. 'It's tough for him with a wife and two kids at home – that's a massive sacrifice,' he said, speaking at the start of 2006. 'I'm sure that Murray's fully aware that he's making that sacrifice, which must add to their relationship, because Murray must know that in some ways it's tougher for Petch to be on the road than for someone who isn't married and doesn't have a family. I just see a great, very tight working relationship, quite similar in some ways to the relationship Tim Henman had with David Felgate in the early days when Felgate was coaching him. Tim always said about Dave that one of the reasons why he wanted to work with him was that he went to India for ten weeks with him, went to all the bad places and went through eating rice and chicken for weeks on end, and that brought them closer together. I'm sure it's had the same effect on Petch and Murray: going away together, living in a hotel room together, training together. It's all part of building up a very strong bond, and you have to have that in this type of environment, because there will be people throwing stones at you all the time.

'Travelling together, sharing the same room, as they did when they were in the States last summer: they have pretty much been living in each other's pockets. They had Christmas together down in South Africa, and they spent the previous four weeks at Mark's house. That could be harmful in the long run, but right now it's a great bonding experience, and I'm sure that's how they view it. I'm sure there are times when Andy is sick to death of seeing Petch every morning, just as Petch probably has his moments with Andy, but it's the best way of bonding. It is a very intense relationship between player and coach, but I do think that he's the right person for Andy at this stage of his career.'

The success Murray and Petchey enjoyed together at Queen's and Wimbledon meant that speculation over their future had reached feverish intensity during the second week of the 2005 Championships, as Murray prepared to go to Newport. Rumour and counter rumour circled round the Wimbledon press room, though the general consensus at the time was that Petchey would have been mad to have walked away from what seemed destined to be a winning partnership.

The suggestion rankled with Petchey, though. 'I think it's easy for people to sit back now and say, "Yes, it was an easy decision, he was always going to be a good player," but there are a hell of a lot of people in tennis and in the business who didn't think he was going to be all that special,' he said, with some passion. 'He won the Open, but I can tell you I spoke to someone a few weeks before that that was quite high up in the tennis world and he was like "whatever" and there were a few clothing companies who were very blasé about him.

'Obviously, he's still got a long way to go . . . and it's a long difficult road, but, like I said, he was 357 when I started working with him and nobody believed he was going to make the top 100. I spoke to some of the press boys, and they were very sceptical. It's very easy for people to sit back and say it was an easy decision, but it wasn't, because there are no guarantees in life. He was [the] only one I felt that had a genuine chance to make it, having been around him the little that I had been and having been to Barcelona and seen him play. I genuinely believed he was going to be a top 100 player, and from there on in it's about how good a job we both do and, more importantly, how much he can make of himself.

'Hindsight is a wonderful thing, and people can look back and say it was a given. My situation was slightly different because I do have a good career with Sky as well, which I cherish, and you don't go throwing away solid careers like that. So it was and it will be a tough decision. I wanted to give him everything that I could and help him be everything that he wanted to be, and, fortunately, everything has turned out well.'

There were those who suggested, often with a jealous, self-serving agenda, that he was underqualified and, at 34, too young to take on the responsibility of nurturing Britain's only decent young player. Yet a glance at Petchey's CV reveals plenty of preparation for the job.

Born in Essex in 1970, Petchey had developed from a promising junior into a solid but not exceptional pro-player. By the time he retired in 1998 after ten years on the circuit, he had reached a career-high ranking of eighty, won one ATP Tour doubles title (at Nottingham in 1996 with fellow Briton Danny Sapsford), played eleven Davis Cup ties and could claim big-name scalps like Michael Stich, Pat Rafter, Michael Chang, Greg Rusedski and Alex Corretja.

'I stopped and I didn't know what I was going to do, to be honest,' he admitted. 'It sounds crazy now when I look back on it, but my wife was just about to have our first child, and I had no plans. I just knew I didn't want to play any more. That was the easy decision, though in some ways it would have been easier to just have kept playing. Tim Henman and Greg Rusedski were coming up then, and I could have maybe jumped on them for a couple of years in Davis Cup, and what have you, and been around. But it just didn't feel good to do that, so I spent four months playing golf and waiting for my first child and then needed to do something very rapidly. That was when I got involved with Kim McDonald at his management group – he sadly died a couple of years after I met him – and he gave me the chance to coach those two girls.'

The two girls in question were Croatian Silvija Talaja and Slovenian Tina Pisnik, who he worked with for two years with some success, particularly in the case of Talaja, who climbed into the world's top 20 under Petchey's guidance.

'Coaching was always something I was interested in, but it wasn't necessarily my first port of call. I'd done a bit of commentary for Eurosport, but there wasn't going to be enough work there, and, fortunately, he [McDonald] gave me the chance to work with them,' said Petchey. 'It was a great two years. I learned a lot about coaching, I learned a lot about myself and, fortunately, they were fairly successful with Silvija breaking into the top 20. It kind of gave me an air of respectability, but after two years, I just didn't want to do it any more.

'Those two years gave me a nice head start coming into the job with Andy, which was important. I don't think I would have felt comfortable taking the job with him had I not had those two years, because I think I would have felt very unsure about what perhaps I should have done. I learned a lot in those two years about what I felt didn't happen with me when I was coming through, especially at a young age. I've certainly tried to put that into practice, both with the girls and, even more so, with Andy, because he's British for one and also because of the age that he is. I think there are certain things that I feel I could have done better as a player and ways that I think I could have been guided a bit better and, hopefully, he's reaped some of the benefit of that early on.'

After he stopped working with Talaja and Pisnik, Petchey went back to work as a commentator with BBC Radio Five Live and Sky TV, who have the rights to show the ATP Masters Series in the UK, a job which gave him the perfect opportunity to bone up on his knowledge of men's tennis.

'Sky is one of the reasons why I got the job in the first place, because I know when Andy was off with his knee injury he sat and watched a lot of tennis and listened to my commentary – he was one of the few who thought I was talking at least half sense,' said Petchey. 'I think also, having been fortunate to work for Sky, I have spent three years now watching top-100 players, and that's been a big benefit, because I haven't come into matches unsure of who he's playing and how they play. There have been a lot of upsides in those preceding years.'

Throughout his tenure with Murray, Petchey remained loyal to Sky – whose cooperation he needed in order to accept the job offer from the teenager in the first place – and he continued to provide commentary for them as and when he could. While Petchey's refusal to turn his back on his television career gave him a job to fall back on when he stopped working with Murray, it was also in Sky's interests to keep him on, for not only did they have the coach of Britain's most talked-about player at their beck and call, but they occasionally got the player himself. On more than one occasion, Murray accompanied Petchey to the Sky studios and was an impromptu studio guest, often recording his on-screen performances in order to critique them afterwards.

Bailey, who is Sky's lead presenter, is a good enough friend of

Petchey's to have conceded that both coach and player are men who speak their minds, something which may have made their relationship somewhat volatile at times: 'If Petch has a problem with you, he'll sit you down, tell you exactly what it is, leave it on the table and move on. He's never been the sort of person to hold grudges. He [Petchey] certainly has opinions, and he's not afraid to say them. I think that's probably a valuable commodity these days when a lot of people are afraid to say what they think.'

Petchey's work in the media offered many benefits for Murray. For one thing he came to the job having spent three years being paid to watch and assess players as part of his commentary and thus had a comprehensive knowledge of most ATP Tour players. He also had an understanding of the machinations of the written press, television and radio, a hugely valuable insight for Murray as he tried to come to terms with the attention now focused on him. 'Hopefully, that's one of the areas I can help with,' said Petchey in January 2006. 'When a player is 18, it's always about so much more than hitting tennis balls. Hopefully, I'm helping him manage the media to a point that he is comfortable with it, I am comfortable with it and we don't lose sight of what it's all about. When there's only one person to write about, it is difficult for him, and I think everyone has to understand that. If there were four or five players, then the media would be out looking for stories from other people. One of the hardest problems that the press has had with Tim Henman is just how many times can you write about the same person and make it readable, sell it, make it interesting? So sometimes things have been put in papers which aren't exactly fair or just, but you've had to take a different angle on it. I guess that's another area, and maybe it's about helping Andy understand that if he sees something he doesn't like, then that's probably why it's in there.'

Bailey agreed that Petchey was well qualified to help Andy with his media commitments: 'Because Petch has worked in the media, he

understands that side of the tennis world. He knows the
requirements of a newspaper, a radio station, a TV channel. He
knows that they need to have access to the player and, at times, the
coach, so Murray will have a very good understanding of what is
required of him as a hot prospect. That will help him to learn it
quicker than if he didn't have such a media-savvy coach.'

If the decision to set aside many of his commitments to Sky TV in
favour of working with Murray wasn't an easy one, it's probably safe
to say that Petchey didn't feel the same wrench when it came to
leaving the LTA. Having been a frequent and trenchant critic of the
organisation during the last few years of his playing career and into
his retirement, Petchey was often viewed as a noisy thorn in the LTA's
side. He was seen as a rebel who refused to toe the party line, though
many of his thoughts and criticisms were shared by plenty who had
seen the machinations of the LTA close up and been unimpressed by
its failure to turn an average income of more than £30 million a year
into world-class players.

Having been one of the first appointments made by performance
director David Felgate, who took up his post in March 2003 and
appointed Petchey in July of that year, Petchey worked as manager
of men's national training for two years but was already feeling
disillusioned when he got the call from Murray. 'I wasn't excited at
the LTA at the end,' he admitted. 'It wasn't going in the way I wanted
it to go, and from that perspective, Andy gave me a new lease on
tennis, in many ways, and a way to get back at the coal face and get
involved again. That's been a huge boost – to get energised by it all
again. It's been great. I know more about every area now than I did
before: whether it's nutrition, fitness – everything. I think in life you
learn constantly, and if you think you know everything about one
subject, then it's probably an area of life that you should get out of
because you get a bit blasé. I've certainly spoken to a lot of people
who've taught me a lot over the last few months. You've got to just

keep learning and being excited about it, and Andy gave me that.'

Petchey has been openly critical of the LTA's decision to spend £40 million on a new National Training Centre in Roehampton, his outspokenness, as ever, going down like a lead balloon with his ex-employers. 'It's one of the reasons I was starting to get a bit disillusioned at the LTA,' he admitted. 'I just felt like, "Where are the players? Who's actually going to be there to be part of this?" If you look back three years when it was first talked about, I said I thought it could potentially be a white elephant. Has it been thought out in terms of performance or has it been thought out in terms of the LTA as a whole? I'm all about performance. I don't really give a stuff about the LTA as a whole. How the LTA looks or whether it's got a nice big centre doesn't interest me at all. If we're not producing the players, then what's the point in putting the thing there. If they are not being produced now, then surely you need to address that problem rather than build a National Training Centre, [especially if] you've only got five good kids that are actually going to use it.'

His time at the LTA did give Petchey greater life and professional experience, which helped when it came to his coaching job, though he admitted that he learned plenty by being back on the road with Murray, much of which would have been handy in his previous, office-based job with the governing body. 'When I look back even to being in charge of men's training at the LTA, there were certainly gaps in my knowledge that have been filled since I've been with Andy, which potentially could have been beneficial while I was there,' he said. 'I came out of the LTA with a bit of a reputation for kicking people out and being that way inclined, which is probably not a bad thing, but one of the things I learned is that if you spend a lot of time talking about anything but tennis with a player, then you're probably wasting your time with that player. There was far too much of that going on there.

'With Andy, tennis isn't the only thing we talk about, but we do talk about it a lot: how other players play, different strategies, things like that. We don't spend a lot of time talking about whether he wants to play this game or not – he's always just been immersed in it and obsessed by it and just wants to be the best that he can possibly be. That's why when I was at the LTA, he was the only one who I thought probably had it. There are a couple of players who were similarly inclined, to be fair to them, but when you add his obvious ability on a tennis court, the overall package was going to be good enough to make it.'

It wasn't long into their coaching relationship before criticisms about Murray's fitness began to surface. The columnists and commentators sharpened their laptops again when Murray cramped up at the US Open, some openly blaming Petchey for the player's supposed lack of fitness and even calling for him to step aside and allow a more experienced coach to take over. It must had been particularly hard for Petchey to stomach, given that, together with physio Jean-Pierre 'J.P.' Bruyere, he had committed plenty of time and effort alongside his player in the gym, on the running track and on the practice court, all the better to supervise Murray's fitness regime close up.

The hands-on approach to fitness was something that Petchey learned from Nigel Sears, who now works with top-20 player Daniela Hantuchova and looked after another one, South African Amanda Coetzer, for many years. Sears, a renowned fitness fanatic, was in charge of the Laing Squad, a group of young players in the mid-'80s which included Bailey and Petchey. Sears is still on hand to offer advice to Petchey – and to Murray as well – and his family hosted the Petcheys and the Murrays during their working holiday in South Africa over Christmas 2005.

'We all had that with Nigel when he was coaching us on the Laing Squad, and that was invaluable, because you almost trained that little bit harder because you wanted to beat the coach – you wanted to be better than him,' explained Bailey in January. 'Invariably, because Nigel was a triathlete, he used to end up beating us, but it just spurred us on. Now Petch is being that person for Andy. Petch has lost loads of weight, and he's in great shape from doing all the training with Andy. We're all a bit jealous, to be honest.

'That's one of the advantages of having a coach Mark's age as opposed to someone older: he can say to Andy, "We're doing a five-mile run today, and I'm coming with you. I'm going to try and beat you, and I'm going to go through the pain barrier as much as you are." Or when Andy is doing weight sessions on legs, on arms or whatever, Petch will be in there with him. On days when you really don't feel like doing it, having someone to work out with, who probably feels like doing it even less than you do, is such a good motivator for Murray – to be able to look across and see someone he respects working that hard and being in as much pain as he is. Petch works very, very hard with him, and that builds their relationship.'

Petchey did, though, draw the line at becoming Murray's punching bag – as Murray explained in Adelaide: 'We have got a pair of boxing gloves and pads, but we haven't used them yet – I think Mark's a bit scared.'

In December, at the annual Lawn Tennis Writers' Association dinner dance and the LTA's annual awards, Murray was named Player of the Year. The award for Coach of the Year wasn't given but it would surely have gone to Petchey and no one else.

Murray, who, it had been noted by the stuffier elements present, dared to wear trainers and no tie, let alone a black one, was a shoe-in for the Player of the Year and duly accepted his prize with an understated but sincere speech of thanks to Petchey – his coach, friend, room-mate and the man who had not just helped his career immeasurably but had also been a surrogate 'big brother'.

'I owe all this to Mark,' said Murray. 'I couldn't have done it without him.' In the months that followed, the success continued on the court, yet Murray and Petchey would never seem quite as close again.

16

NEW YEAR, NEW CHALLENGES

MURRAY ARRIVED IN ADELAIDE, A COUPLE OF DAYS BEFORE THE START OF THE New Year, full of enthusiasm after a productive time in South Africa. He was anxious to get his first feel of the idiosyncratic Rebound Ace surface that he was about to make his debut on and ready to experience the hot, dry conditions Australia is famous for.

Within seconds of leaving the hotel that morning, he knew it was a heat unlike anything he had experienced before, and, as is customary on what the Australians call 'fire days', the temperature rose as the day went on. By the time Murray went out to practise with Serbian Boris Pashanski at the Next Generation Club, home of the Adelaide International, it was 43 °C and the wind felt like a hairdryer at full power. Feeling the heat, in all its various forms, was set to become something of a theme for Murray's Australian trip.

Tennis can be a hard taskmaster, with only a handful of weeks off between the end of one season and the beginning of the next. Most players will tell you that the off-season is far too short and offers scant time to both relax and get in training for the punishing year ahead. Finding the right balance in that preparation becomes even more important when a player is getting ready for his first full season on the ATP Tour and is still feeling his way as a fully fledged professional.

Long before Murray had asked Mark Petchey to work with him, Petchey had arranged to spend Christmas with his wife and children, and fellow coach Nigel Sears and his family, in South Africa. It made perfect sense for Andy and Judy to join them there, and for just over two weeks, they combined fun, relaxation and training in a warm climate. Sedgefield, the resort where they stayed, was on the coast and offered all the facilities they would need plus all the benefits of a beach holiday.

'It was great to see him surfing, messing about on the beach and being really relaxed,' said Judy. 'The weather was great most of the time, and they could go up to practise at a place called Knysna, where they had a great gym and a running track. He got to do everything he needed to do, and he had lots of company for when he wasn't training. It worked out really well.'

That company included Sears's daughter Kimberly, an 18-year-old A-level student whom Murray had got to know during the US Open the previous summer when she had visited New York with her dad, who coaches Daniela Hantuchova. The teenagers had become increasingly close.

'It was a good Christmas [with] plenty of hard work to get ready for the season,' said Petchey, who highlighted volleying as one of the areas worthy of particular attention during the daily hours of practice. 'It was off time, but it wasn't really that off in terms of how hard Andy worked to get ready. I think the first two or three weeks it's a bit of challenge to see how you can put that into practice. You can practise as much as you like, but, at the end of the day, it's the matches that get you feeling good about your tennis.'

Petchey did not shy away from putting Murray through his paces in South Africa, because, holiday or no holiday, he needed to be ready for what lay ahead. 'I was actually running hard on Christmas Day,' said Murray. 'When Mark told me we were going to do sprints, I laughed at him, but he was being serious. I took one day off when I was over there just to take a rest after five weeks of training, but I didn't take much time off at all.

'I really enjoyed South Africa. It was the perfect way to get ready to come down to Australia, and it cuts the flight in half. It was great. I really enjoyed it over there because I didn't go on the internet, I didn't speak to anyone except my family and only one of my friends. I got away from everything, went to the beach a lot and it was really relaxing. I just tried to get myself in the right frame of mind for the start of this year.'

Murray's first task in Adelaide, apart from practice, was to attend the draw. After he was drawn against a qualifier, he spoke to the local media and the one British journalist who had come to cover his first match of 2006. He ingratiated himself with the locals before he had even sat down for his press conference when co-tournament director Peter 'Johnno' Johnston asked him about The Ashes cricket series, expecting the typical crowing response from a smug Pom. 'I'm Scottish,' said Murray, flatly. 'I wanted Australia to win.'

Having earned his brownie points, Murray outlined his goals for the year ahead, starting with a place in the top 50 but looking ahead to getting inside the top 20 by the end of the year. Having come good on his prediction that he would make the top 100 the previous season, he spoke with the same air of certainty this time around. 'I think the top 100 was a pretty realistic goal,' he said. 'This year, it's just about winning the big matches, because if you're going to get into the top 20, then you've got to do well in the Masters Series and the grand slams.'

Murray was keen to emphasise the five solid weeks of fitness work he had just put in, a work rate which might have surprised those who had rushed to criticise his conditioning after his loss to David Nalbandian at Wimbledon. The widespread discussion and plethora of so-called expert opinions aired on the issue clearly still rankled. 'It was quite difficult for me last year because nobody came to watch any of the Challengers and nobody came to watch me practise away from a tournament. You can't comment on something like that unless you've actually been to see me practise, seen me in the gym and seen how hard I'm working,' said Murray. 'I've always worked hard. I don't enjoy practising as much as I like competing, but just because I don't enjoy practising, doesn't mean I can't work hard when I'm doing it. I don't see my fitness as being a problem, but I know what it's like. As soon as somebody has a slight problem in Britain, everyone is going to say it's a problem for the next five years until you prove that you don't get tired during long matches. That's just something I'm going to have to do.

'When I played Nalbandian, I had only just turned 18. When there is that much pressure on you to do well at something, it does take its toll. It can get really difficult, because everybody is expecting you to do well, everybody is wanting you to win and there is a bit of added pressure, which you might not think about at the time but which does affect you subconsciously. At Wimbledon, that was one of the reasons why that happened.'

Pressure was to be a recurring topic over the course of his time in Australia, where he seemed to feel the burn of the spotlight more acutely than he had done during 2005 when he was still regarded as an emerging player and expectations were therefore lower. In 2006, Murray was having to adjust to playing against better, stronger players week in and week out, something which those who had clamoured for early success from him sometimes failed to take into account.

The size of the furore he had unwittingly caused at the Aberdeen Cup, by mentioning that he thought the LTA had 'ruined' his brother Jamie, had surprised him. Unfortunately, there was more of the same to come. 'Obviously, I realise that for the next five or six years, or until another British guy starts to do well, it's always going to be there, and so I'm just going to have to get used to it,' he said. 'I have to be careful about what I say, because I've learned that if I say something slightly wrong, like what I said about my brother, then it just goes from being one little sentence into being this huge thing. It's always the same in Britain: they make a big deal out of things which are so small.'

The qualifier Murray was due to play on his 2006 debut was Italian Paolo Lorenzi, whom Murray had easily beaten en route to qualifying for the US Open the previous summer. Lorenzi was ranked No. 252 in the world, and the fact that he was studying to be a doctor of sports medicine in between tournaments suggested he didn't harbour ambitions on the same scale as Murray. On paper, it looked like a snap, but the man from Dunblane had not played a competitive match since losing to Fernando Gonzalez in Basel the previous October – compared to the three matches Lorenzi had won in qualifying – and had never played a match on Rebound Ace before. Both of those factors rendered the 188 ranking places between them irrelevant.

Murray eventually won 3–6, 6–0, 6–2, but it was a performance stained with the rust that comes with not playing. He seemed to be unsure of himself tactically, making half-hearted forays to the net only to retreat to the baseline mid-point, and his timing, not surprisingly, was less than crisp. There was an overeagerness in his play, too, as if he was anxious to show off the hard work he'd done during the off-season.

'I just need to get used to playing matches again, because it's been quite a while, and once you remember how to win, it keeps happening,' said Murray. 'Obviously, I'll need to play a little bit better against Thomas Berdych in the next round, but it's not the end of the world if I don't win against him, because it's just another match in getting ready for the Australian Open.'

Murray stayed true to his word and played far better against Berdych. Though Murray had beaten him in Basel, the tall Czech had taken himself to the fringes of the top 20 the following week by winning the Masters Series event in Paris. Even before that he had been touted as one of rising stars of the ATP Tour. He was a far classier proposition than Lorenzi, and though it was close, Berdych was physically and mentally stronger and won 7–6, 4–6, 6–1.

Despite the huge improvement from the Lorenzi match, Murray still didn't seem to be quite himself. While his play sometimes suggested he was trying too hard, his demeanour was subdued, a flatness which often spread to his shot making. It prompted the teenager to warn that meeting players of Berdych's calibre would be the norm now that he was a regular on the ATP Tour and that expectations should be tempered accordingly. 'Everyone is expecting me to have a great year, and I hope I do, but it's not the end of the world if I don't,' said Murray. 'It's not that easy just to jump straight away, because you need to get used to playing in the big tournaments week in and week out and get used to winning against the big players. I'll still only be 19 at the end of the year, so I've got a long time to improve.'

It may not have been the glorious start to the year that he had hoped for, but Murray could head for Auckland feeling that he had made some progress, albeit limited, in his first two matches. What mattered was performing well at the Australian Open in Melbourne, by now just ten days away. 'You want to make sure that you are better and getting closer and closer to your best with each match,' he said. 'For me, the most important tournament of this trip is the Australian Open, and I'd rather play my best tennis there than in Adelaide.'

At least he made a good impression with the tournament staff during his time in Adelaide. One courtesy-car driver, herself the mother of an 18 year old, offered him the highest praise after having helped to ferry him around. 'He is a sweet, well-brought-up boy, that one, and so grown up for his age,' she said. 'He's a credit to his mother.'

Having stopped off in Melbourne to change planes, Murray and Petchey made the three-and-a-half-hour journey across the Tasman Sea to Auckland, where organisers had been so keen to get Murray to play their event that they had offered him appearance money. Such fees are standard for the sport's bigger names – and in some cases can be into six figures – but it was the first time Murray had received such an incentive. It was a sign of his rising profile around the world.

Auckland is a city which, for most of the year, is obsessed with yacht racing, and even away from its bustling harbour, it's hard to escape the nautical emblems and references everywhere. However, once a year, it finds time to focus on tennis. The somewhat eccentric design of the tournament's 3,200-seater stadium means many punters – predominantly well heeled and over 40 – watch the matches from the restaurant tables which make up the first tier of seating behind the baseline. Serving players often have to ignore the presence of ducking waiters and waitresses – doing some serving of their own – in their eye line.

It was in this relaxed, convivial atmosphere, amidst the clanking of plates and cutlery, that Murray took on Danish veteran Kenneth Carlsen in the first round. The first set was uneven stuff. Murray, who seemed just as unsure of himself as he had been on court in Adelaide, repeatedly went up a break only to be pegged back. After seven breaks of serve, he eventually wrapped up the first set 7–5 and thereafter seemed to relax. When Carlsen hurt his foot late on in the second set, it was only a postponement of the inevitable, although the injury break did give Murray a chance to entertain the crowd

283

with an impressive display of keepy-uppy with a tennis ball, for which he got a sustained round of applause.

Once Murray had wrapped up the 7–5, 6–2 win, he trotted over to do his post-match interview on court with New Zealand television. With the cheers of the crowd still echoing around the stadium, he responded to a light-hearted opening question about the number of breaks of serve there had been in the first set. 'I know,' said a smiling Murray, without skipping a beat. 'We were playing like women.' At that point, some female voices in the crowd jokingly chided him for his cheekiness with a 'whoooooo', the sort of noise a pantomime audience might make at the villain. At the same time, many of the men in the stands clapped and laughed. The interviewer grinned and said, 'Well you've got one half of the crowd on your side . . .'

'Yeah,' said Murray, smiling and looking around. The interview continued in a similar vein, with Murray being asked about his skills at kicking a tennis ball. 'I'm really glad I managed to do that, because normally when I try and show off like that, it goes all wrong,' said Murray, to another warm chuckle from the stands. When it was over, Murray got a round of applause and wandered off court, racket bag over his shoulder, oblivious to the trouble he had just caused himself.

During the post-match press conference, he was jokingly teased by a female journalist about his comment. 'I was watching one of the matches on TV from the Hopman Cup. Svetlana Kuznetsova was playing, and there was something like nine breaks of serve in the first set, so that's why I said it,' he explained, keen that his remark would not be misinterpreted.

Anyone who has watched women's tennis to any extent – be they players, coaches, journalists or WTA Tour staff – will happily admit that women's matches tend to have more breaks of serve than men's. Those whose job it is to promote the women's game would probably be delighted to think that an 18-year-old male took enough of an interest to spend a spare afternoon watching a rather poor-quality match.

NEW YEAR, NEW CHALLENGES

With a former pro-tennis player for a mum, who also happens to be one of the most accomplished coaches in the UK, Murray is hardly likely to share an opinion once aired by a young Richard Krajicek, who said that all women players were 'lazy, fat pigs'. That did not stop some British columnists and commentators equating Murray's and Krajicek's comments in their rush to condemn the teenager for his perceived slight on female athletes.

The two British journalists who were in Auckland covering Murray's matches had both been on or near the court – close enough, certainly, to hear if there had been any sustained booing. Yet it seems unlikely that it would have merited much more than a light-hearted mention in either of their stories had it not been for the intervention of a reporter who had watched the match on television in Wellington – which, incidentally, is nearly 620 miles away from Auckland.

He immediately wrote a story, based on what he had seen on television, reporting that Murray had been 'loudly booed' and giving the impression of a rather more extreme reaction from the crowd than the genial response which those on-site had heard. By that evening, Auckland time, the story, which had been filed to a reputable news wire service, had landed on the sports and news desks of UK newspapers, radio stations and TV broadcasters. Faced with news from what appeared to be a reliable source that one of Britain's most exciting young sportsman had dropped what seemed to be a sexist clanger, the UK media reacted with a raft of stories, columns and discussion programmes.

As storms in teacups go, it was a category-five hurricane. When Tim Henman had joked to reporters sitting courtside during a match in Monte Carlo in 2004 that he ought to 'put on a skirt' because he was serving so badly, he was praised for showing a sense of humour. Murray was vilified for doing much the same thing.

Early the next morning, Auckland time, after 12 hours of the story being repeated and rebuffed and discussed back in the UK, Murray's phone rang. It was a radio station asking him for a comment. It was the first of many calls and texts which made him only too aware of the hullabaloo back home.

Murray later revealed that he was angry and perplexed that such an innocuous remark could backfire on him so horribly, and coming a few weeks after his comments about Jamie being ruined by the LTA, he felt he could barely open his mouth in public without incident. His hurt, anger and confusion at the fuss in New Zealand was to linger for days afterwards, to the extent that it arguably contributed to his defeats not just to Mario Ancic in the second round in Auckland but also to Juan Ignacio Chela in the first round of the Australian Open.

Despite his state of mind, Murray played well against Ancic – well enough to have at least won the second set, which he served for and had two set points in. It was by no means a perfect performance – his uncertainty about the surface and his lack of matches left him unable to take advantage of the opportunities he created – but a 6–3, 7–6 defeat to a former Wimbledon semi-finalist ranked No. 21 in the world was not disastrous.

After the match, downcast by defeat and irritated by the distraction of the previous days, it didn't take long for Murray to let his feelings out. 'I have to watch every single word I say,' he said. 'I make one small comment which is a joke and it gets completely taken out of context. It's hard for me, because I don't know what to do: if I have to be serious the whole time or if I'm not allowed to joke. So there's a few things I'm going to have to change a little bit and not be myself as much as I have been so far, 'cause it's a little bit unfair how I was treated. I'd rather I wasn't getting phone calls telling me that people are making a big deal of it back home. If you explain everything that happened, then it wasn't a big deal. I thought I was making a joke, but I guess other people didn't think so. I'll have to try not to worry about things like that.'

NEW YEAR, NEW CHALLENGES

He had other concerns as he prepared for his first Australian Open. He still didn't feel comfortable playing on Rebound Ace. It is a surface only used during the Australian summer tournaments, on which the ball bounces high and spins and which feels different underfoot to conventional hardcourts. He wasn't happy with his on-court demeanour either, which he felt was still too flat. Despite all his hard work in South Africa, his trip Down Under was not going as well as he'd hoped.

Once he got to Melbourne, he received the news that he had drawn Juan Ignacio Chela, a consistent and obdurate Argentine with a reputation for gamesmanship, earned at the previous year's Australian Open when he had appeared to spit at Lleyton Hewitt in their third-round match. Murray had avoided any of the more stellar names in the draw – though he had a potential second-round match against Hewitt in prospect if he got past the Argentine – but Chela was never going to be a pushover.

'I'm still going to go into a lot of matches as the underdog,' he told a pre-tournament press conference. 'I think people have gone a bit over the top in expecting me to win matches against guys who are much higher ranked than me, especially when I've hardly played any ATP tournaments.'

With Greg Rusedski back in London awaiting the birth of his first child and Tim Henman losing in the first round to Dmitry Tursunov (who'd also been his conqueror at Wimbledon) on day one, Murray took to the court against Chela knowing that, for the third grand slam in succession, he was the last British representative in the draw. The knowledge didn't help him, although it was hard to think what might have, given that he put in arguably his worst display since he had risen to prominence the previous June. Yet again he seemed subdued and out of sorts, and even the presence of St Andrew's Crosses, a sign saying 'Guan Yoursel Andy' and a banner from the Innerleithen Tartan Army failed to gee him up. Forehands were sprayed, volleys were dumped into the net and his movement was sluggish. In short, like thousands of players in countless tournaments down the years, he was having a nightmare of a match.

Chela, who played well throughout, humiliated Murray 6–1, 6–3, 6–3 in front of a bemused crowd in the Vodaphone Arena. They must have wondered when the promising young Scotsman they had heard so much about was going to show up.

The Australian Open's press-conference room, known as the 'theatrette', can be an imposing place to take questions in. While the player sits behind a large desk at the front, with TV cameras directly in front and blinding spotlights in his or her eyes, the journalists sit in steeply banked seats like inquisitors peering down at their prey. It is the sort of arrangement which can be intimidating, particularly to an inexperienced teenager whose ego has recently been bruised by defeat and disappointment.

Within 20 minutes of walking off court after losing to Chela, Murray found himself sitting behind that desk, with his head in his hands at times, trying to explain what went wrong. As he was to observe later, 'You have to analyse every single match when you go into the press room. If you didn't do something so well, it's not just you and your coach talking about it, the press are also asking you questions about it. So, that's pretty difficult.'

The emotions bubbled near the surface and, before long, began to spill out into his words. 'You know, if you guys expect me to play well every single match and every single tournament, then, you know, it's not going to happen. Everybody has a bad tournament sometimes. Unfortunately, it came here,' he said. 'You guys are expecting me to win matches like this. The guy's ranked 20 places in front of me and is a much better player than me. It's difficult for me to go out there and try and perform to the best that I can when, you know, I'm expected to win all these matches.'

When a journalist countered that he had consistently enjoyed a good press, he only succeeded in infuriating Murray further. 'You don't think there's any pressure on me? Well, if you don't think that, then, you know, I'm obviously going to disagree on something,' he snapped. 'If you guys don't think you're putting pressure on me, then that's fine. I'll forget about it.'

Most of the travelling tennis writers, frequently sent around the world to feed the demand for information about one of the country's most exciting young sportsmen, put his remarks down to him lashing out in the wake of disappointment. Murray's comments, though, attracted interest from the local and international press. Brad Gilbert – former coach to Andre Agassi and Andy Roddick – was prompted to chastise Murray in his column in *The Age*, Melbourne's daily broadsheet. He wrote:

> I was really disappointed in Murray saying the media put too much pressure on him. As tennis players we put pressure on ourselves but, when it's over, don't put it on anybody else. He had the chance to go out there and win or lose – he lost. Give your opponent credit and move on. Don't blame the media, don't blame anybody.

A few days later, Murray gave a calmer and far friendlier press conference, following his first-round doubles match with his good friend and fellow 18-year-old Novak Djokovic. Speaking to a tiny room packed full of the British tennis press and a smattering of interested local and international journalists, he said, 'To be honest, I think it's good for British tennis that everybody's here, but, at the same time, it's maybe not good for me that so many people are all having their opinion about my game and trying to find other people's opinions on me.'

Afterwards, he arranged to meet up with the British journalists – most of whom he has a warm and easy-going relationship with – in private and had a long and largely convivial chat with them to clear the air and exchange insights into the different pressures borne by press and player. 'I think I got everything off my chest in Australia,' he said later. 'I spoke to all the journalists. I let them know my feelings, they told me theirs. It helped a lot. I had a few problems off the court with a few different things, and I sorted that all out when I got home. It's quite difficult when you've got so many different things going on.'

There was no doubt that the incident in Auckland continued to play on his mind long after he left New Zealand, and he was still smarting when he looked back on it a good two months later. 'It's quite difficult when I'm making jokes and I'm getting in trouble for it and people are taking things the wrong way,' he said. 'Yeah, I was little bit caught up, but, at the same time, I couldn't not be because I was getting in trouble for things that I shouldn't have been. Things that were just little jokes. I want to try and be myself, but if I'm going to be myself and it's going to cause me extra problems, and I'm going to have to worry about what people think, then I'd rather just not say anything and be boring. I can just concentrate on my tennis. It's kind of up to the media to decide – if they do a couple more things like that then I'm just going to be dull.'

Mark Petchey said, 'It's very easy, because it's been such an incredible run, not to realise just how difficult it is to change from where he was, which was literally doing no media, to all of a sudden doing what he has to do now. It's every week now, and because of who he is and what he's done and where he comes from, there is always someone wanting something. That is difficult for an 18 year old to have to deal with. I think he's done an incredible job of dealing with it and still played the tennis that he has done. Obviously, he's got people around him who are hopefully guiding him in the right direction, but he's still got to find his own path. He knows it's going to be part of his life, so it's not a question of ignoring it; it's a question of dealing with it.'

NEW YEAR, NEW CHALLENGES

Like everything else about his trip Down Under, his encounters with the media had provided another learning experience. The four weeks may not have been the most enjoyable of his career, but they proved to be a precursor to the biggest high of his professional life, just a month later.

17

DO YOU KNOW THE WAY TO SAN JOSÉ?

ANDY MURRAY HAS PROBABLY NEVER HEARD DIONNE WARWICK'S 1960s' CLASSIC, AND unless Fallout Boy or the Black Eyed Peas choose to record a cover version of it, that is unlikely to change anytime soon. He does, though, know the answer to Warwick's harmonious question, and in February 2006, he proved it. Not only did he know the way to San José, he knew exactly what to do when he got there.

Winning your first tour title at the age of 18 is not something that happens to many players, particularly not ones who have to beat two former grand-slam champions back to back to do it. He arrived in San José after a difficult and confusing start to the year and having never beaten a top 10 player before. A week later, he had beaten Andy Roddick and Lleyton Hewitt on consecutive days, become the youngest British man ever to win an ATP Tour title and got his ranking inside the top 50 for the first time.

Murray had not played like himself in Australia, and distractions off the court had not helped his mood. A week back in London plus long talks with Mark Petchey and Tim Henman made him feel much better about life and his tennis.

'Tim, especially after Australia, was fantastic with him,' said Petchey. 'They practised a lot, and Andy and I sat down and talked about things that could have been better, where his game was at.' The confusion and disagreement about match tactics which had initially surfaced in Australia would eventually return later in the trip, ensuring that it was Petchey's last journey as Murray's coach. Yet the conversations in early February with Petchey and Henman meant Murray headed to his first indoor event of the season in Zagreb with renewed optimism. It was almost as though the year was starting all over again.

Zagreb's co-tournament director, the 2001 Wimbledon champion Goran Ivanisevic, had had no hesitation in offering a wildcard to Britain's newest and most exciting player. 'Andy's got something inside him which I really like, an attitude on court that not many players have,' said Ivanisevic. 'He's an emotional guy on court, and I really like guys like that. I'm almost certain he's going to be a top 10 player.'

It was Murray's misfortune that he was drawn to play another Croatian, the then world No. 5 Ivan Ljubicic, in the first round. It was another reminder – as if one was needed – of just how difficult life on the ATP Tour can be. Despite the testing circumstances and the quality of his opponent, Murray won the first set and created opportunities to cause what would have been a huge upset. Ljubicic proved too strong in the end, running out a 4–6, 6–2, 6–3 winner, but there was plenty for Murray to take heart from. For the first time in weeks, he had played the way he wanted to. It wasn't quite enough to beat Ljubicic, but things were getting better.

With his tennis back on track, Murray packed his bags for

America. The plan was to take in five tournaments – San José, Memphis, Las Vegas, then the Masters Series events in Indian Wells and Miami. Petchey opted to stay in London and spend a precious week at home with his wife and two young children while they were on half-term holiday from school and would meet up with Murray in Memphis, though they would remain in contact as much as the eight-hour time difference between California and London would allow. At the time, there appeared to be nothing sinister about Petchey's decision to stay at home, but, in retrospect, enjoying the most successful week of his career in Petchey's absence might have increased the doubts in Murray's mind about whether the Englishman was the right coach for him.

Murray was not alone – he had flown his girlfriend Kim Sears, who was on a half-term break from her A-Level studies in Brighton, out for support. He also had his good friend and sometime doubles partner James Auckland there to cheer him on.

Sears was also called upon for a bit of impromptu hairdressing. Murray hadn't had a haircut in over a year (despite his mother's entreaties) and by now was sporting a wild mop of auburn curls. Up until then, he had ignored teasing about it from family and friends, but when *The Sun* ran lookalike pictures of him and Coco the Clown, it was the last straw. Sears trimmed her boyfriend's hair with nail scissors, which meant he played San José with a new look to match his new, more upbeat frame of mind.

The $1 million indoor SAP Open is played in the 17,496-seater HP Pavilion in downtown San José, a huge, glass-fronted venue which has an ice-rink underfoot, courtesy of its day job as home to the San José Sharks ice-hockey team. Day one of the event saw Murray, now ranked 60, up against American Mardy Fish, whom he had lost to in Indianapolis in July 2005. This time, armed with what he had learned then, Murray played Fish off the court, beating him 6–2, 6–2.

Next up was 21-year-old Yeu-Tzuoo Wang of Taipei. On paper it looked like a far easier match than the one against Fish, since Wang was ranked 88 and had only ever reached one ATP Tour quarter-final. Wang, though, was like a human backboard, trapping Murray in marathon rallies which tested both his patience and his stamina. 'I've actually burnt a hole through my insoles, running so much,' said Murray after his 6–4, 6–2 win.

Despite the fact that he had reached something of an understanding with the travelling tennis writers in Melbourne, he was relishing flying under their radar somewhat in America. The US media were simply interested in finding out who this straggly haired kid from Scotland was rather than passing judgement the way Murray felt some sections of the British media were apt to do. 'It's always difficult to say, because it sounds like you're knocking the press, but he likes being away from it all,' explained Petchey. 'He likes to be away at a tennis tournament and just practise and work hard and not have to deal with too much of the other stuff.'

In what was only his third ATP Tour quarter-final, Murray would face Swede Robin Soderling, the man he had beaten in Bangkok the previous October to break through to the top 100 for the first time. Murray's hopes of a bright start were not helped by the fact that the match against Wang had finished late, and he began the contest against Soderling feeling tired and sluggish. Before he knew it, Murray was a set and a break down, and he was in severe danger of being bounced out of the tournament, yet unlike in Australia, where he had felt irretrievably flat, this time he managed to rouse himself.

He did so with a technique that 47-year-old John McEnroe (who was in San José to play doubles with Jonas Björkman), would have been proud of. Murray gradually worked himself into a fury about the perceived injustice of a couple of close line calls, smashing his racket four times and earning himself a code violation after he appeared to swear in the hearing of umpire Norm Chryst.

'I was trying to get myself going, because I started the match so sloppily,' said Murray afterwards. 'It obviously worked.' Soderling, though, was unimpressed and complained to Chryst about Murray's behaviour. He then voiced his unhappiness after the match as well. 'He was talking before the point was over a lot,' said Soderling. 'Before the umpire had made calls, he was screaming, "Yes!" I didn't like that.'

'I wasn't trying to put him off, and I didn't do it at any other time except when the ball was already past him when he was at the net,' countered Murray. 'You don't want to be unpopular on tour, but when you are on the court, you have to do what you have to do to win.' Murray's manufactured surge of adrenalin came flooding through into his shot making at 1–3 down in the second set, when a ferocious forehand winner screamed across the court, giving Murray the break back and turning the match irrevocably in the Scot's favour. It put him on course for a 4–6, 7–5, 6–4 victory and a semi-final against Roddick.

Roddick was the world No. 3, a former No. 1, the 2003 US Open champion, had won San José the previous two years running and boasted an enviable record in front of his home crowd – 13 of his 20 ATP Tour titles had come on American soil. He also owned a record-breaking serve and a forehand that could strip paint. 'I don't have much of a chance of winning,' said Murray. 'These sorts of matches are the ones you want, because you really see where your game is.'

Murray was 'almost sick' with nerves before what was only his second ATP Tour semi-final, but, fortunately, it didn't show in his tennis. After battling on nearly every service game, he succeeded where many an opponent has failed by breaking Roddick's serve at 5–5, winning two games on the trot to put himself a set up. Murray earned another break to go 3–2 up in the second set, but the American hit back straight away, breaking to love in the next game.

It was the sort of change in momentum that can undo inexperienced players, but Murray was determined not to let Roddick bully his way back into the match the way other top 10 players had done against him. 'There was definitely momentum,' Roddick said. 'To his credit, he stayed tough.'

At 5–5, Murray hit a searing cross-court backhand to earn a break point and knew the moment Roddick's forehand sailed wide in the next point that he had the match in his hands. A double fault on his first match point must have had the nerves jangling, but two points later, a 125-mph serve and a crisp volley gave him his first career win over a top 10 opponent.

On the other side of the draw, Hewitt, the 2002 San José champion, beat Vince Spadea 6–3, 6–4 to earn his place in the final. Beating Hewitt would be arguably even more difficult than beating Roddick. The Australian had reigned for two years as world No. 1, had won the 2001 US Open and the 2002 Wimbledon titles, and was renowned as one of the most obdurate players ever to pick up a racket. He had long been a hero to Murray, who admired his tenacity and his fieriness. 'I like the way he plays and his attitude,' said Murray. 'I think we have the same kind of never-say-die attitude, and we don't give up. I've learned quite a lot from watching his matches.'

The euphoria after beating Roddick made preparing for Hewitt all the more difficult. Murray slept badly that night, waking at 3 a.m., which contributed to a slow start from the teenager. Hewitt had never lost a final to a player ranked outside the top 50, and after winning the first set 6–2 courtesy of three breaks of serve, he didn't look likely to. Murray, though, buoyed by the self-belief the win over Roddick had given him, was not about to fade away.

Apart from a deliberate decision to get pumped up when he needed to against Soderling, Murray's matches in San José had all been characterised by his calmness on court. The wildly fluctuating emotions of Queen's and Wimbledon had been replaced by an altogether more controlled, steadier on-court demeanour. There was certainly no hint of panic against Hewitt despite the loss of the first set.

Murray earned himself the break in the opening game of the

second set with the help of an artful lob and a wayward backhand from Hewitt. Two audacious backhand passing shots gave him a double break for 3–0, and with Hewitt's attempts to play outside his baseline comfort zone making Murray's task even easier, the young Scot took the set. The 18 year old was always ahead in the third set and would have won it more easily had it not been for Hewitt's typically dogged resistance. The Scot was twice a break up (at 2–0 and again at 4–2) but the Australian has made a career out of clawing his way out of trouble and did so on both occasions. At 5–4, Murray forced a match point only to be aced. When the same thing happened again at 6–5, Murray must have begun to wonder if he would ever be able to put Hewitt away.

Murray's performance in the tiebreaker dispelled any thought of failure, though. He led it all the way with a mixture of aggression, penetrating serving and Hewitt-esque resilience. At 6–3, three more match points arrived, and he took the first of them with a gorgeous cross-court backhand return winner. Murray looked stunned. Not only had he won his first ATP Tour title at the age of 18, the win was also enough to see him break into the top 50 of the world rankings, making it a doubly significant moment.

Kim Sears, who had been on the edge of her seat throughout, screamed 'Yes'. Murray put his hands up to his face in disbelief then went over to shake Hewitt's hand before running across the court and climbing up into the stand where Sears was. In a tender moment that was being shown live on television in the UK, US and Australia, and would be photographed and splashed across almost every newspaper in the UK within hours, the teenagers embraced and kissed.

'It was kind of emotional. It's the first time she came to a tournament with me, and it felt like it was the right thing to do,' said Murray. 'This has been the best week in my life so far, so it was quite nice to share it with someone.'

'I think it was great that his girlfriend was there and that she was able to share that very special moment with him,' Judy told Sky TV. 'For him to have a friend along to chat about it with – another teenager – that's really important, too.'

The hotel in Sheffield where Judy had been on a work trip didn't have Sky TV so she hadn't been able to watch a ball of her son's debut ATP Tour title win. She slept through the whole thing but woke up and realised he'd won the moment she picked up her phone to find it full of text messages. Had he lost, she surmised, her inbox would have been empty.

Through the on-court formalities, Murray stared straight ahead, glassy-eyed, as if he couldn't comprehend the events of the previous two days. He looked almost in a daze as he went up to collect his trophy. 'To win against Lleyton 7–6 in the third is a dream come true,' said Murray. 'It's an honour to play against someone who's won two grand slams and been No. 1 in the world, and to win against you is amazing.'

Only four players (Hewitt, Björn Borg, Roddick and Rafael Nadal) had been younger than Murray when they won their first ATP Tour titles. Henman had been twenty-two years and four months old, and Roger Federer and Pete Sampras had both been nineteen years and six months. 'I guess there haven't been too many eighteen year olds in the last five years or so with that kind of skill,' said Hewitt. 'I think he's a guy who's confident out there, and that's what it takes to make it on the tour at a young age.'

There is no doubt that Murray headed to Memphis with both his self-belief and his reputation enhanced, even though he insisted it wouldn't go to his head. 'I don't see why you should change just because you won a few tennis matches,' he said. 'I've still got the same family; I've still got the same friends. Maybe now there's going to be more people who are wanting to be close to me, but I haven't changed.'

As Judy put it, 'He's still his usual laid-back, grumpy self.'

With all that he had been through in California, it would have been both predictable and understandable if he had lost his opening match in Memphis against Rainer Schuettler, the 2003 Australian Open runner-up. When the German whipped through the first set 6–1, no other outcome seemed likely, yet Murray rallied, determined to prove that he wasn't just a one-week wonder. He battled to a 1–6, 7–5, 6–2 win, then, despite creeping fatigue, put in a similarly stubborn performance to beat South African Rik De Voest 7–6, 3–6, 7–5 and earn his fourth ATP Tour quarter-final berth. Only when he ran into Soderling (yet again) in the last eight did his resistance finally run out, the Swede beating him 6–1, 6–4.

'To keep it going is mentally very tough,' said Murray. 'I don't think winning the whole thing was the most important thing for me this week. I didn't go out and tank any of my matches. I think I showed that my feet are still on the ground.'

His two wins in Memphis were enough to push Murray's ranking past those of Henman and Greg Rusedski, making him British No. 1 for the first time. As much as it caused a stir and threw up the threadbare clichés about the passing of the baton from one generation of British tennis to another, Murray insisted it meant little to him. Henman, whose chronic back injury had contributed to his slide down the rankings, was similarly uninterested. Only Rusedski, who had played a Challenger in Ukraine at the end of the previous season in a doomed bid to overtake Henman in the rankings, seemed remotely bothered.

'For me, Tim's still the best player in Britain,' said Murray. 'If you're No. 1 in America or Spain then that's a huge achievement, because you've got ten guys in the top 100, but in Britain, when there's only three or four guys who are near the top, it's not really that huge an achievement. I'd much rather get into the top 10. And if I was ranked 10 and Tim was ranked 2 and Greg was 4, I'd much rather that than all of us be around 40 to 50.'

It was back across the US again for Murray's next tournament, the inaugural Tennis Channel Open in Las Vegas. Unlike San José and Memphis, the tournament was played outdoors, although the plummeting evening temperatures and the icy gusting wind that greeted Murray's first-round match against world No. 18 Tommy Robredo cast doubt on the wisdom of playing outside in March. Most of the sparse crowd looked like they were wearing everything they owned, and one lady even wrapped herself in a carpet. In vile conditions, Murray lost 6–2, 6–2 in a match that was best forgotten.

As exciting as Las Vegas looked, being under 21, and therefore not allowed to gamble, was something of a trial. With almost every hotel and restaurant housing a casino he wasn't allowed into, Murray needed a chaperone just to check in to his room. He didn't appear to care much about his gaudy, neon-lit surroundings – he had an exploding volcano outside his hotel, yet when asked what he had seen of Las Vegas, he answered, 'Not much . . . Starbucks.'

From Las Vegas, he and Petchey drove down to southern California to the picturesque desert retirement-resort city of Indian Wells, a place full of elderly golfers, where the average age is in the 70s, dinner is eaten at 5.30 p.m. and the entire population is in bed by 9 p.m. It wasn't exactly a teenager's paradise.

Masters Series events are arguably more competitive than ATP Tour events and even the grand slams, and the draw in Indian Wells had been kind and cruel in equal measure, pitching him against qualifier Vasilis Mazarakis from Greece in the first round but setting him up to play world No. 5 Nikolay Davydenko in the second.

Having been delayed all day by rain – the cold, inclement weather seemed to have followed him from Nevada – Murray dispatched Mazarakis 6–2, 6–1 in 47 minutes. Davydenko, though, proved much more troublesome. The Russian delights in drawing his opponents into long, punishing rallies and is one of the most consistent performers on the tour. Murray said before the match that he thought Davydenko probably had the best ground strokes in the men's game and learned, to his chagrin, that he was right. Murray had chances to win but couldn't find a way to put Davydenko away in the third set, and the Russian won 6–1, 3–6, 6–3.

Murray remained in Indian Wells for a few days to practise, time which gave him a valuable opportunity to relax and get to know some of his fellow pros a little better. Like any 'new boy' in an unfamiliar environment, Murray had needed time to settle in socially to life on the ATP Tour, but by March, he was a familiar face to his colleagues in the locker-room. In Indian Wells, he spent several evenings playing soccer with the other players on a patch of grass by the practice courts, even taking part in a South America versus Europe clash, during which Petchey somehow ended up in goal for the South Americans.

The fact that the Scot and his coach had played on different sides on the football field was somewhat apposite since, privately, tensions were beginning to surface between Murray and Petchey. They were spotted arguing fiercely on the practice court in Indian Wells, and they had gone from being constantly (and happily) in each other's company at tournaments a few weeks previously to eating meals separately and appearing distant with each other between practice sessions.

The Nasdaq-100 Open in Miami would turn out to be their last tournament together. Murray's first-round opponent was Stanislas Wawrinka, who had been so dominant in their previous match during Great Britain's Davis Cup tie against Switzerland the previous September. Wawrinka got the better of him again, although Murray lead the first set 5–3 and did not go down without a fight. He lost 7–5, 3–6, 6–4, his chances of turning things around in the third set not helped when he twisted his left ankle and fell after trying to change direction too quickly. Had it not been for the ankle brace he was wearing, he might have sustained a serious injury. As it was, it was the kind of tweak which players often suffer when their legs are weary from week upon week of tournaments.

In his post-match press conference, remarks Murray made about how punishing his recent schedule had been were interpreted in some quarters as thinly veiled criticism of Petchey. 'It's been quite a long trip now, and I just didn't quite have enough left in the tank to kind of sustain a high level. It's really hard playing or being away for kind of six, seven weeks at a time. And I know if I do well here, I've got Davis Cup straight after, which is a week of practice and then possibly three five-set matches. Then I've got to go and practise on the clay before Monte Carlo. Then you've got Monte Carlo, Barcelona, Estoril, Rome, Hamburg, St Polten and the French Open. It's quite tough when you're coming to the end of a trip like this and you know if you do well, you've still got another kind of six, seven weeks of hard work before the next grand slam'. When asked who set his schedule, Murray said, 'It's up to my coach to make the schedule. That's one of the things that I leave him in charge of.'

It had been a gruelling, exhausting trip and one which would prove to be crucial for Murray's career. When he set out for San José, even he cannot have expected it to be quite as glitteringly successful, quite as quickly, nor could anyone have predicted that it would mark the beginning of the end of his partnership with Petchey. 'There were quite a lot of question marks when I was in Australia. I'd pushed all the best players close, but I never won against them. Once I won San José, by beating Roddick and Hewitt, I think I kind of showed people, yeah, I can play, and I can play really well,' said Murray. 'I'm not going to play like that every single week just now. It's going to take me a while to get my consistency. I'm going into every match trying to play my best, but if I don't, it's not the end of the world. To be ranked in the 40s at 18 is not a bad position to be in.'

Not a bad position at all. Twelve months earlier, he had been ranked 419, was British No. 15 and had never played a match on the ATP Tour. It had been a difficult journey to get to San José, but Murray knew the way.

18

BRAEHEAD AND BEYOND

ON THURSDAY, 24 NOVEMBER 2005 IT WAS OFFICIALLY ANNOUNCED THAT SCOTLAND would host its first Davis Cup tie for 36 years. It was a significant moment for Andy Murray and a remarkable testament to the impact that the 18 year old had made on the game. Without Murray it seems unlikely that the Davis Cup tie against Serbia and Montenegro would have been staged north of the border. Such was the massive interest in the return of the country's newest sporting hero to his homeland, nine major venues throughout Scotland bid to host the match with the 3,900-seater Braehead Arena in Renfrewshire, on the outskirts of Glasgow, winning the race, and the first batch of tickets sold out within a few hours.

The Europe/Africa Zone Group I second-round tie was to be the first Davis Cup match on British soil since September 2002, when Great Britain beat Thailand. The last time Scotland hosted a match was in 1970 when Great Britain played Austria in Edinburgh.

Tennis Scotland said that the interest in Murray and the decision to stage the tie in Scotland had given the sport its biggest boost for years. In 2004, there were 27,285 members of the 202 registered tennis clubs in Scotland. In 2005, these figures had risen by up to 5 per cent on the back of Murray's success, but these statistics did not include the occasional pay-as-you-go player who uses local authority facilities.

Jim Campbell, chief executive of Tennis Scotland, said, 'Andy's achievements have been incredible and have had a major impact. Hopefully, we can find another Andy Murray in the future, and the key word for us is support as we want to give any youngster as much chance to make it as we can. Tennis is the seventeenth most popular sport in Scotland among the adult population, while it is the tenth most popular in the 8–15 age group. In Australia and France, it has a much higher profile. We believe we can make it more popular in Scotland, and what Andy has done will help us do that.'

Two weeks before the tie, which was scheduled for 7–9 April, Murray called on the crowd to forget they were at a tennis match and shout and scream their support for the British team. He had been to Braehead only once before with his friend Alex Arthur, to watch a boxing match involving Amir Khan, who was another good friend. Murray watched from a front row seat as Khan, whom the Scot had visited at his training camp in Manchester beforehand, dispatched Walsall journeyman Steve Gethin 49 seconds into the third round of a thoroughly one-sided contest.

'The crowd chanted my name when I was at the boxing, so I know I will get really good support,' said Murray. 'I have good memories of Braehead, and I'm sure the crowd will get right behind the Davis Cup team and be really noisy, which will help us.'

Murray made his comments as Jeremy Bates announced that Murray's teammates to play Serbia and Montenegro would be Greg Rusedski, Arvind Parmar and doubles specialist James Auckland.

Belgrade-born Alex Bogdanovich turned down the chance to join the team as he felt he was still mentally scarred by his bad experience in Tel Aviv the previous year when he had lost his opening singles rubber against Israel.

Tennis can be as cruel and unpredictable as any other sport, and plans for a glorious homecoming for Murray were dealt a massive blow when the niggling ankle injury which he picked up during his three-set, first-round defeat to Stanislas Wawrinka at the Nasdaq-100 Open in Miami, took longer to heal than expected and made him a doubt for the tie. On Wednesday, 29 March, Murray had a scan on his injured ankle to evaluate whether he would be fit enough to play.

'The results of my scan confirmed damage to ligaments in my ankle suffered during my first round match in Miami,' said Murray in a statement issued through his manager Patricio Apey. 'The ligaments have not fully healed, so we will need to monitor my progress on a daily basis. I will practise with the team and continue the rehabilitation with caution so as not to aggravate it any further and will reassess the injury to determine whether or not I am fit to play.'

If that was not bad enough, Murray picked up a bacterial infection five days before the start of the match. The portents for the tie were looking increasingly ominous. He had begun to feel ill at his home in Dunblane on the Sunday while watching Hibs play Hearts in the Scottish Cup semi-final at Hampden Park. He lasted up until half-time, when Hibs were 1–0 down, but felt so ill he had to go to bed and miss the rest of the match. Hibs lost 4–0. It seemed that it wasn't going to be his week.

Both Murray's injured ankle and his bacterial infection put his appearance in the Davis Cup tie in severe doubt. Missing the match would have been a huge blow to the proud Scot, who had dreamed of leading a Great Britain team in his own country. As the tie drew near, Murray felt his ankle get better but the virus had drained him of energy.

Jeremy Bates arrived in Scotland on the Tuesday in the run-up to the tie and, speaking after walking round the Braehead Arena, said he would not gamble with Murray's fitness. 'Andy is better than he was,' said Bates. 'We had the results of the blood test, and it is a pretty severe bacterial infection which he is in the process of fighting off. In saying that, he hit some balls for 40 minutes on Monday and that was the first time he's done that since last Thursday. He's been hitting and moving around, and there are no visible signs of the ankle being a problem, but the more important issue is his health.'

Murray had talks with Bates about his fitness, and the Great Britain team captain made it clear that it was vital to his plans for the match to have the young Scot in the team. 'There is nothing I would like more than to have Andy playing through the weekend,' said Bates. 'He's our No. 1 player, he has caught the imagination of everybody and he is world class. We'd like him to be involved from the first moment, but when you are recovering from something like this, nobody really knows how long it will take. He has had a pretty severe illness which doesn't just disappear in 48 hours. I can't jeopardise his health, and I am not prepared to do that. The final decision will be up to him.

'In saying that, he is vital enough to us that I would pick him to play only on Sunday, if he were not fit enough for Friday and Saturday. We have to ask if he can play on Friday, and if not, can he play on Saturday or Sunday? We'll try to get him to play Friday, and if he can't, we'll try Saturday, and if he can't do that, we'll try Sunday.'

Bates said the crowd would have a big part to play in the match whether Murray played or not. 'Having good backing is like having an extra man, particularly if somebody from the other side is a little bit fragile and things aren't going their way,' said Bates. 'If the match starts to swing our way and the crowd can get at them, it just puts another nail in their coffin. This arena is what I've always wanted for a Davis Cup match. I've always wanted everybody right on top of the tennis, and the stands here are steep and the crowd will be very loud.'

The draw for the order of play for the tie was made on Thursday, 6 April and saw Murray being left out of the opening singles matches, although he would play doubles with Greg Rusedski the following day. His presence in the side at some stage of the tie was vital for Britain as the Serbia and Montenegro team, whose members turned up at the draw all wearing Scotland football strips, were hailed by their young star Novak Djokovic as the best side they had assembled for 15 years.

Murray revealed that he had defied medical advice to take part in the Europe/Africa Zone Group 1 match and that his own doctor had advised him against taking part. However, the lure of playing in front of a Scottish crowd proved too much of a temptation for the 18 year old, who was adamant he would participate in at least part of the match.

'Obviously I would have loved to have played the singles on Friday, but I still get the chance to play on Saturday,' said Murray. 'I'm sure Arvind is going to play very well in my absence. Everyone loves to play Davis Cup and to play in Scotland would be great, but I'm still going to get my chance.

'I would rather not risk my health and be out for three months and just miss one day's play. The doctor's advice would be not to play because of what can happen with infections if you come back too quickly. He told me if it was his son, he would say not to play, but it was obviously my decision if I wanted to play. I think if I played a long five-set singles match it could have been a problem, but by Saturday, I'll have had four or five days of feeling better, and doubles is obviously not as physically draining.'

The first match on the Friday would involve Rusedski, who would play Janko Tipsarevic, the Belgrade-born right hander in a contest the British player was the favourite to win. That match would be followed by Arvind Parmar, who had yet to win a singles match in the Davis Cup in five attempts, against Novak Djokovic.

Rusedski and Murray would face Nenad Zimonjic and Ilia Bozoljac in the doubles on Saturday, and if Great Britain still had a chance to win the match, the pair would take part in the singles on Sunday, provided the young Scotsman was fit enough.

Just in case Murray wasn't fit, Bates nominated Rusedski to play Djokovic on the Sunday and Parmar to take on Tipsarevic in the final game of the tie.

Bates refused to be drawn on whether Murray would also play on Sunday, but Dejan Petrovic, the Serbia and Montenegro team captain, fully expected the Scot to play on the final day, provided the tie was still alive. 'We will have to see how Andy reacts to playing on Saturday before we decide what happens on Sunday,' said Bates. 'The more involvement he can have the better it is for everybody, but I have to listen to what the doctors and Andy say. I have said all along I'm not prepared to put Andy in a position that jeopardises his health. He is well on his way to recovering from a pretty serious infection, and it's a question of letting that run its course. To expect three days out of him is a little much, and it's a question of being sensible.'

The doom and gloom increased further when Djokovic confirmed that it was a huge boost to his team that Murray was not playing in the first round of singles matches. 'This is bad for the British team as Andy is a very good player,' said Djokovic, who at eighteen years and five months was the youngest player in the world top 100 by the end of 2005, finishing in eighty-third spot.

Although the tie was a sell-out, there were plenty of empty seats on the opening day. Part of the reason was that tickets set aside for the ITF to distribute to corporate clients had not been taken up, and the Serbs had hardly sold any tickets, handing back four hundred for each day's play only six days before the tie was due to start.

Not having Murray play on the opening day was a huge disappointment to the crowd, which had hoped to see him in action. The atmosphere seemed to reflect that sense of anticlimax. Although the match was being played in Scotland, there was no overt nationalism on show with the hall being full of Union Jacks and only a few Saltires in evidence. Murray spent his time on the sidelines cheering on the Great Britain team and signing autographs for the Scottish fans. Some of the non-playing members of the Serb squad turned up in Scotland football tops again and one of them was wearing a Rangers football team away top and hat.

Once the pleasantries were over and the teams introduced to the crowd, Greg Rusedski gave Great Britain a perfect start with a gutsy performance against Janko Tipsarevic, one of the few tennis players in the world who wears glasses on court. The 32-year-old Briton had to work hard for his win, and the Serb saved five match points before finally relenting 6–3, 6–7, 7–5, 7–5. The second match was won easily by Novak Djokovic against Arvind Parmar 6–3, 6–2, 7–5, which left the Brit with the unenviable record of having lost all six Davis Cup matches he had played in.

Afterwards, Parmar said he expected to be dropped in favour of Murray for the second round of singles matches on Sunday, provided the tie was still alive and the young Scot was fit. 'It was made clear that Andy was the No. 1 player, and if he was fit and ready to go, there was no question of him not playing on Sunday,' said Parmar.

There was some good news when Bates revealed that Murray had hit on court after the singles matches were finished and was fit and ready to go in the doubles on the Saturday: 'He is getting better day by day and he is sharpening up all the time. In saying that, there is a big difference between practising and playing an actual game, but he is ready. One thing in his favour is the fact that Greg will be his partner in the doubles, and he is playing with confidence after his singles win.'

After the first day's play, Bates said he was disappointed at the support the team had received from the crowd and hoped it improved over the weekend. 'There were quite a lot of empty seats, and the crowd were a bit too docile and not what I expected, and I don't understand why,' said Bates. 'I was a little bit disappointed and hope it won't be like that again.' The atmosphere did improve on the Saturday, but that was not surprising considering Murray was due on court.

It was going to be a difficult match as Zimonjic was a world-class doubles player who won the Monte Carlo Masters Series title with Tim Henman in 2004. On paper, Bozoljac was the weaker player of the two, but he did partner Zimonjic to a doubles title in Belgrade in 2003.

Rusedski, who played Davis Cup doubles with Murray when they were beaten by Roger Federer and Yves Allegro of Switzerland in October 2005, admitted having his young colleague fit in time for the doubles and possibly the final-day singles was vital. 'Andy coming in on Saturday and possibly Sunday gives us a much better chance of winning,' said Rusedski, sounding typically upbeat. 'He looks fine, he is smiling, happy, playing football in the locker-room and eating junk food as usual. He also had two practice sessions on court, which was one more than the rest of us, and he is confident and looking good for the rest of the tie.'

Murray may have looked confident – though pale – but it was clear from the start that the British duo were struggling to play well as a team. Both played well in spells but unfortunately never at the same time. They also failed to take their chances with the British pairing squandering the first fourteen break-points they had, while the Serb team took four out of the five break points they engineered. Zimonjic and Bozoljac played more steadily and consistently, but the match, arguably, turned on a bad line call at a crucial time, which greatly upset Murray in particular. His reaction to it would have serious repercussions for the British team and for the teenager himself.

In the first game of the fourth set, and down 30–40 on Rusedski's serve, Zimonjic played a passing shot which Rusedski decided to leave as it was heading out of the court. It looked long to everyone in the arena, but it was called in by the line judge, a decision which gave the Serb pairing the best possible start to the set. Murray, frustrated, swore in anger at the decision and was furious at umpire Adel Aref from Tunisia for not overruling the line judge.

Up until then, the game had been evenly poised with the Serbs winning the first set 6–3 and the Brits winning the second by the same 6–3 scoreline. Zimonjic and Bozoljac won the third set 6–3 and the bad line call allowed them to take full advantage of their good fortune and run out 6–4 winners in the fourth to clinch the match and put their country 2–1 up in the tie.

The dubious line call had not been forgotten by Murray, who let rip at Aref again at the end of the match, using the F-word at least once. His outburst was born of frustration and disappointment, and he was hardly the first teenager – or the first tennis player – to vent at an official. However, the presence of a television microphone by the umpire's chair ensured that every word was relayed to BBC television viewers. Andrew Castle, who was commentating on the match, was prompted to remark that it 'wasn't the sort of language' which should be heard on a tennis court.

Afterwards, Murray tried to explain why he had lost his temper with the umpire. 'We got an absolutely shocking call in the first game of the fourth set,' he said. 'The mark shows it was an inch and a half out. I told the umpire how bad he was during the match. I swore at the umpire. It's tough because you see footballers swearing after every foul, or after every mistake by the referee, but it's picked up here because there is a microphone underneath the umpire's chair. I'd have preferred it if everyone had not heard it, but that's what happens sometimes when you get angry. Hopefully, not too many people heard it. After all, it was only on interactive television.'

Unfortunately, Norbert Pieck, the German match referee, heard it and said he was in the process of reviewing the incident and would announce the size of the fine after the final match of the Davis Cup tie on the Sunday afternoon. The Sunday papers, meanwhile, seized on Murray's use of the expletive on afternoon television and concentrated more on the outburst than the match. There was even speculation that Murray might receive a three-year ban from Davis Cup competition.

Judy, who had been in the crowd when Andy swore at the umpire, took a mature approach to her son's misdemeanour. 'He is sorry for what he said and will have to live with the consequences,' she said.

With Great Britain 2–1 down after the doubles, the home side were in a precarious position, and there was now huge pressure on Rusedski to beat Djokovik in the first of Sunday's singles games to keep the tie alive. A defeat would mean Great Britain would lose the tie. It said a lot for the 32 year old that he was willing to try and play three matches in three days for his adopted country.

'I'd better get some good sleep before the match,' said Rusedski. 'I'll be in bed by 8.30 as I'll be required to play at 11.00 in the morning against a very good 18 year old who has had a day's rest. It's going to be tough, and I'll have to give my all.'

The Serbs were so confident they would secure the match that the minute Marks and Spencer opened at the Braehead shopping centre on Sunday morning a member of their coaching staff was in the queue to buy champagne. And their prediction came true after Rusedski, visibly flagging having been forced to play so much tennis, lost to Djokovic. In the end, Murray's absence on the opening day and the 14-year age gap between Rusedski and Djokovic had taken its toll, the younger man's 6–3, 4–6, 6–3, 7–6 win clinching the tie for Serbia and Montenegro. It ended a thoroughly miserable weekend for Murray and his teammates.

Statistics showed that Rusedski had spent nine hours on court over the previous two days, while Djokovic had played for only one hour forty-five minutes in his first match on Friday against Parmar and had had Saturday off. It had been a brave performance by Rusedski but circumstances conspired against him, just as they had done to his team.

Murray would have played the final match if the tie had still been alive, but because it wasn't, he spent his time on the sidelines once again cheering on the British players and signing autographs. Arvind Parmar played the meaningless rubber instead, winning his first Davis Cup match in seven attempts, beating Bozoljac 7–5, 6–4. That victory made the final score 3–2 and gave the impression that the tie was closer than it actually was.

Afterwards, Bates revealed he had tried to have Sunday's 11 a.m. start put back to allow Rusedski more time to recover from his doubles match with Murray but was rebuffed by the BBC who demanded the start time fitted in with their schedules. 'I am very frustrated because we had to play the Davis Cup at 11 a.m. on a Sunday morning,' said Bates. 'That was no help to us as a team.'

Both Bates and Rusedski defended Murray following his verbal outburst at the umpire and made it clear that the whole thing had been blown out of all proportion. 'I had a chat with Andy about what happened, but what was said remains between him and me,' said Bates. 'Footballers say that kind of thing all the time but they don't get picked up on microphones. In tennis, the microphone is right on the umpire's chair. It was a mistake, but he's not the first to make one, and he won't be the last.'

Rusedski also sprang to Murray's defence, making the point that he was no saint himself when it came to swearing on court and had done it many times, most notably at Wimbledon when he too had fallen foul of the courtside microphones and had inadvertently treated the BBC's viewers to a string of expletives. 'I think some of the things written about him have been a bit harsh considering he is just 18,' said Rusedski. 'I have sworn on Centre Court and said every bad word imaginable. Andy is an interesting person and has character. Last year, he was 450 in the world and nobody had heard of him. Now he is the British No. 1. He will have a few difficult moments to deal with, but he is very mature, and this has been another learning experience for him.'

After the tie was over, it was announced that the British team had been fined £1,500 because of Murray's verbal outburst, but, in truth, by the Sunday afternoon, the hasty moral indignation shown by some people had subsided. It was easy to sympathise with Murray and understand how his frustration had boiled over. Twisting his ankle before the tie then contracting a bacterial infection meant he was not able to perform to his full capabilities in front of his home crowd.

Roger Draper, the chief executive of the LTA, also defended Murray on the issue. 'Andy recognises he made a mistake,' he said. 'I have been around in sport a long time, and if I had a bank account for every professional sportsman who swore, I would be a billionaire by now. We are not in nursery school, we are in professional sport here and that is what happens. At the end of the day, whether it is Wayne Rooney or Andy Murray, it is that passion and controlled aggression that makes them the great sports people they are.'

There were bigger issues brought to the fore by the defeat, the main one being how much Great Britain already relied on Murray to be fit and playing on a regular basis. Tim Henman had retired from Davis Cup tennis, and although Rusedski was brave and determined at Braehead, age was beginning to catch up with him. Rusedski expressed his concern at the lack of support for Murray in future Davis Cup ties: 'Hopefully we will get some good younger players coming through. I am 32 years old, and I don't know for how long I will be playing. Andy must find somebody to join him in the team for the next ten years.'

The importance of Murray to the British side was summed up by Djokovic, who explained the relief the Serbian and Montenegro players had felt when they had discovered that the young Scot had only been fit enough to play doubles. 'This was a big win for us, but they were at a disadvantage because Andy did not play on the first and last days,' said the Serb. 'It would have been difficult for our player to play Andy in front of 4,000 of his own people in the last match. It is a good thing we won before the fifth match and he did not play.'

Murray's closest confidant at the Davis Cup tie had been Leon Smith, the man who coached him during his junior years. The pair sat next to each other on the second row of the team benches during the matches in which Murray was not playing and looked relaxed in each other's company. There had been no sign of Mark Petchey, the coach who had done so much for Murray over the preceding ten months.

Late on the afternoon of Good Friday, 14 April, five days after the Davis Cup tie had ended and at a time when most people were heading away for the Easter weekend, Murray issued a joint statement with Petchey through the player's management company, announcing their split.

Murray said, 'Mark has been a big part of my success in the last ten months, and we had a great run together, but we have had a difference of opinion regarding some aspects of my game. It was a very difficult decision.'

Petchey was full of praise for his young charge and said, 'I am very proud of what we have achieved together, which includes getting Andy into the top 50 and winning his first ATP title at the age of 18. I have no doubt that Andy will be a grand-slam winner in the future and wish him every success.'

Petchey, in an interview with Sky TV, admitted that their parting had not come as a total shock: 'I have to say, although it only happened in the last couple of days, I'm not completely surprised. All I can say is we were talking a lot this year about his best way to play and perform consistently against the best players in the world so he could reach the top 10 as quickly as possible. I felt that we made a lot of progress in the months we'd been together, and I thought the process would take another year until he was playing his best tennis consistently.

'In relationships like this, there are bound to be differences of opinion at some stage, and it's Andy's prerogative to find someone who sees it the way he does, not just strategically but in all the elements that end up making a great player. We can't lose sight of the fact Andy is an exceptionally talented player, and there's no doubt in my mind, and many people's minds, that he was destined for a huge amount of success anyway. Last year at Wimbledon, there were probably a lot of questions surrounding Andy, and I feel as though I've guided him well through the first stage of his career. I'm proud of our achievements together, and I'm going to enjoy watching his many successes in the future.'

Murray's first match without Petchey was in the first round of the Monte Carlo Masters Series, four days after the split was announced. It was an inauspicious start to the latest chapter of his tennis career as he was beaten in three sets by wildcard Jean-René Lisnard 4-6, 7-6, 7-5, an opponent ranked over 100 places below him. It was not the way he wanted to start the clay-court season but such minor disappointments are as much a part of professional sport as the success which greeted Murray's first year on the ATP Tour.

Murray is not just one of the most charismatic young sportsmen in the country, he is also the best hope for the future of British tennis. Thankfully, those closest to him believe he can continue his rise up the rankings and has the talent and self-belief to stay at the top for a long time to come.

Tim Henman, the man who has been an inspiration and a mentor to the Scot, has faith that Murray has what it takes to spearhead British tennis after he retires. 'I think his mental strength has been evident in his progress in the time since Queen's, and it's such an important element of any top-level sport. Everybody's good, everybody plays well and there are some good athletes out there, but the mental aspect is so important. Andy is going to have endless challenges ahead of him and to have that fortitude is going to serve him very, very well.'

Petchey believes the British public should enjoy Murray's joie de vivre and give him all the encouragement they can in the coming years, through the good times and the bad. 'At 18 years old, Andy is experiencing life as well as he's experiencing tennis,' he said. 'We're all flawed, to a certain degree, and we all have our little foibles, and that's what I tried to say to Andy. At times I would say to him, "Hey listen, you're not going to get it perfectly right all the time", but for an 18 year old, he's pretty much got things perfect most of the time.

'Sport is tough. It's very, very difficult, and even if you are doing well, then you are playing five tennis matches in a week. Unless you are Roger Federer or Rafael Nadal, it is inevitable that you are going to have ups and downs, and you have to be resilient and accept that this is the life you've chosen and get on with it.'

Tennis is indeed the life that Andy Murray has chosen and graced since he broke through onto the world stage. Britain's top player is set to go from strength to strength as he grows older and gains more experience. He has had an incredible rise up the tennis rankings so far, and the boy from Dunblane has the potential to go much, much further. Tennis fans throughout the world should sit back and enjoy the ride.